New Ideas About Eating Diso

369 0285695

2012

**This book is to be returned on or before
the last date stamped below.**

X

In th   life
instin   sh,
rage,   ger
drive   ard
eatin

New   di-
vidua   ers,
a ne   ind
preve

This   ing
for   ing
theo   of
inter   one
want   and
eatin

Cha   ley,
Calif   and
1977   vith
staff   on-
duct   ren,
adol

D1350172

New Ideas About Eating Disorders

Human emotions and the hunger drive

Charles T. Stewart

Routledge
Taylor & Francis Group

LONDON AND NEW YORK

First published 2012
by Routledge
27 Church Road, Hove, East Sussex BN3 2FA

Simultaneously published in the USA and Canada
by Routledge
711 Third Avenue, New York NY 10017

Routledge is an imprint of the Taylor & Francis Group, an Informa business

British Library Cataloguing in Publication Data
A catalogue record for this book is available from the British Library

Library of Congress Cataloging-in-Publication Data

Stewart, Charles T.
  New ideas about eating disorders : human emotions and the hunger drive /
Charles T. Stewart.
      p. cm.
  Includes bibliographical references and index.
  ISBN 978-0-415-55469-5 (hardback) – ISBN 978-0-415-55470-1 (pbk.)
    1. Compulsive eating–Psychological aspects. 2. Compulsive eaters–
Psychology. I. Title.
  RC552.C65S74 2011
  616.85'26–dc22

                                                              2011007109

ISBN: 978-0-415-55469-5 (hbk)
ISBN: 978-0-415-55470-1 (pbk)
ISBN: 978-0-203-80222-9 (ebk)

Typeset in Times by Garfield Morgan, Swansea, West Glamorgan
Paperback cover design by Andrew Ward
Printed by TJ International Ltd, Padstow, Cornwall

To Matilda B. Stewart
Bon appétit

Contents

    subject Helen   134

9   Primary prevention of eating disorders: Interest and Joy
    in infancy   152

    References   165
    Index   172

Tables and Figures

Tables

Figures

Preface

They are not usually described as such, but eating disorders are quintessentially psychosomatic disorders, in the sense that they bring psyche and soma together, often to a malignant degree. My interest in psychosomatic disorders that illustrate the power of mind over body began in medical school, continued during four years as a pediatrician, and never left me during another four years of psychiatric training, during which one was tempted to leave body behind in favor of what one was learning about mind. Nor did my interest in the mind-body interface wane during a 50-year career as a child psychiatrist. Realization of the full implications of my interest, however, awaited the construction of a model of the most bodily and simultaneously psychological of phenomena, the Archetypal affect system, that would do justice to the way feelings support or destroy physical life. Now, after two books that have illustrated how fundamental that model is to the understanding of both normal ego development and destructive, life-threatening behaviors, I feel ready to address the psychosomatic interface conundrum of eating disorders.

The method I have constructed for analyzing these conditions is grounded in contemporary affect theory but is founded on the statements made by C. G. Jung as long ago as his 1907 monograph, "The Psychology of Dementia Praecox" (in CW 3, *The Psychogenesis of Mental Disease*) to the effect (a) that the essential basis of our personality is affectivity and (b) that every affective event experienced by the individual is structuralized as a feeling-toned complex. Despite the fact that this monograph seemed to link his view of emotion to Freud's psychoanalytic theory of drives and their derivatives, Jung's was a theory of emotion itself, not a theory of emotion as the derivative of drives. Over half a century later, in the first volume of his seminal study of the innate affects, published in 1962, Silvan Tomkins said as much of his own theory when he declared that the affects were the primary, and the drives the secondary, motivational systems in humans. These propositions by Jung and Tomkins are Copernican in their implications, because they suggest that affects are the suns around which the earths of our instinctive behaviors revolve. The centrality of affect has become the basic idea informing my own method. Not surprisingly, it was both Jung and Tomkins who also emphasized the importance of the emotions in conditioning the Hunger–Satiety drive in ways that result in its optimal or pathological functioning.

A further contribution to my understanding was made by James Hillman, the Jungian analyst and theoretician of affect, who presented a review in 1960, *Emotion*, of all of the extant theories of emotion and concluded this monumental work with his formulation of an integrated theory based on Aristotle's four types of cause. In that monograph, Hillman noted that emotion is the key concept in psychosomatic medicine, long recognized as playing a crucial role in the body–mind relation.

Finally, in a series of articles published in the 1980s, my own brother, L. H. Stewart, also a Jungian analyst and theoretician, presented his formulation of the Archetypal affect system, which was also grounded in the work of Jung, Hillman, and Tomkins. Lou was ahead of me in formulating the thinking I had been reaching for to bring these viewpoints together, and his theory provided the linchpin for my research approach.

The method has proved its value not only by supporting the research presented in this study, which includes rethinking the affective course of a number of classic eating disorder psychotherapies, but also by leading to the discovery of a new theory of the etiology of Anorexia nervosa and Bulimia nervosa in adolescence and adulthood. These conditions, as well as Failure to Thrive in infancy, have needed such a theory. Let me share it with you here.

Foreword

A book by Charles Stewart, though a great help to practicing psycho-therapists like myself, is never an ordinary explanation of how to keep in mind the deep and perplexing issues that our child, adolescent, and adult patients bring to us when they present themselves for psychological help. Rather, it is an exploration of the *central* feature of all such work, the emotion that is being communicated – or cannot be without professional help. For that reason, his books (and this is the third I have engaged with as his personal editor) are demanding of the reader but, in the way they repay our engagement with them, satisfying. His first book – about the positive role emotion plays in normal development when self and other come together in symbolization – and his second – about the negative role emotion takes up when, instead, it drives people to negate self and other through lethal behaviors – demonstrated emotion's centrality in both the healthiest and the most pathological instances of what it can lead to. Now Stewart has chosen to focus on demand and satisfaction themselves, which he does through an examination of what is either the happiest or the most dismal aspect of many lives, the way eating is felt and symbolized.

He leads us to re-imagine Anorexia nervosa and Bulimia nervosa, so often mystified, as a unitary syndrome, one that expresses our relation to both Hunger and Satiety. He makes us see that a disorder that interferes with someone's normal ability to hold the tension of these opposites is always a pointer to how that person has been taught, in earliest development, to regard the feeding situation. Stewart's command of the archetypal field in which a baby, through daily contacts with parents, can develop a disturbed understanding of his or her eating enables him to understand what patients who later turn out to suffer from Bulimia, Anorexia, or both have been trying to tell their therapists about what their feeding or not feeding themselves feels like. This is learned behavior that can also be unlearned in the right therapeutic environment. The present small volume actually offers such an environment to the reader, who may have learned the wrong things from some of our previous literature on eating disorders. Before I worked on this book, I always felt like an outsider to these disorders. Now I see that they are inside me and all of us, and I am as hungry to learn more about them as I am satisfied by this book's approach to such learning.

For the reader for whom psychological treatment is not just a technical pursuit but can still find ground for the understanding of psychotherapy in the dictum offered by Terence, the Berber playwright from Carthage, in a play that the Roman Republic held dear, *The Self Tormentor: Homo sum: humani nil a me alienum puto* ("I am human, I consider nothing human alien to me"), Stewart's new book will be especially precious. Its feeling re-reading of previous accounts of disordered eating makes us much more empathic toward human conditions that have sometimes seemed, when described without Stewart's unblinking compassionate gaze, alien and (in the words of many a person who suffers from the syndrome he describes) "too heavy." In the literature on psychotherapy, it is a rare author who can motivate us to take up the burden of emotion in a region of experience like eating, where many of us would simply prefer to be unthinkingly happy, but because Charles Stewart does so in a way that makes difficult emotions actually easier to hold, reading his work has the paradoxical effect of actually lightening our load.

John Beebe

Acknowledgments

I want to thank my editors at Routledge – Kate Hawes, Jane Harris, Sarah Gibson, Dawn Harris and copy editor Alison Jones – for their invaluable assistance in bringing my book to publication. Their thoughtful responses to each of my questions, from book proposal to book production, helped me during each stage of the publishing process.

I want to thank my professional editor, the Jungian analyst and author, John E. Beebe, MD, who had worked with me to edit my two previous books. It was a pleasure to meet with him regularly to review the manuscript and to experience his artistry in directing me toward greater clarity in expression of my ideas and to revisions that made the book more readable. Then, when we had completed the editing, he generously agreed to my request to write the Foreword.

I want to thank my wife Matilda, as well as my friends and colleagues Joan Chodorow, Sylvia and Earl Shorris, Lise and Neal Blumenfeld, Jean Harasemovitch and Gary Truax, Mary Brady and Carey Cole, Robert Tyminski and Gady Heinic, Millicent Dillon, Judy Rascoe, and Jill Fischer whose lively interest in my research helped sustain me as I was writing this book. I want to thank Susan Jamison, my personal trainer, for her creative thoughts about the title of my book.

Acknowledgments are due to the publishers of the following works for permission to quote extensively: Jung, C. G., *The Structure and Dynamics of the Psyche, Vol. 8 of the Collected Works* © 1960 by Bollingen Foundation, New York, NY Second edition © by Princeton University Press and Routledge. Reprinted by permission of Princeton University Press and Routledge; *Existence* © 1958 Rollo May. Reprinted by permission of Basic Books, a member of the Perseus Books Group © 2006 by the American Psychological Association; Knudson, Roger M. (2006) Anorexia dreaming: A case study, *Dreaming*, 16 (1): 43–52; Sechehaye, M. (1951) *Symbolic Realization*, International Universities Press. By permission of International Universities Press, Inc. © 1951.

All reasonable efforts have been made to contact copyright holders but in some cases this was not possible. Any omissions brought to the attention of Routledge will be remedied in future editions.

Abbreviations

Sources in the text identifying quotations from the *Collected Works* of C. G. Jung as listed in the bibliography include author, year of publication by Princeton University Press, and the page number, e.g. (Jung 1968a: 54).

Introduction

A crash course in Affect Theory (before applying it to eating disorders)

The goal of this study is to highlight the part played by archetypal affects or emotions in the psychogenesis of certain eating disorders and in their psychological treatment. The purpose of the Introduction is to acquaint the reader with the author's view of the emotions as rooted in a complex system of archetypal affects, because that is the view that informs this research. My primary sources for this conviction about the essential nature of human affects are: *The Expression of the Emotions in Man and Animals* by Charles Darwin (1872); C. G. Jung's *Collected Works*; *Emotion* by James Hillman (1992); Volumes I, II, III of *Affect Imagery Consciousness* by Silvan Tomkins (1962, 1963, 1991); *Exploring Affect: The Selected Writings of Silvan S. Tomkins*, edited by Virginia Demos (1995); and my late brother Louis H. Stewart's formulation of his theory of the Archetypal affect system (1984, 1985, 1986, 1987a, 1987b, 1988, 1992). This developing theory of emotion, as based in a system of archetypal affects that have evolved along with everything else that makes us human, informs my previous works, *The Symbolic Impetus: How Creative Fantasy Motivates Development* (2001) and *Dire Emotions and Lethal Behaviors: Eclipse of the Life Instinct* (2008). The reader should be aware that these books do not stint on, and in fact underline and amplify, the role of development in infancy, childhood, and adolescence in determining how archetypal affects end up motivating human behavior. In the present book, this theory will be applied to what we already know about the development of eating disorders.

Affects as primary motivators

By postulating a theory of archetypes as the psychic representations of the instincts, C. G. Jung grounded his analytical psychology on the motivational primacy of innate emotions: "The essential basis of our personality is affectivity. Thought and action are, as it were, only symptoms of affectivity" (Jung 1960: 38). Throughout his *Collected Works*, Jung reiterates this view and discusses the implications of this basic fact for both normal and abnormal development.

Silvan Tomkins, in his revision of psychoanalytic theory, which had always been weak in its approach to consciously expressed affect and in differentiating underlying basic emotions, also arrived at the view that innate affects form the primary motivational system in humans, and went so far as to postulate that the drives are only secondary motivators: "In our view, the primary motivational system is the affective system, and the biological drives have motivational impact only when amplified by the affective system" (Tomkins 1962: 6). What distinguishes Tomkins from Jung is that Tomkins focuses on the typical ways we experience and express emotion, whereas Jung is more interested in differentiating the archetypal images that enter the mind at the time that emotional expression starts to occur. Both, however, would agree that the basis of such ways of experiencing and imaging en route to emotional expression is innately determined by an a priori affective system that has evolved over millennia.

The postulate that the innate affects are the primary motivational system in human beings is a foundation stone for this book, as it was for my previous works. I consider it a heuristic fact from which further theory can usefully proceed.

Specifying the affects

In *The Expression of the Emotions in Man and Animals*, Charles Darwin (1872) identified the following emotions as forming the prototypical expressive behaviors in human beings and many animals – Joy, Surprise, Fear, Sadness, Anger, Contempt, and Shame. He took it for granted that such emotions were innate: "That the chief expressive actions, exhibited by man and by lower animals, are now innate or inherited, – that is, they have not been learnt by the individual, – is admitted by every one" (Darwin 1872: 350). He contrasted these innate affects, which his extensive observations convinced him were evolutionary products, with what he referred to as complex emotions that could be developed and cultivated within a single lifetime – Jealousy, Envy, Avarice, Revenge, Suspicion, Deceit, Shyness, Guilt, Vanity, Conceit, Ambition, Pride, Humility, etc. – and that he noted are not revealed in typical ways "by any fixed expressions, sufficiently distinct to be described or delineated" (ibid.: 261), but always show an individual character.

After his own even more extensive studies of the affects, Tomkins (1962) affirmed Darwin's list of a specific set of primal emotions and added only one innate affect that Darwin had omitted, perhaps because it so characterized his own most typical expression of emotion – Interest. Helen Lynd (1958), meanwhile, had demonstrated that Contempt and Shame are in fact essentially the same emotion, the only difference being that it is directed, in the case of Contempt, toward another and, in the case of

Shame, toward oneself (she was the first to say that Shame can be formulated as self-Contempt).

With these studies and our own in mind, L. H. Stewart and I arrived at a system of seven innate affects: Interest, Joy, Surprise, Fear, Sadness, Anger, and Shame/Contempt. It is quite possible, of course, that this categorization of the innate emotions will be revised by others in the future. What is important for the present study is that eating disorders make so much more sense when the specific emotions that seem to condition the eating behaviors involved are identified and explored.

The question of "universal" affects

Darwin wrote: "I have endeavoured to show in considerable detail that all the chief expressions exhibited by man are the same throughout the world" (1872: 359). By man, Darwin of course meant mankind, and he was not excluding women from that designation. And Jung was following Darwin when he stated: "Emotions have a typical 'pattern' (fear, anger, sorrow, hatred, etc.); that is, they follow an inborn archetype which is universally human and arouses the same ideas and feelings in everyone. These 'patterns' appear as archetypal motifs chiefly in dreams" (Jung 1975: 537). Ekman and Friesen (1971), who conducted cross-cultural studies of the facial expression of the primary emotions, are close to the spirit in Jung confirming the universality of certain affect patterns. More recently, Ekman (1994) and Carroll Izard (1994) have updated the evidence for the universal distribution of the expression of what appear to them to be innate emotions.

A corollary of the specificity and universality of emotions is the fact that recognition of others' affects is definitely an innate capacity. Darwin, again, had already expressed his opinion on this topic in the nineteenth century:

> As most of the movements of expression must have been gradually acquired, afterwards becoming instinctive, there seems to be some degree of *a priori* probability that their recognition would likewise have become instinctive. There is, at least, no greater difficulty in believing this than in admitting that, when a female quadruped first bears her young, she knows the cry of distress of her offspring, or than in admitting that many animals instinctively recognize and fear their enemies; and of both these statements there can be no reasonable doubt.
>
> (Darwin 1872: 357–8)

Similarly Jung wrote: "Emotional manifestations are based on similar patterns, and are recognizably the same all over the earth. We understand them even in animals, and the animals themselves understand each other in this respect, even if they belong to different species" (Jung 1977: 234). Jung also suggested that a specific mechanism accounted for this capacity:

> We have a highly differentiated subjective system for recognizing and evaluating affective phenomena in others. There is present in each of us a direct instinct for registering this, which animals also possess in high degree, with respect not only to their own species but also to other animals and human beings. We can perceive the slightest emotional fluctuations in others and have a very fine feeling for the quality and quantity of affects in our fellow-men.
>
> (Jung 1970a: 14)

This innate capacity is referred to by Ernst Cassirer (1957) as the "perception of expression," and by Heinz Werner (1957) as "physiognomic" perception.

In their article, "Selection for Universal Facial Emotion," Waller, Cray, and Burrows introduced their study of facial musculature with these comments:

> Facial expression is heralded as a communication system common to all human populations, and thus is generally accepted as a biologically based, universal behavior. Happiness, sadness, fear, anger, surprise, and disgust are universally recognized and produced emotions, and communication of these states is deemed essential in order to navigate the social environment.
>
> (Walter et al. 2008: 435)

What puzzled these investigators was how individuals are capable of producing similar facial expressions when facial musculature is known to vary greatly among individuals. This is what their research revealed:

> Here, the authors show that although some facial muscles are not present in all individuals, and often exhibit great asymmetry (larger or absent on one side), the facial muscles that are essential in order to produce the universal facial expressions exhibited 100% occurrence and showed minimal gross asymmetry in 18 cadavers.
>
> (ibid.: 435)

They concluded their investigation with this statement: "This explains how universal facial expression production is achieved, implies that facial muscles have been selected for essential nonverbal communicative function, and yet also accommodate individual variation" (ibid.: 435).

How affects are brought into play

There are three ways that an innate affect can be activated: (a) by contagion from the emotions of others, (b) in response to a life stimulus and primal image working in tandem to become an efficient symbol keyed to evoke that very affect for life-development, and (c) through continuous activation of a complex carrying an archetypal feeling tone that has been constructed in the course of development. I will now examine these three routes of activation of emotions associated with the Archetypal affect system.

Contagion from the affects of others

Contagion is that involuntary process whereby emotion is transmitted from one person to another. It is a remarkable phenomenon. Nothing is as infectious as affects: "When you are in a crowd which is moved by an emotion, you cannot fail to be roused by that same emotion . . . somebody makes a joke and people laugh, then you laugh too in an idiotic way, simply because you can't refrain from laughing" (Jung 1977: 138). Indeed, contagion is a fundamental consequence of affectivity itself:

> All affects, with the exception of startle, are specific activators of themselves – the principle of *contagion*. This is true whether the affect is initially a response of the self, or the response of another. By this we mean that the experience of fear is frightening, the experience of distress is distressing, the experience of anger is angering, the experience of shame is shaming, the experience of disgust is disgusting, the experience of joy is joying, the experience of excitement is exciting.
>
> (Tomkins 1962: 296, original emphasis)

It is understandable, then, that Jung and Tomkins would both accept the perception of someone else's emotional state to be a primary activating experience for all of us and that they would postulate this process in the shaping of our social being:

> The characteristic of contagion is critical for the social responsiveness of any organism. It is only when joy of the other activates joy in the self, fear of the other activates fear within, distress of the other activates distress within, anger of the other activates anger within, excitement of the other activates one's own excitement that we may speak of an animal as a social animal.
>
> (ibid.: 296–7)

James Hillman, during a discussion of the therapeutic process, arrived at a similar conclusion:

The primary contact with the soul of another person is emotion. . . . In short, emotion is wholeness and the affective contact is the first level of healing, of making whole. Therefore the patient continually provokes the emotion of the therapist, involving him in anger, in love and desire, in hope and anxiety, in order to get a whole reaction. It is only this wholeness perhaps which works a cure.

(1960/1992: 275)

The susceptibility to affect contagion is maximal at birth, because the infant's relation to the world is still one of "adualism" (Piaget), "primary unitary reality" (Neumann), and "unconscious identity" (Jung). Susceptibility to contagion, however, persists throughout life, even though progressive differentiation of the ego-complex enables the individual to some degree to "gate" incoming emotions and certainly to determine, with ever increasing clarity, the origin of affective events that impinge upon the self. The experience of affect contagion calls for discrimination from within. We learn to notice the frequency, intensity, and duration of our contagious episodes as well the effectiveness of our parents and others in modulating and integrating these episodes. We naturally gravitate toward people who enable us to manage our affects and avoid people who stir us up and leave us vulnerable to continuous contagion. One way to understand the decision to enter therapy is the search for another person who can turn potentially pathogenic affects into developmental and adaptive channels. And perhaps the most common complaint in therapy is about some significant other who continuously leaves us upset, that is, affectively over-stimulated without relief.

Constellation in oneself of archetypal affects

From the perspective of Jungian affect theory as first circumambulated by Hillman and then elaborated more systematically by L. H. Stewart, the efficient cause of emotion is a symbol, which always involves a conscious element – usually some life stimulus – linked to an unconscious prototype for perceiving and reacting to a stimulus like that in a particular way. It is the unconscious prototype that Jung originally called the primordial image, which he saw as innate, leading him eventually to select the term archetype. The archetype however is never experienced except when it slips into the natural setting of some actual life event, whether internal or external to the subject of the emotional episode. It was Louis Stewart's contribution to show just how such a combination of particular life stimulus and evoked primal image could result in the constellation of each of the innate affects that Tomkins had identified. The result was a highly specific key to the genesis of emotions, which is summarized in Table I.1.

Table I.1 Constellation of archetypal affects

Symbol		
1 *Life Stimulus* +	*Primal Image* →	*Innate Affect*
2 Novelty	Focused Insight	**Interest**
3 the Familiar	Diffuse Illumination	**Joy**
4 the Unexpected	Disorientation	**Surprise**
5 the Unknown	the Abyss	**Fear**
6 Loss	the Void	**Sadness**
7 Restriction	Chaos	**Anger**
8 Rejection	Alienation	**Shame/Contempt**

This is a model of how the Archetypal affect system works in relation to the vicissitudes of life. Although it can be demonstrated that activation of the innate affects recurs throughout the whole of life, it is those constellations that first occur during infancy that have particularly interested developmental theorists, because they provide the first evidence that there is in fact a healthy affective basis to the personality:

The first year of life sees the constellation of all the innate affects in the infant's daily experience . . . [and] it is the empathic responsiveness of the "good enough" parent that provides the modulating effects which make these eruptions of the innate affects bearable and containable.
(L. H. Stewart 1988: 15–16)

It is, therefore, the effectiveness of parents in modifying their infants' affects that allows the latter to integrate them; otherwise they become split-off affect complexes that take on a more pathological character.

The chronic activation of particular complexes

Another source of the individual's experience of emotion is the continuous activation of already structured complexes: "The persistence of a feeling-toned complex naturally has the same constellating effect on the rest of the psyche as an acute affect" (Jung 1960: 43). Even if the innate affect associated with a complex is of such intensity that it cannot be repressed, it may have still either a normal or a pathological effect on the total psychic economy of the person experiencing the complex. When emotion is felt in a normal way it can contribute to a robust and creative affective life; when it is experienced as a debilitating intrusion, it may interfere with the integration of affect and even block or arrest psychological development.

Dynamic properties of archetypal affects

It is important to recognize that the separate innate affects are not identical, either in their dynamics or their content. Each of the archetypal emotions exhibits its own range in level of potential activation, which is always on a continuum that measures the amount of psychological energy associated with the activation (Table I.2).

Table I.2 Intensity of innate affects

Low	Intermediate	High
Interest	Excitement	Fascination
Enjoyment	Joy	Ecstasy
Surprise	Startle	Astonishment
Fear	Terror	Panic
Sadness	Anguish	Agony
Anger	Rage	Fury
Embarrassment/disapproval	Shame/contempt	Humiliation/disgust

The level of emotional energy attained depends on the frequency, intensity, and duration of the activation of the archetypal affect.

The magnitude of the energy charge of the innate affects is expressed in their *autonomy* and *numinosity*, terms that did not originate with Jung but which he emphasized in his writings about complexes and archetypes to emphasize the dynamic emotional qualities of these structures of the psyche.

> It is important to remember that my concept of the archetypes has been frequently misunderstood as denoting inherited ideas or a kind of philosophical speculation. In reality they belong to the realm of instinctual activity and in that sense they represent inherited patterns of psychic behaviour. As such they are invested with certain dynamic qualities which, psychologically speaking, are characterized as "autonomy" and "numinosity."
>
> (Jung 1977: 541)

It is important to realize that as the intensity of emotion increases, so does its autonomy and numinosity, both of which pose a significant threat to the integrative capacities of the individual, because the emotion begins to assume, for the ego, the character of a commanding other that in a sense can't be integrated, but rather must be feared or obeyed. Autonomy, in Jung's usage, refers to the ability of affect-toned complexes to assert themselves irrespective of the wishes of the ego. Numinosity refers to the archetypal character of the affects involved, which have a capacity to grip, thrill, and fascinate, and to evoke such profound emotions as wonder and awe.

Affects in complexes

Jung's formulation of the relation between affects and complexes was straightforward: *"Every affective event becomes a complex"* (Jung 1960: 67, original emphasis). Viewed from the standpoint of their developing structure and dynamics, however, the psychology of complexes is far from simple, particularly in infancy. In his paper "On Psychic Energy," Jung summarized the findings of his first quarter century of thinking about this structuralization of emotion:

> The feeling-toned content, the complex, consists of a nuclear element and a large number of secondarily constellated associations. The nuclear element consists of two components: first, a factor determined by experience and causally related to the environment; second, a factor innate in the individual's character and determined by his disposition.
>
> (Jung 1970a: 10–11)

Eventually, he would speak of the innate factor as the archetypal core of the complex, which for him included evolved capacities for particular emotional expressions of the kind that Darwin had described. From the standpoint of a theory of archetypal emotions, the nuclear element is composed of an Innate Affect and its Primal Image (see Table I.1). Various Life Stimuli can both evoke that image and combine with it to form a symbol, which activates the associated affect. The complexes that result can be described in relation to the archetypal affect involved. There are Interest-complexes, Joy-complexes, Surprise-complexes, Fear-complexes, Sadness-complexes, Anger-complexes, and Shame/Contempt-complexes.

There are also cultural and personal complexes, the nuclear emotion in the former being an archetypal affect assimilated to a cultural form and in the latter an emotion composed by blending of the archetypal affects. These two types of complexes will not concern us in my analysis of eating disorders, but the reader will find in Marjorie McDonald's 1970 article an example of a musical complex in a 5-month-old infant and in L. H. Stewart's 1988 publication a discussion of the blended emotions, Jealousy and Envy.

The difference between normal and pathological complexes can be understood by placing them on two continua. Complexes composed of Interest and Joy would inhabit a continuum with *optimal* (for development) numbers and intensity at the normal end and a critical *decrease* in numbers and intensity at the pathological end. Complexes composed of Fear, Sadness, Anger, and Shame/Contempt would lie along a bell-shaped continuum with optimal numbers and intensity in the middle and a *critical increase* or *decrease* in numbers and intensity at the left and right pathological ends. This is in line with Tomkins's view that the two most general goals or images of human beings with respect to affect are that (a) Positive affect should be maximized and that (b) Negative affect should be minimized.

In another approach to assessing the normality and pathology of organizations of affective experiences, Tomkins has proposed an affect theory with the following types of organizations or models (see Table I.3).

Table I.3 Tomkins's affect theory

Affect theory: Moment of time (Synchronic)	Has the developmental analog of the	Affect theory: Across time (Diachronic)
Monopolistic model	"	Snowball model
Intrusive model	"	Iceberg model
Competition model	"	Co-existence model
Integration model	"	Late bloomer model

Source: Tomkins 1963: 302–4.

The healthiest pattern of emotion organization is achieved through the integration model. In that model, the emphasis is on achieving balance and harmony between the affects.

> In the integration model no single affect theory is permitted to dominate the personality monopolistically, to be suppressed or relegated to the mode of intrusion or permitted to oscillate in competition with alien affect theories. Instead, a modus vivendi is achieved in which there is mutual accommodation between the affects in the interests of a harmonious personality integration. In its analog across time, the late bloomer model, the elements of the past personality may have continued to compete with each other unhappily, in an early competition model which continued into a co-existence model. At some later point in development there is a confrontation of the warring affect theories out of which a harmonious integration is achieved by the late bloomer.
>
> (Tomkins 1963: 303–4)

The most pathological model, by contrast, occurs when the monopolistic model is adopted for the understanding and management of emotion. As I have shown in *Dire Emotions and Lethal Behaviors* (C. T. Stewart 2008), the monopolistic model disrupts the psychic economy by casting other emotions that it cannot accept into shadow. Jung describes the power of emotions when they become powerful complexes that can be activated by chance stimuli to compromise consciousness:

> We see how the psychic energy applies itself wholly to the complex at the expense of the other psychic material, which in consequence remains unused. All stimuli that do not suit the complex undergo a

partial apperceptive degeneration with emotional impoverishment. . . . On the other hand the slightest remark even remotely touching on the complex instantly arouses a violent outburst of anger or pain which may assume pathological proportions.

(Jung 1960: 48)

In other words, the complex, with its one emotionally charged issue and particular affective tone, has taken over the ego, making the normal flexibility of thinking and feeling and a range of emotional options impossible. This formulation allows an assessment of complexes that is at one and the same time, qualitative and quantitative, that is, a monopolistic complex, which may have any of the archetypal affects as its nucleus is also, by definition, of great intensity.

The nuclear element has a constellating power corresponding to its energic value. It produces a specific constellation of psychic contents, thus giving rise to the complex, which is a constellation of psychic contents dynamically conditioned by the energic value. The resultant constellation, however, is not just an irradiation of the psychic stimulus, but a selection of the stimulated psychic contents which is conditioned by the *quality* of the nuclear element. This selection cannot, of course, be explained in terms of energy, because the energic explanation is quantitative and not qualitative. For a causal explanation we must have recourse to the causal view. The proposition upon which the objective estimate of psychological value intensities is based therefore runs as follows: *the constellating power of the nuclear element corresponds to its value intensity, i.e., to its energy.*

(Jung 1970a: 12, original emphasis)

It is the socialization of the innate emotions, first in the family and then in the community and society, that determines both the pattern of complexes and the magnitude of particular complexes (for a comprehensive survey of how each of the innate affects can be socialized both positively and negatively see Tomkins in Demos 1995: 168–95).

During the first year of life, facial expressions, accompanied by vocalizations and body movements, are the clearest indicators of emotional states. We are just beginning to be able to reliably determine when complexes have been constructed during infancy and can anticipate that their nuclear archetypal affects will appear in expressive behaviors. During the second year of life and beyond, the individual's symbolic play, fantasies, and dream reports become the primary source of information about the structure and dynamics of complexes. Jung's use of the Word Association Test led to his initial discovery of feeling-toned complexes and their indicators. Jung comments on the results of the Word Association Test with a schizophrenic patient:

> The most striking thing is the enormous number of perfectly clear complex-constellations. With a few exceptions all the associations are thinly veiled expressions of complexes. . . . From this we can conclude that the psychic activity of the patient is completely taken up by the complex: she is under the sway of the complex, she speaks, acts, and dreams nothing but what the complex suggests to her. . . .
>
> (Jung 1960: 109)

It is not clear at what age a modified Word Association Test might be expected to detect complexes that are being formed during a child's development.

Affects in development

To integrate, rather than be possessed by a complex, to use Jung's deliberate reversion to medieval imagery to describe the regression involved when the ego is no longer stronger than its affect based-complexes, one has to understand and regulate the affects involved. That is actually what occurs, without the need for any assistance by a psychotherapist, in the course of normal development. The developing child goes through a series of stages in which affects come up strongly that are at first unfamiliar to the child (and often as well to the parent, at least as parts of that child) and then are accepted and integrated. The self-healing play of the child is the natural process through which the more troublesome emotions are brought to consciousness and managed. In this way the developing child becomes, in a sense, an affect theorist, having learned to recognize and modify archetypal affect states, thus getting as much of each affect complex into the ego as possible, so as to be able to deal effectively with that affect complex ever after.

In the unconscious at birth there is an ego germ composed of elements that are the nuclei of the higher functions of the ego-complex. One aspect of L. H. Stewart's theory of the Archetypal affect system that contributes to its comprehensiveness is his view that the relation between the innate emotions, the components of the ego germ, and the structures and functions of the ego-complex is the warp and woof of development (see Table I.4, Archetypal Affects and Ego Development).

Table I.4 indicates that the negative or "crisis" affects that inevitably are evoked by the difficulties of human life are put to good use in childhood to provide the motivational dynamic for the development of the functions of consciousness, the cultural attitudes, and the will to engage life with these cognitive and symbolic tools.

In a citation which I have heavily edited, L. H. Stewart made suggestions concerning the relations of the specific crisis emotions to the development of each of the Jungian ego functions:

Table I.4 Archetypal affects and ego development

Archetypal Affect	Ego Function	Cultural Attitude
Joy	Play	Anima
Interest	Exploration	Animus
Surprise	Orientation	Psychological
Fear–Terror	Intuition	Religious
Sadness–Anguish	Sensation	Aesthetic
Anger–Rage	Thinking	Philosophical
Shame/Contempt	Feeling	Social

[I]n the narrowed and concentrated focus of attention caused by a [crisis] affect, one may identify a potential for the development of the [Jungian] ego functions, as follows: the unknown possibilities [that are found] in Terror [foster the development of] Intuition; in Anguish, the once known object of loss [that is missed in ways that can no longer be seen, tasted, touched, heard, or smelled, accelerates the differentiation of] Sensation; the strategies to remove the frustration [involved] in Rage [force us to utilize] Thinking; and the [necessity to engage in the] evaluation of others] to discover whether they can be relied on or are more likely to disappoint can of course lead the child to turn to the strong . . . antipathies of Disgust/Humiliation [but this very turn requires the child to do some] Feeling.

(L. H. Stewart 1986: 201)

Implicitly emphasizing the fact that the crisis affects have another factor of meaning, L. H. Stewart wrote the following about the way typical cultural attitudes arise when crisis affects are activated:

As we know, however, there is another realm in reference to which the system of archetypal affects has evolved, namely the subjective realm of the Self. With respect to the Self, these archetypal affects evoke the age old categories of the Holy, the Beautiful, the True, and the Good, [which were] Kant's Ideas of Reason. As psychological structures these may be thought of as the fourfold Categories of the Imagination. [All four of them] are represented by Henderson's Cultural Attitudes: the Religious, the Aesthetic, the Philosophic and the Social.

(1987b: 137)

The reader will note that the crisis affects of the archetypal system not only foster the development of the individual ego functions but also the kinds of cultural attitudes the person is likely to take up. This is important, because it is the cultural attitudes that shape what the person is willing to introject from the consciousness of others (someone with an aesthetic attitude is willing to listen to music and learn from the experience something about how to develop affect that she/he never would have been able to figure out for herself/himself). Stewart contrasts the cognitive and symbolic development the crisis emotions generate:

> It is not, of course, immediately self-evident just how such highly differentiated systems as Ego Functions and the Cultural Attitudes could possibly have developed from the primary archetypal affective system of apprehension. . . . but we can suggest that the distinction between Ego Functions and Cultural Attitudes is related to two basic aspects of the archetypal experience, namely the *noetic* and the *expressive*. It would appear that the Ego Functions have evolved from the noetic aspect and the Cultural Attitudes from the expressive.
>
> (L. H. Stewart 1987b: 137, original emphasis)

What is less clear in Table I.4 are the developmental functions of the affects of the life instinct, Interest and Joy. In *The Symbolic Impetus* (2001), I demonstrated that these life-enhancing emotions advance development itself. Development of what Jung calls the four functions of consciousness occurs under the aegis of Interest, which includes curiosity and exploration or what a particular consciousness can bring us closer to in the world. The development of cultural attitudes, L. H. Stewart believes, is much more supported by the archetypal affect of Joy, which is behind the kind of fantasy/play that involves making use of opportunities provide by the culture, starting with toys, stories, games, and the like. At the same time, the relationship between Interest and Joy is dialectical, so that we can expect both cultural attitudes and functions of consciousness to develop together as a consequence of that dialectic. In *The Symbolic Impetus*, I presented empirical evidence showing the development from infancy through adolescence of both ego functions and cultural attitudes in psychotherapeutic and normal developmental contexts.

Affects in symbols

From the perspective of Jungian affect theory, the efficient cause of emotion is a symbol, which is composed (very like the word symbolon from which it derives) of two interlocking parts, a conscious component – some life stimulus demanding response – and an unconscious propensity for perceiving and reacting to a stimulus like that in a quite particular way – this is what Jung means by archetype, an innate primal image of a situation that also suggests the way to feel and behave in that situation (see Table I.1).

In his discussion of what he calls in Aristotelian language the "formal" cause of emotion, Hillman foregrounds the symbol: "The primary language of the soul as a whole, the primary way the soul grasps reality, is as symbolic reality. An emotion is the psyche symbolized; it is like a rite, a ceremony. . . . (1992: 274). What this carefully worded definition suggests is that the symbol links conscious and unconscious, ego and archetype, into some kind of wholeness through which the entirety of psyche may be expressed. He elaborates, helpfully, on the correspondence between the form of the evoking symbol and the form of emotional expression:

> Analysis of the forms of emotional behaviour shows appropriate symbols; an encounter with a symbol corresponds to a specific quality and pattern of emotional behaviour. This correspondence of symbol and form is more exact the less the emotion is coloured by subjective consciousness. The more universal the symbol, the more collective the behaviour pattern.
>
> (ibid.: 274)

There are certain parallels between these thoughts of Hillman and Jung's view of the soul, which comes alive when experiencing emotion, as a function of relation between the subject and the inaccessible depths of the unconscious:

> The determining force . . . operating from these depths is reflected by the soul, that is, it creates symbols and images, and itself is only an image. By means of these images the soul conveys the forces of the unconscious to consciousness; it is both receiver and transmitter, an organ for perceiving unconscious contents.
>
> (Jung 1971: 251)

What consciousness perceives, therefore, are symbols of the archetypes expressing the formal qualities of the latter, and also their energy: "But symbols are shaped energies, determining ideas whose affective power is just as great as their spiritual value" (ibid.: 251).

In *Complex/Archetype/Symbol*, Jacobi makes the following distinction, as do other Jungian theorists, between the archetype per se and the symbol that expresses it. The former is what she calls an ectopsychic structure, meaning that it is not within the psyche but actually outside it, though life events can induce it to undergo psychic assimilation, in which case it appears in the form of a symbol:

> As a structure of indefinable contents, as a "system of readiness," "an invisible center of energy," . . . it is . . . a potential symbol, and whenever

a general psychic constellation, a suitable situation of consciousness, is present, its "dynamic nucleus" is *ready to actualize itself and manifest itself as a symbol.*

(1959: 74, original emphasis)

The "energy" of the ectopsychic archetype that drives it into the psyche originates in a "dynamic nucleus" composed of innate affects associated with a primal image. Jung has gone so far as to equate emotion and symbol as co-equal expressions of the archetype when it enters the psyche, and to emphasize that a revitalization of the unconscious itself occurs when this happens: "Instead of observable details with clearly discernible features, it is life itself that wells up in emotions and symbolic ideas. In many cases emotion and symbol are actually one and the same thing" (Jung 1977: 249). Affects, therefore are essential companions of symbols if the archetypes are to do their job of replenishing the self (Jung says "the archetypes appear when the instincts are in danger") and they are essential for psychological development, which is a socialization of the archetype, but impossible without the energy of the archetype. At the same time, they are the basis for all ability to gain insight into these processes that must appear first of all in an unconscious that gives them place: "The unconscious can be reached and expressed only by symbols and for this reason the process of individuation can never do without the symbol" (Jung 1968b: 28). Or, I would add, without the emotional energy that accompanies the symbol. Jung defines an archetype this way: "Archetypes are systems of readiness for action, and at the same time images and emotions" (Jung 1970b: 31).

Finally, a caveat: I wish to express my apology to other theories of affect for an almost total omission of their points of view. I feel that much work is urgently needed to bring into some more workable relation the findings attained from these quite divergent standpoints. My apparent neglect of them here is not a statement of my lack of interest in them or lack of respect for them, but a necessary delimitation of the discussion for the sake of clarity.

In Chapter 1, in consonance with the title of this study, I will set forth my view of the relation between the innate or archetypal emotions and the Hunger–Satiety drive as it pertains to the etiology of those eating disorders discussed in Chapters 2–8.

How emotions condition the Hunger–Satiety drive

Affect–Drive complexes

Is there any other psychic factor, any other basic drive except hunger and its derivatives, that has a similar importance in human psychology? I could not name one.

(C. G. Jung, *Freud and Psychoanalysis*)

To survey the research on eating disorders is to discover that there is no single agreed upon basis for them. The existing findings, however, do permit us to postulate one. I believe the Ariadne thread that can lead us through the labyrinth of the literature on eating disorders can be found in the emotions that the individual patients reported on have unconsciously attached to their eating. If we pick up on the clues as to what these emotions are by following their affective tracks, just as we must do with any complex influencing behavior at an unconscious level, we will discover not only the affects involved, but the way they have pathologically conditioned the normal Hunger–Satiety drive that is part of these patients' biological birthright. We also will be able to understand how the therapies that worked managed to release this innate, natural Hunger–Satiety drive from the crimp of conditioning. This is the way this book will read the literature on eating disorders. We need at the outset, therefore, to unpack what is meant by emotional conditioning of the Hunger–Satiety drive. We assume that the common basis of both pathology and normality are the affects that are brought to bear on the developing individual's feeding situation, and that this can be uncovered by (1) taking a developmental history of the patient's emotions when eating and (2) studying the same emotions when they are displayed in the presence of a therapist. Often we have to read between the lines of what is in the literature to reconstruct either of these, but it can be done. With an understanding of the innate affective system of the infant, which we would designate as the "Archetypal affect system," we can begin to identify which innate affects are being expressed and which are suppressed in the emotions a patient displays around eating. We still need to show, however, how these have affected the functioning of the Hunger–Satiety drive.

Like all drives, the Hunger–Satiety drive is originally a biological structure that is psychologically modified during its functioning so that it becomes an eating complex capable of shaping both feelings and behavior. This is an empirical example of such a process:

> When the nurse took my first child and put him to my breast his tiny mouth opened and reached for me as if he had known forever what to do. He began to suck with such force it took my breath away. I began to *laugh* [emphasis added]. I couldn't help myself. It seemed incredible that such a tiny creature could have such force and determination . . . *Tears of joy* [emphasis added] ran shamelessly down my cheeks while he sucked. I thought back to my past conviction that only when I had a baby would I *know* whatever it was I had to know. Now I *did* know. It is the only important thing I have ever learned, and so ridiculously simple: love exists . . . *There in the midst of all that clinical green and white, I had discovered what love was all about. It was a meeting of two beings* [emphasis added].
>
> (Stevens 1990: 78–79)

In other words, the very being of the child manifested itself to his mother in the process of feeding. Any failure of the mother to respond as she actually did to the expression of his self in the feeding role would have produced a very different complex than the positive one which emerged as a consequence of her reaction. During this infant's early nursing experience, we can postulate that his Hunger–Satiety drive was being conditioned by the mother's Joy at the force of his appetite, and that this helped him to begin to feel his own innate affect of Joy. From then on, his feeding experiences would be structuralized around an unconscious perception that feeding could be a joyous experience. This was the nucleus of this particular child's eating complex.

Here is a contrasting example of another mother feeding her 5-week-old daughter, which presents a rather different emotional patterning. The mother, a bit daunted by her daughter's appetite, is trying to cut down her feedings to the adult cultural standard of three meals a day and has decided to start introducing solid foods so that her baby could go longer between feedings.

> The baby detested this, and with great determination mobilized her tiny forces against it, while her mother, with equal determination, overpowered her and shoved the food into her mouth. . . . Mrs. Portman would hold Belle in her left arm, the baby's right arm pressed against Mrs. Portman's abdomen so it could not move, while Mrs. Portman's left hand held down the baby's left arm. Now, with a baby spoon, Mrs.

Portman pushed food into Belle's mouth, but Belle pushed it out with her tongue. Mrs. Portman would then scrape it off the baby's face with the spoon and shove it back. For every mouthful that Belle finally swallowed, Mrs. Portman had to do this five or six times. . . . As the shoving continued the baby would try to turn its head away but Mrs. Portman was able to partially control this by stiffening the muscles of her left arm. Meanwhile, the baby's entire body would grow stiff and arched *in a state of maximum counter-mobilization against the invasion*. As soon as the bottle [delivering liquid nutrition] was substituted for the shoving process [required to introduce solid food into the baby's digestive system], the baby relaxed.

(Henry 1963: 333–4, original emphasis)

Given the level of her need to control the feeding situation with skillful physical actions, it is more difficult to identify the specific emotions evoked in this mother by feeding, but they are surely present and are conditioning her baby's feedings. It is reasonable to conjecture, that crisis affects, such as Fear, Anger, and Humiliation were constellated respectively by the life stimuli of Unknown expectations, Restriction of autonomy, and Rejection of the baby's own attempts at relatedness. Although the mother may be satisfied at achieving her agenda, it is hard to believe that Joy is present for Belle in these mealtimes.

Jung: psychization of the Hunger–Satiety drive

C. G. Jung uses the term *instinct* in a way that invites a consideration of emotion as well as behavior, but it is not always clear what his own focus is. At times he is referring to behavior-shaping drives, on other occasions to motivating affects, and sometimes to both of these. Although he thinks of the separation of psychology from biology "is purely artificial, because the human psyche lives in indissoluble union with the body" (Jung 1970a: 114), he considers drives as arising originally from outside the psyche, and only secondarily undergoing psychic assimilation. There is thus an internal move from physiology to psychology: "Instinct as an ectopsychic factor would play the role of a stimulus merely, while instinct as a psychic phenomenon would be an assimilation of this stimulus to a pre-existent psychic pattern" (ibid.: 115).

That pre-existing pattern is the archetype, which guides the development of all psychological life. Jung assigns a name to this process: "I should term it *psychization*. Thus, what we call instinct offhand would be a datum already psychized, but of ectopsychic origin" (ibid.: 115, original emphasis). He believes that this formulation makes it possible "to understand the variability of instinct within the framework of its general phenomenology" (ibid.: 115). Because the psyche is not only archetypal but also self-regulating,

> The psychized instinct forfeits its uniqueness to a certain extent, at times actually losing its most essential characteristic – compulsiveness. It is no longer an ectopsychic, unequivocal fact, but has become instead a modification conditioned by its encounter with a psychic datum.
>
> (ibid.: 116)

Referring specifically to psychization of the hunger drive, Jung goes on to say, "For example, no matter how unequivocal the physical state of excitation called hunger may be, the psychic consequences resulting from it can be manifold" (ibid.: 115). He summarizes this perspective as follows:

> Under these circumstances the immediate determining factor is not the ectopsychic instinct but the structure resulting from the interaction of instinct and the psychic situation of the moment [feeding, eating, mealtime]. The determining factor would thus be a *modified* instinct. The change undergone by the instinct is as significant as the difference between the colour we see and the objective wave-length producing it.
>
> (ibid.: 115, original emphasis)

This is a good analogy, for one of the critical attributes of any psychized instinct is that it has affective coloration. Jung noted this in relation to the sexual instinct, in a useful gloss on what Freud had offered in his writings: "The sexual instinct enters into combinations with many different feelings, emotions, affects, with spiritual and material interests to such a degree that, as is well known, the attempt has been made to trace the whole of culture to these combinations" (ibid.: 116–17). During psychic assimilation, the hunger drive is similarly conditioned and generalized by the innate affects, so that eating in effect becomes everything to those who focus on it. Another way of understanding this totalizing phenomenon that accompanies the integration of the hunger instinct into everyday eating psychology is Jung's insistence that psychization means assimilation of the instinct into a pre-existent psychic pattern. Thus the archetypes, the patterns for behavior that are already present in the individual, are ways of digesting the experience of the instincts, and they contribute to the structure of the complexes that are our way of biting into the empirical experience of the world that feeds us. Psychic assimilation, therefore, involves imaging of the instinct: "Every psychic process is an image and an "imagining," otherwise no consciousness could exist and the occurrence would lack phenomenality" (Jung 1970c: 544). When a drive such as hunger undergoes psychization the images formed may be more generally mythological or more idiosyncratically personal, but they are definitely always fantasies that have an archetypal character:

> Hunger makes food into gods. Certain Mexican tribes even give their food-gods an annual holiday to allow them to recuperate, and during this time the staple food is not eaten. The ancient Pharaohs were worshipped as eaters of gods. Osiris is the wheat, the son of the earth, and to this day the Host must be made of wheat-meal, i.e., a god to be eaten, as also was Iachhos, the mysterious god of the Eleusinian mysteries. The bull of Mithras is the edible fruitfulness of the earth.
>
> (Jung 1970a: 155)

The same mythological process accompanies the psychization of any instinct:

> Like the physical conditions of his environment, the physiological conditions, glandular secretions, etc., also can arouse fantasies charged with affect. Sexuality appears as a god of fertility, as a fiercely sensual, feminine daemon, as the devil himself with Dionysian goat's legs and obscene gestures, or as a terrifying serpent that squeezes its victims to death.
>
> (ibid.: 155)

Indeed, as Hillman has noted, "Whatever we know of instinct in ourselves has already been through the process of psychization. We have only those perceptions of instinct which have been filtered through the prism of our psyche" (1972: 32–3).

Walter B. Cannon: appetite and the Hunger–Satiety drive

The great physiologist, Walter B. Cannon, first became interested in the emotional states associated with the hunger drive during a series of researches on the mechanical factors attending digestion: "The conditions favorable to proper digestion are wholly abolished when unpleasant feelings such as vexation and worry and anxiety, or great emotions such as anger and fear, are allowed to prevail" (1929/1970: 8).

This recognition led Cannon to consider the difference between hunger and appetite. He concluded that hunger originates in the internal experience of gastric contraction, which for many people is the unmistakable signal that it is time to eat again. Appetite, on the other hand, is aroused by external stimuli associated with the preparation and presentation of food:

Careful observation indicates that appetite is related to previous sensations of taste and smell of food. Delightful or disgusting tastes and odors, associated with this or that edible substance, determine the appetite. It has, therefore, important psychic elements in its composition. Thus, by taking thought, we can anticipate the odor of a delicious beefsteak or the taste of peaches and cream, and in that imagination we can find pleasure. In the realization, direct effects in the senses of taste and smell give still further delight.

(ibid.: 269)

From my standpoint, however, it is the psychic assimilation of the hunger drive that accounts for the fantasies associated with appetite. This is not to deny the importance of external stimuli, but it is to insist on the psychic elements involved in their reception by any individual. The hunger drive, in its fullest definition, might be designated as the Hunger/Appetite/Start Eating–Satiety/Fullness/Stop Eating Drive. On the other hand, the subjective experience of "Fullness" or "Emptiness" that usually controls individual decisions to eat is shaped by the way the hunger drive has been psychized. When we refer to the hunger drive as the Hunger–Satiety drive it is important for the reader to remember that this drive is only identified indirectly on the basis of experience.

Emotional conditioning of the Hunger–Satiety drive

We have, therefore, to examine how both the hunger drive and the feeling of having had enough to eat to satisfy it are conditioned by emotions. In the 1920s, Cannon reviewed all the extant research to date and expressed his conviction that hunger results from contractions of the alimentary canal. Direct proof for this hypothesis, however, was still lacking. His own research into the temporal association between gastric contractions and sensations of hunger at the same time was able to provide the scientific proof he was seeking: "The close concomitance of the [gastric] contractions with hunger pangs, clearly indicated that they are the real source of those pangs" (Cannon 1929/1970: 292). He could conclude: "Hunger, in other words, is normally the signal that the stomach is contracted for action; the unpleasantness of hunger . . . leads to eating; eating starts gastric digestion and abolishes the sensation" (ibid.: 296).

Now he could turn his attention to appetite. Cannon examined the influence of the affects on the Hunger–Satiety drive by recording their effects on gastric contractions: "They cease during intense emotional states such as joy, fear and anger" (ibid.: 293). He cited an example published by Muller, which describes the case of a young woman whose lover had broken the engagement of marriage: "She wept in bitter sorrow for several days, and during that time vomited whatever food she took" (ibid.: 344). It is reasonable to assume that, in common with many who feel betrayed by a loved one, the archetypal affect, Humiliation/Disgust, had overtaken her psyche making it impossible to find any form of food other than nauseating. Cannon concluded:

> From the evidence just given it appears that any high degree of excitement in the central nervous system, whether felt as anger, terror, pain, anxiety, joy, grief or deep disgust, is likely to break over the threshold of the sympathetic nervous division and disturb the functions of all the organs which that division innervates.
>
> (ibid.: 344–5)

Tomkins: drive–affect interactions

Tomkins introduces his discussion of drive–affect relations with this statement: "We begin our examination of the drive system with the assumption that what has passed for drive for centuries was in fact a drive–affect assembly" (Tomkins 1962: 88). Although Tomkins does not identify the process by which a drive–affect assembly is constructed, it is reasonable to assume that he has a process similar to psychization in mind. He writes that it is the structurally based generality of affects that makes it possible to co-assemble with drives: "One can invest any and every aspect of existence with the magic of excitement and joy or with dread or fear or shame or distress" (Tomkins 1991: 71).

Tomkins stated categorically that the drive system must be amplified by the affect system before it has sufficient motivational power. This is because affects are capable of much greater generality of intensity than drives; "The affect system is therefore the primary motivational system because without its amplification, nothing else matters — and with its amplification, anything else *can* matter" (ibid.: 6, original emphasis). The urgency of the sexual drive is created by its affect amplifier: "Sexuality without the affective amplification of excitement, however, makes a paper tiger of the penis" (Tomkins 1981: 53). He suggests that the information gained in the affective response that accompanies the drive is general in nature:

> We are suggesting that affect serves the purpose of a general amplifier in the motivational system, intensifying the drive which it accompanies. The drive mechanism ordinarily is conceived to lack nothing essential in intensity and motivational urgency. However, part of the seeming urgency of the drive state is, in fact, a consequence of an affective response, which ordinarily amplifies, but may under certain conditions modulate, attenuate, interfere with, or even reduce, the primary drive signal.
>
> (Tomkins 1962: 45–6)

In his discussion of the affect–hunger drive assembly, Tomkins notes that amplification of the drive may be positive or negative. If the drive is amplified by Interest, it produces an overall experience of delight rather than distress. "If, while waiting for a slow waitress in a crowded restaurant, such impatience is replaced by conversation which instigates positive affect, the hunger pains lose much of their urgency" (ibid.: 49). These are Cannon's *pleasant feelings*.

Amplification by crisis emotions can interfere with or reduce the Hunger–Satiety drive: "Disgust, fear, distress and apathy, depending upon their intensity, will either modulate, mask, attenuate, interfere with or completely inhibit the hunger drive" (ibid.: 50). Fear-induced "butterflies" in the stomach attenuate the stomach contractions or salivation characteristic of hunger. It has been demonstrated that in depressive psychoses the digestive process is long delayed.

Whether the amplification of the hunger drive is accompanied by positive or negative emotions, a complex is formed:

> Last and not least of the earliest of social communion is the enjoyment of the eating complex. We say eating complex rather than eating, because it is the combination of the relief from the pain of hunger, the relief from the cry of distress, and the pleasure of eating which combine with the presence of the loving, feeding mother which evokes the smile of enjoyment of this complex. Theoretically, either the reduction of hunger pain or the cry of distress is sufficient to make the act of eating not only pleasurable in its stimulation of the receptors of the mouth, but also enjoyable with no social reference whatever. In earliest experience, however, the presence of the feeding mother guarantees that for some time the smile of enjoyment is to the whole eating complex, which includes both social and non-social objects of enjoyment as well as both positively enjoyed objects and the reduction of negative experience. Thenceforth, eating together may become a primary mode of social communion, and even solitary eating may serve as a symbol of such communion and serve to reduce the distress of loneliness.
>
> (Tomkins 1962: 424–5)

Tomkins contrasts the affective amplification of the hunger drive in Anorexia and Bulimia: "In pure anorexia, terror is restricted to the act of taking in, to becoming full" (Tomkins 1991: 551). In the binge–purge cycles of Bulimia, on the other hand, "there is combined both terror and disgust at taking in as well as at having taken in and therefore vomiting forth – what one wanted but also did not want" (ibid.: 551). Tomkins suggests that when Bulimia and Anorexia are cyclical "there are many different types of reciprocal magnification of fear and nausea and disgust" (ibid.: 552). He has also emphasized the importance of Positive and Negative affect ratios in drive amplification.

Affect ratios and conditioning of the Hunger–Satiety drive

Tomkins has stated that two of the most general goals of human beings with respect to affect are (a) to maximize Positive affect (PA), Interest and Joy, and (b) to minimize Negative affect (NA), Fear, Sadness, Anger, and Shame/Contempt. [It is necessary to qualify (b) by indicating there must be a minimum level of these emotions as they are the raw materials for construction of the ego-complex.]

Demos

Virginia Demos, who has edited the most comprehensive review of Tomkins's works (1995), has realized the importance of affect ratios in parent–child interactions. In "Empathy and Affect: Reflections on Infant Experience," Demos (1984) has presented her operational view of these principles in infancy. Her subjects were mother–infant pairs videotaped biweekly in their own homes, two pairs beginning at two weeks and four pairs beginning at six months. She is in agreement with Tomkins "that the human organism strives to maximize opportunities for positive experience and to minimize opportunities for negative ones" (Demos 1984: 14). Her results will contribute to our understanding of the significance of PA/NA or NA/PA ratios during the first year of life.

Of the six types of caregiver–infant exchanges that Demos identified, only the most and least ideal will concern us here. She reports this of the Type 1 pattern:

> In the ideal paradigm the mother correctly perceives and understands the stimulus, the infant's affective state, and the intention or plan represented in the infant's behaviors; she then responds in a way that communicates her empathy — facilitating or prolonging the infant's positive states of interest and enjoyment, or trying to reduce and end the infant's negative states of distress, fear, shame, or anger by comforting the infant or removing the offending stimulus.
>
> (ibid.: 19)

Parents who behave in this way are intuitively following the two principles just enunciated. Parents are in the best position to establish and maintain this type of field when they are bonded with their infant and experiencing a spontaneous flow of Interest and Joy to the baby. A PA/NA ratio then exists in which Positive affects predominate over Negative affects.

The most salient characteristic of the Type 6 pattern, which is less fleshed out, was the caregiver who "does not seem to notice or respond to the child, although the child is present in the room and may be seeking a response" (ibid.: 30). For a parent not to notice their baby, parent–infant bonding, that is the parent–infant Interest–Joy field, must be at a minimum. Under these circumstances, a NA/PA ratio in which Negative affects predominate over Positive affects will exist.

In "A Prospective Constructionist View of Development" (1989a) and "Resiliency in Infancy" (1989b), Demos drew upon parent–infant interactions in subjects who had participated in a longitudinal study to analyze affect sequences. She indicated that although a number of sequences are possible her focus would be on positive–negative–positive and positive– negative–negative sequences. She found that when the former pattern predominates, the child learns PA can be reestablished and NA can be managed, through integration into the developmental process, I would add.

> The four families in our longitudinal sample that produced the most well-functioning, resilient children all shared two characteristics that were either not present or were present to a more limited degree in the other families. They maximized opportunities for the shared experience of positive affects, and they were quick to reestablish shared positive affect whenever there was a break, e.g., an angry scolding, or an experience of negative affect by the child. Thus they were frequently engaged in creating positive–negative–positive affective sequences.
>
> (Demos 1989a: 300–1)

The ratio of PA/NA in these conditions favors Positive affects.

There were six families on the other hand, who produced predominately positive–negative–negative affective experiences.

> By contrast, families 2, 4, 8, 12, 13, and 19 consistently interfered with or failed to support their children's interests and enjoyments, and compounded and intensified their children's negative states with shaming, punishment, abandonment, or lack of support. Thus, for all of these children, positive affects in interaction with parents almost always led to negative consequences; all of these children, in their own way, gradually constricted and inhibited their interests and enjoyments in an attempt to control, prevent, or minimize the possibilities for experiencing distress, anger, shame, or fear.
>
> (Demos 1989b: 21)

For these children, the NA/PA ratio favors Negative affects. Those children with positive–negative–positive sequences would be more likely to construct complexes with Positive affects as their nuclei and to have reduced the magnitude of complexes with Negative nuclear affects. Infants' habitual restriction of Interest and Joy would inevitably lead to a general stunting of psychological development and pathological psychization of the Hunger–Satiety drive by NA.

Tronick and Gianino

The studies of mother–infant interaction by Gianino and Tronick (1988) and Tronick (1989) demonstrated patterns like those of Demos. These researchers referred to the positive parent–child interactions as "matches" and negative ones as "mismatches." These sequences were followed by repair or non-repair of the mismatches:

> During a normal interaction, positive affect is generated by well-regulated exchanges, and negative affect is generated by mismatched exchanges. Both positive and negative affect manifest themselves in affective expressions and, motivationally, in interactive behavior. Specifically, the infant's expressions of joy and interest indicate his positive emotional evaluation of the ongoing interaction and communicate to the partner that she should interact or continue to engage in what she is doing (Tronick, Als, & Adamson, 1978). The infant's negative appraisal of a mismatched interaction (Campos et al., 1983) — manifested in distress, anger, and sadness — signals to the partner to change her behavior. Together, positive and negative affect enable the infant to regulate the interaction to achieve mutual regulation. As noted earlier, however, this is true with one qualification. The infant's affective displays regulate the interaction when he is with a sensitive partner who is willing to modify her own behavior to match her reading of his communications.
>
> (Gianino and Tronick 1988: 50)

It was clear to the researchers that the patterns with repair and non-repair have different effects:

> In normal interactions, the infant experiences periods of interactive success and interactive error and frequent reparations of those errors. Emotionally, the infant experiences periods of positive affect and negative affect and frequent transformations of negative to positive affect; hence, experiences of negative emotion are brief. In abnormal interactions, the infant experiences prolonged periods of interactive failure and negative affect, few interactive repairs, and few transformations of negative to positive affect.
>
> (Tronick 1989: 116)

Let us recall, "Every affective event becomes a complex."

Gottman and Levenson

John Gottman and Robert Levenson (1999) referred to one of the models they developed to predict the deterioration of affective marital interaction and divorce over a 4-year period as a ratio model.

> [This model] predicts that, to the extent that there is a low ratio of positive to negative affect at Time-1, there will be evidence of a Time-2 of the cascade toward divorce. This is a balance theory of marriage, which suggests that since negative affect is endemic to all marital conflict (regardless of marital quality), the marriage will work to the extent that this negative affect is balanced by positive affect. Gottman (1994) reported that, in three different marital types, stable marriages had a 5:1 ratio of positivity to negativity during conflict, whereas in unstable marriages the ratio was .8:1.
>
> (Gottman and Levenson 1999: 145)

Robert W. Levenson carried out research that found support for the value of the positive–negative–positive affect sequence at the physiological level: "Results indicated that the cardiovascular arousal associated with fear did in fact dissipate more quickly when it was followed by the contentment film than by the sad or neutral films. Thus, the notion of positive affect as an efficient autonomic '*undoer*' received some preliminary support" (1994: 257, original emphasis).

Nielsen

Tore Nielsen (1991) set out to find if Positive and Negative affect sequences in dreams were or were not random. This is what he concluded:

> The sequencing of N and P affects in dreams is not random. NN affect pairs in dreams are relatively more frequent – and much more frequent than in waking event reports. Moreover, within scenes in dream reports, an N affect is more likely to follow a P affect than to precede it. This suggests that, in some respects, dream reports may be even more structured than waking event reports. The relative prevalence of PN pairs in dreams may reflect an organizational propensity to introduce negative affect scene-wise into a narrative structure.
>
> (Nielsen 1991: 163)

We know that one of the functions of dreams is to bring to consciousness positive and negative emotions that require conscious attention and at the same time facilitate their integration into the developmental process.

In Chapter 2, we will observe the results of psychization of the Hunger–Satiety drive by both positive and negative emotions in an infant suffering from the eating disorder known as Failure to Thrive.

Thriving and not thriving during earliest infancy

Parent–infant bonding

A life-threatening eating disorder of infancy is psychogenic or nonorganic Failure to Thrive (PFTT). The syndrome is characterized by the infant's growth curve falling below the third percentile of what is normally seen. At times this grave nutritional state is irreversible and may result in death of the infant due to starvation. Its psychogenesis is most often attributed to a lack of "good enough" parental care.

In this chapter, I will discuss a case report drawn from Selma Fraiberg's (1980) *Clinical Studies in Infant Mental Health*, which concerns an unmarried, 17-year-old mother, Beth, and her infant daughter, Trudy. When Trudy was four and a half months months old, she was diagnosed with PFTT characterized by unhappy feedings, frequent vomiting, lack of vitality, and a growth curve below the third percentile. I will show that Trudy's eating disorder resulted from a lack of emotional conditioning of her Hunger–Satiety drive by Positive affects coming from her mother and that this deficit resulted from a more basic failure of parent–infant bonding. The cure of Trudy's eating disorder during one month of psychotherapy, which included both of them, resulted from regeneration of a symbolic mother–infant bond. My analysis of this case will consist of an amplification and specification of the therapist's views from the standpoint of affective consequences.

In discussing how it was possible in one month to help Beth establish happy feedings for Trudy, her therapist explained the work as having two phases: In the first period, she was able to help Beth integrate the negative emotions resulting from past traumas and feel herself valued by her therapist. In the second phase, doors were opened which made it possible for Beth to sustain her expressions of positive affect toward Trudy.

Birth to six months: the onset of Trudy's failure to thrive

Trudy was a healthy, seven pound infant when she was born after a normal pregnancy and delivery. Since Beth was unmarried, she had planned to place Trudy up for adoption, but changed her mind and, after her adoptive mother refused to let her return home with her granddaughter, moved with Trudy into low-cost housing.

This was heroic on Beth's part, but it didn't enable her to bring an adequately secure level of mothering to Trudy. At one month of age, Trudy was already eating and sleeping poorly, crying and vomiting. At two months, she was placed in a day-care nursery so Beth could return to high school. There was a progressive decline in her growth curve, so that by the time she was four and a half months old it had fallen below the third percentile, the cut off for diagnosis of PFTT. There was now concern about Trudy's very survival and Trudy was placed in the hospital. During this ten-day hospitalization, Beth was sullen and defiant in relation to the doctors who had called her ability to care for her child into question and seldom visited Trudy. When feedings by the hospital staff were no more successful than Beth's in helping Trudy gain weight, she was returned to Beth and both were referred to the Child Development Project. Her prospective therapist, Ms A, had difficulty making initial contact with Beth, whose high school never knew when she might be showing up to drop off or to retrieve Trudy. Contact was finally made when Trudy was six months old. When her pediatrician let Ms A know that Beth and Trudy had a clinic appointment, Ms A was able to get there before they left.

First treatment visit: Beth begins to develop rapport

In the first therapy visit in the Pediatric clinic, this is what Ms A observed: "Trudy was a desolate sight. Her tattered clothes were damp from vomit. Scraggly hair framed a gaunt, weary face. Beth was cornered, glowering at the hospital staff . . . who could even take her baby away" (Adelson and Fraiberg 1980: 223). Although Beth felt cornered, furious, and mistrustful, Ms A's ready acceptance of her feelings enabled Beth to make two office visits in the next week. With Ms A's help, Beth has begun to integrate the crisis affects evoked by the adoptive mother's Rejection.

Second and third treatment visits: Trudy's "awful smile"

The prelude to these sessions required Ms A to further demonstrate her acceptance of Beth's negative transference – Beth changed meeting times, asked for Trudy's hospital records, had Ms A summon the hospital social worker so she could rebuke her, and even insisted on bringing the day-care counselor to the therapy appointment as a witness.

Ms A passed all these tests by staying open, flexible, and available, but Trudy continued to be in dire straits. At each visit, Trudy lay on the couch vomiting and drifting to sleep with open, glassy eyes. Because Beth's rough handling of Trudy tended to make her cry, Beth took to leaving her daughter alone and untended even when she vomited or soiled herself. Beth appeared to be in a thoroughly negative state in the face of her daughter's inability to thrive, which was always underscored by the therapist's witnessing that this was the case. As Beth's fear increased and she became despairing, she became confused and, at times, her thinking verged on the bizarre. The day-care counselor could sometimes calm Trudy briefly, but at such times she smiled with the awful smile of a baby with Marasmus, Renee Spitz's (1951) term for the child who has managed to survive but has the unchanged expectation of continuous emotional deprivation, and has learned to grin and bear this. Ms A gave no advice but expressed her wish to understand how this situation had come about and said Beth could talk to her and she would listen.

Fourth treatment visit: Beth's numinous moment of "awe"

This time Beth came alone and when Ms A encouraged her to talk about her early years, she learned that Beth herself had once been a starving child. She had been abandoned on the street, without food, in a country ravaged by war. She was placed in an orphanage and, when two and a half years old, adopted by an American couple. She was described as unhappy and difficult: "She ate poorly and vomited. She was fearful and cried a good deal, but she could not be held or comforted. There were sleeping problems, then behavior problems, and eventually learning problems" (ibid.: 222).

Near tears, Beth went on to relate to Ms A the reactions she had on becoming a mother, her decision to keep Trudy, and her devastating Rejection by her adoptive mother, who yelled at Beth that she had nothing to give her daughter and would not be allowed to keep her. Although deeply hurt, Beth had hidden her anguish, taken Trudy, and moved out. With Ms A's support of her ego, Beth has begun to integrate and resolve the archetypal crisis affects – Terror, Anguish, Rage, Humiliation/Disgust – evoked by both her biological and her adoptive mothers. This is the "opening of the doors" that Ms A thought enabled Beth to begin to express positive emotions toward Trudy.

Beth was then able to think about her decision to keep her baby. She had not intended to, but found that she could not repeat what had been done to her by both her mothers. Another experience had also contributed to her decision not to abandon Trudy. After making sure Ms A was accepting of her continuing need to talk, she reviewed the delivery of the baby: "As she spoke, she seemed to glow; her voice was touched with awe. She said that when the baby was born and she heard the baby cry, it was a feeling too hard to describe, a feeling she would never forget" (ibid.: 225). Ms A thought that through her very existence and her cry, Trudy had made a compelling claim on Beth.

The "awe" that Beth recalled being evoked by Trudy's birth had been Beth's first step in bonding with Trudy as a "Wonder-child," but this event had been buried beneath the negative emotions evoked by her adoptive mother's Rejection of her. This meant that the emotional components of such a symbolic image, the affects of the life instinct, Interest and Joy, which are the source of the numinous "glow," or aura, and the numinous "awe," that accompany the image of the "Wonder-child," were not embracing Beth and her daughter. In Chapter 1 of *The Symbolic Impetus* (2001), I analyze the way the development of the parent–infant bonding process in pregnancy culminates with this image of the "Wonder-child" and the archetypal affects of the life instinct, Interest and Joy, that enliven it.

But in Beth's case, the constellation of the archetypal affect of awe had soon been followed by a recognition of how her own birth had been handled by her mother, and she was soon caught in the traumatic discrepancy between the ideal she had briefly glimpsed in Trudy and the bitter reality of her own remembered infancy. Beth ended this fourth visit by asking Ms A if she would help her deal with Trudy's screaming, which made her very tense and almost beside herself. Ms A agreed to her request, and thought this a further indication that Beth was developing a positive transference to her as someone who might be able to help Beth find her "awe" again in Trudy.

Fifth treatment visit: a first happy feeding

Beth, however, was not home at the time of the next visit and the hospital called to tell Ms A that Trudy was losing weight. Ms A, recognizing that a crisis was looming, went immediately to Beth's apartment. Beth was there and let her in. There were trash bags in the living room. Beth was evidently cold toward Trudy to the point of ignoring her. There were some friends of Beth in the room and Ms A learned that the doctor had told these friends that he wanted Trudy to be given whole milk. There was no sign that the order was being carried out, and Ms A sensed that Beth was often not troubling to feed Trudy. When she did follow her own idea of a proper regimen, Ms A realized that Beth was diluting Trudy's milk in an attempt to stop her vomiting, but ended up starving her baby. Ms A became even more alarmed when she asked Beth when Trudy had eaten last and discovered Beth was completely out of touch, for she vaguely suggested maybe yesterday or the day before. Trudy is now 6 months, 22 days old.

One of the male friends of Beth who was visiting said that one of Beth's brother's had told him that Beth herself had screamed and screamed when she was a baby. Hearing this, Beth became furious. She described the long, terrible trip from the orphanage to her new home in America, when she was only two years old. She didn't know anyone in this new setting and nobody could understand her – she was terrified. Ms A responded to him with a comment that was intended to establish a link "between that screaming child who was now a mother and her screaming, neglected baby" [who was Ms A's other patient] (Adelson and Fraiberg 1980: 226). She thought Beth heard her and understood the double reference. Whether because of Ms A's comment or for another reason associated with Ms A's enabling presence, Beth began to reflect and asked Ms A: "Could memories from long, long ago, memories that are forgotten, still be in the back of someone's head?" (ibid.: 226). She asked if a mother's tension and past anxieties could get passed on to a baby. Although Beth was beginning to re-experience some of her own traumatic past and to see how it was affecting her behavior in the present, and in the previous visit had begun to experience a symbolic bond with Trudy, she was still having great difficulty feeding her.

At the heart of Beth's inability to master the feeding of the difficult Trudy was her own inability in getting past her own Disgust, Anguish, and Rage. These archetypal affects had been activated by her adoptive mother's Rejection and were still very much alive in the form of acute complexes. The adoptive mother's Rejection had also reactivated the Disgust, Anguish, and Rage complexes resulting from Rejection by her own mother when she was two years old. Because both the acute and chronic Rejection–Humiliation/Disgust, Loss–Agony, and Restriction–Rage complexes were still roiling in her unconscious, she could not nourish her child. In terms of life-enhancing affect, what she could not do was access the Interest in feeding her child and the Joy in discovering how to do so. Trudy's Hunger–Satiety Drive, in turn, was being poisoned by these Negative affects that she was imbibing from her mother, and so the infant too was not accessing Joy and Interest in feeding, and instead could only throw up. We can assume that Ms A was also struggling with intense affectivity as she came upon a terrifying clinical situation that could easily have resulted in Trudy's death. It was to her eternal credit that she chose to appear on this scene unannounced to see for herself what was happening. Jung often emphasized that developmental realization cannot be successful if the recognition of the intention of the unconscious does not lead to meaningful action:

> [T]he therapeutic method of complex psychology consists on the one hand in making as fully conscious as possible the constellated uncon-scious contents, and on the other hand synthesizing them with con-sciousness through the act of recognition. Since, however, civilized man possesses a high degree of dissociability . . . it is by no means a foregone

conclusion that recognition will be followed by appropriate action. On the contrary, we have to reckon with the singular ineffectiveness of recognition and must therefore insist on a meaningful application of it.

(Jung 1969: 40)

This is precisely what Ms A did with her understanding of the dilemma faced by both Beth and Trudy. When Trudy wakened, although it was clear that Beth could not read her hunger signals, Ms A could, and acted accordingly. She told Beth that the baby must be very hungry, as she had not eaten for a long time. She observed negative emotions rise in Beth as she began to feed her daughter, and how ready Trudy was to give up and go back to sleep without eating.

> I crouched beside them and worked to prevent a disruption, to help the essential exchange continue. I spoke aloud for mother and for baby, playing both parts. I provided the signals, established the rhythm, named the delicious pleasure. It was a silly mundane monologue: "Mom, I liked that and I'm ready for some more." "Isn't that a good baby, to open her mouth so wide?" "Won't she grow to be beautiful, eating all the good food that Mommy gives her?" "Such a good girl!" I sensed that Beth took all these comments as being addressed to her. Toward the end of the feeding, I became quiet because Beth was starting to imitate me. She called the baby "good girl" and made small "num num" sounds to her. Beth opened her own mouth with each spoonful she gave to Trudy. She was joined [with Trudy] in the act of feeding and was enjoying her baby's satisfaction, if only for these few brief moments. Beth kept going through the pitiful remains in three encrusted jars, about half a cup altogether. Trudy ate it all, with no spitting up.
>
> (Fraiberg 1980: 227–8)

What Ms A catalyzed in this effective intervention was the "meaningful application" of her intuitive understanding that Trudy's Hunger–Satiety drive needed to be psychized through the parent–infant bond by Positive affects. Ms A's modeling mediation of this need resulted in a major advance: Beth's first successful feeding of Trudy. Ms A does not identify the speech register she used in addressing Beth and Trudy, but we can almost hear it. Structurally, the "silly mundane monologue" is baby talk, known more formally as Infant-directed speech (IDS). Beth's adoption of this way of speaking to her infant was a major step in this mother's ability to translate into meaningful action her emerging feeling of emotional connection to her infant that surfaced with the previous week's rediscovery of her "awe" at Trudy's birth. Trudy had now become, through Beth's symbolic apprehension and bonding ("num num"), her "Wonder-child."

This was not the only breakthrough. Before this fifth visit was over, Beth told Ms A that Trudy's crying made her so uncomfortable, angry, and even furious, that she wanted to get rid of her. One can hear in this confession several of the emotions all of us experience when we are near the end of our particular ropes: Fear, Sadness, Anger, and Shame/Contempt. These are what theorists of emotion call the "crisis affects," all of which are archetypal. For Beth to verbalize their presence to Ms A was essential to her being able to experience them in a human way. Otherwise she would have gone on enacting her unconscious rejection and abandonment of Trudy by de facto allowing her baby to starve for fear of the negative consequences of trying to feed her. This negative parental behavior had given this mother no pleasure at all: it had left her sad, angry, contemptuous of her child, and ashamed of herself. Yet saying that she felt like giving up on her baby was an essential symbolic communication that was central to Beth's advance beyond this frozen archetypal affective position. Here is how Ms A received the communication. Having heard Beth out, Ms A made her a promise: "I would do all I could to find a way to help her with these frightening feelings, to find relief, to keep things safe for her and her baby" (ibid.: 228).

> I suggested a plan for the rest of the week. I would come at lunchtime each day to help Beth and Trudy have a quiet feeding, to keep the food in Trudy's stomach. The next medical checkup would show us if it worked. If it did not work, we would think of something else. Beth said I was welcome any time.
>
> (ibid.: 228–9)

Sixth to tenth treatment visits: Trudy is cured of failure to thrive

During the next week, with visits occurring on a daily basis, Ms A was able to listen day by day to Beth's fears for Trudy and herself and to help Beth learn to feed her baby more gently, with the happy result that Trudy did not spit up all week. When weighed at the clinic, Trudy had gained nine ounces. Ms A recorded Beth's reaction:

> At first Beth could not believe it. Then as the good news was repeated, she was beside herself with excitement. She came to me to have her long hair brushed from her face. Then, with Trudy sitting high on her shoulders, Beth dashed to the mirror to see herself and her baby together. She said, "Look, Trudy. Say, 'I'm so happy! I feel so good!'"
>
> (ibid.: 229)

It is significant that Beth said this to Trudy, not to Ms A. Beth's symbolic relatedness with her daughter had expanded beyond just feedings: more sharing of Interest, "Look, Trudy" and more Joy, "I'm so happy!" This mother's life-enhancing libido affects were bubbling up from the unconscious, along with the self-portrait of these emotions, the image of the "Wonder-child," who could grow and develop and by doing so reflect her mother's competence. Within this reciprocal field of archetypal affects, Trudy is starting to thrive. The rapidity of her cure suggests that the pathological eating complex she developed during the negative psychization of her Hunger–Satiety drive was of a relatively small magnitude.

Eleventh treatment visit: Beth is cured of anorexia

The eleventh visit came when Trudy was seven months old. At this point, Beth's eating, not Trudy's, was more the focus. Ms A had become increasingly concerned about Beth's self-starvation: "In truth, I was very concerned about Beth herself. She seemed anorexic and often out of touch" (ibid.: 229). Ms A presents the following account of how she had used food as a diagnostic tool during the previous sixth through tenth visits:

> At every visit I brought a variety of baby foods to help us discover Trudy's preferences. I also brought a simple lunch for Beth and myself. Trudy was fed and I ate. But Beth was unable to feel her own hunger; she ate one piece of celery, one slice of green pepper. Each day I left the untouched food with her.
>
> (ibid.: 230)

Ms A was watching for an awakening of Beth's appetite as a further indication of emerging positive affect. During the eleventh visit, the developmental transformation occurred: "Beth welcomed me with a picnic feast. She was humorous, delighted with herself, pleased by my deliberately open pleasure in the food she was giving her therapist. She made a fine sandwich and ate it all" (ibid.: 230). Ms A had helped Beth to associate mealtimes with positive emotions to such a degree that Beth's Hunger–Satiety drive had found a place in her life. Delightful mealtimes now followed for her. Beth's integration into consciousness of both the acute and chronic mother complexes had restored her contact with the healthy emotional basis of her psyche, so we can expect she will begin to "thrive."

During the next weeks, Trudy's progress, though not linear, was unmistakable. Her weight gain continued as did her psychological development: "She became lively, happier, and prettier. Her vocalizations became more normal. In her walker she scooted about after her mother, exploring things along the way. Trudy invited more social responses, and Beth could not always resist" (ibid.: 232). Treatment for Beth would continue, however, until Trudy was three years old, at which time Beth married and the family moved to Europe. But the therapeutic relationship was not over. For the next year, Ms A received letters containing positive reports of Trudy's progress.

Chapter 3

A new view of the etiology of Anorexia and Bulimia

Dissociation of the Hunger–Satiety drive

It is by disease that health is pleasant; by evil that good is pleasant; by hunger, satiety, by weariness, rest.

(P. Wheelwright, 1974, *Heraclitus, Fragment 99*)

The reader noting the title of this chapter may wonder, after all that has been written on the subjects of Bulimia nervosa (hereafter BN) and Anorexia nervosa (hereafter AN), whether a new theory of these conditions is really needed. It will also not have escaped the reader's notice that this chapter not only offers such a theory, but also promises to take care of both conditions with it. Given all the work that has gone into distinguishing BN and AN from each other as separate eating disorder syndromes, whether or not they occur in the same person, can it be credible that the two have a common basis and may even be the same Janus-faced syndrome? This chapter will try to demonstrate to you that they are in fact results of a common etiology and that to argue this is only common sense. As to whether they are the same syndrome, I fully allow for the branching of symptom choice at different moments in the evolution of eating disorders, even if the root is the same. This enables me to continue to learn from all the literature built around thinking of these conditions as separate syndromes. I will argue that these separate clinical pictures are in fact simply branches of one basic syndrome. But even if this chapter should fail to live up to its billing and prove this to every reader's satisfaction, it can hardly shed less light on the etiology of the conditions than recent efforts to clarify them have done. Polivy and Herman (2002) concluded their review article, "Causes of Eating Disorders," with the statement that, although there are certain factors that may be necessary conditions for the development of these eating disorders and that there are certain risk factors that warrant further study, there is (a) no conclusive proof of what causes BN or AN in any one individual and (b) no understanding of the mechanism underlying these eating disorders. In "Risk Factors for Eating

Disorders," Striegel-Moore and Bulik (2007: 183) wrote, "the state of knowledge concerning the risk and causal factors of eating disorders is frustratingly incomplete." They also expressed concern about the neglect of the eating disorder field both by the US Centers for Disease Control and by the World Health Organization:

> We attribute much of this marginalization to pervasive misperception about the *volitional* [emphasis added] nature of eating disorders, which has impacted research; third-party reimbursement; and most tragically, families and sufferers who have known all along that eating disorders are far more grave than merely a choice to pursue thinness.
>
> (ibid.: 194)

Throughout my work, I will assert that a necessary condition of those eating disorders referred to by Polivy and Herman, and by Striegel-Moore and Bulik, and the focus of my investigation, is an unconscious, pathological eating complex resulting from psychization of the Hunger–Satiety drive by negative archetypal affects in early development.

Bulimia nervosa and anorexia nervosa as a unitary disorder: a literature review

The stage has certainly been set for considering BN (stuffing oneself) and AN (starving oneself) as two phases of a common disorder. In their article, "The Anorectic Bulimic Conflict: An Alternative Diagnostic Approach to Anorexia Nervosa and Bulimia," Holmgren et al. (1983) reported finding in their clinical material (79 patients) an "overlap between the anorexia nervosa and bulimia diagnoses and the tendency of patients to alternate between diagnoses in the course of the disorder . . ." (Holmgren et al. 1983: 10). They discovered that previous authors had reported similar observations:

> Sours (1973) pointed out that anorexia nervosa patients may be anything from starving "cadavers" to binge-eaters of normal weight, who gorge on enormous meals three to four times a day. The term "bulimia nervosa" is suggested by Russell (1979) for a symptom very similar to the DSM-III bulimia. Russell, however, thinks that it would be premature to consider "bulimia nervosa" a distinct syndrome; instead it must be seen as related to anorexia nervosa. Three authors proceed further and suggest new syndromes or designations for a disturbance embracing both anorectic and bulimic behavior. Boskind-

Lodahl (1976) proposes the term "bulimarexia"; Ehrensing & Weitzman (1970) think that "anorexia bulimia nervosa" would be an adequate designation; and Guiora (1967) coins the expression "dysorexia."

(ibid.: 10)

Holmgren and his co-authors then set out to determine the common features among the patients with BN and AN and, based on their own observations and the accounts of others, concluded: "All patients have endured a subjective conflict between on the one hand, anorectic efforts to lose weight and, on the other, bulimic impulses threatening to thwart these strivings" (ibid.: 11). This led the authors to propose a model which they called the "Anorectic–Bulimic-Conflict" Model (ABC model): "The conflict between anorectic strivings ('weight phobia') and bulimic impulses is regarded as the central pathognomonic symptom. The contradictory behavior towards food and eating is an expression of the patient's approach to this conflict" (ibid.: 11).

Van der Ham et al. (1997) came upon other authors who had a unitary view of eating disorders:

They consider the eating disorders as one syndrome with a broad spectrum of expressions of manifestations (Bruch, 1973; Lowenkopf, 1982; Holmgren et al, 1983; Vandereychen & Pierloot, 1983; Mickelide & Andersen, 1985; Sunday et al, 1992). According to this view the core symptoms of the eating disorder are the same, but the symptomatology can be differently expressed in the severity of the disorder and in the kind of eating behaviour during the course of the illness. By the term 'core symptoms' we mean those symptoms that underlie the behavioural symptoms and can be considered as 'inner states' which activate the disordered eating behaviour.

(Van der Ham et al. 1997: 363)

This formulation opens the door to the idea that any eating disorder "syndrome" is part of a spectrum of common ways these inner states may express themselves through disordered eating behaviors. To test this hypothesis, Van der Ham and her colleagues studied 55 adolescents,

25 patients with anorexia nervosa (DSM-IV anorexia nervosa, restrictive type), nine with anorexia nervosa and bulimia nervosa (ANBN; DSM-IV anorexia nervosa, bulimic type), 14 patients with bulimia nervosa and a history of anorexia nervosa (BNhAN; DSM-IV bulimia nervosa), and seven with eating disorder not otherwise specified (EDNOS).

(ibid.: 364)

They identified these distinguishing patterns:

> Bulimic and restrictive behaviour turned out to be differentiating symptoms in this study. Patients with varied manifestations of the eating disorders divide into two groups on the component bulimic-versus-restrictive behaviour. Anorexia nervosa patients and EDNOS patients cluster on the restrictive side and ANBN and BNhAN patients on the bulimic side of the component.
>
> (ibid.: 367)

They interpreted their results this way: "In our opinion these results can be considered to support the spectrum hypothesis of the eating disorders" (ibid.: 368).

The question then arises: what determines what portion of the spectrum gets selected by a particular patient? The answer that has been most compelling to recent researchers of these conditions has been the patient's perception of the inner signals that determine whether one is hungry or not and has eaten enough to satisfy that hunger or not. This reasonable notion has only become a focus of attention in the literature, however, in the last 20 years. Halmi *et al.* (1989) began their article, "Hunger and Satiety in Anorexia Nervosa and Bulimia Nervosa," by admitting that the "possibility that distortions in the perceptions of hunger and satiety may occur and be related to the eating behavior in anorexia and bulimia nervosa is a sparsely investigated idea" (Halmi *et al.* 1989: 431). They set out to rectify this deficit, and their findings showed that eating disorder patients do have general disturbances in the perception of hunger and satiety and "that the eating disorder subgroups were distinguished primarily by their differences in before-meal perceptions of hunger and satiety both in the pre-treatment and post-treatment periods" (ibid.: 440). They then formed the following hypotheses to explain the different syndrome pictures:

> There are anorexia nervosa patients who maintain their underweight condition exclusively by restricting food intake. It is reasonable to assume these patients may perceive lower hunger and higher satiety levels than healthy persons or bulimics. Other anorexia nervosa patients do not have this control and alternate severe food restrictions with binge eating. These patients should have lower satiety levels after a meal compared with the anorectic-restrictors. The bulimic patients who are normal weight should have the lowest satiety levels after a meal compared with anorectic patients and healthy controls. These patients are unable to achieve an underweight condition even though they purge.
>
> (ibid.: 443)

The results of their study clearly supported these hypotheses:

> Underweight anorectics had lower hunger levels, higher satiety levels, and less urge to eat than normal weight bulimics and healthy controls. Subjects who binged and purged were more preoccupied with thoughts of food, and normal-weight bulimics had more urge to eat after finishing a meal.
>
> (ibid.: 443)

These differences persisted for some patients after treatment: "When all subjects were at a normal weight, the anorectics continued to have lower hunger levels, and the AN-R [the 'restrictive' type of anorectics who did not also engage in bulimic purging] also continued to have higher satiety levels" (ibid.: 443). For students of emotion, like myself, this is one more example among many that we cannot very well understand why a person is doing something when we leave out how he/she has been feeling before they do it.

Eddy *et al.* (2007) began their article, "Should Bulimia Nervosa Be Subtyped by History of Anorexia Nervosa? A Longitudinal Validation," with this statement: "Research suggests that more than 50% of those with AN will prospectively develop bulimic symptoms, crossing over to the binge/purge subtype of AN or to BN and likewise, that one-third of those with BN have a history of AN" (Eddy *et al.* 2007: S67). They studied a group of eating disordered subjects over a median of 9 years: 144 met criteria for BN at intake and 32 did so during follow-up; 4 had restricting AN and 28 had binge/purge at intake. They described these results: "Women with BN who had a history of AN were more likely to have a protracted illness, relapsing into AN during follow-up, compared with those with no AN history who were more likely to move from partial to full recovery" (ibid.: S67). When the researchers reflected on these results, the explanation they offered appears to support the unitary syndrome hypothesis by assuming that the same syndrome might have different phases:

> Given that eating disorder symptoms, including weight, are apt to fluctuate across time, it is also possible that the transition from AN (particularly ANBP) to BN may not represent a change in disorder but rather a change in stage of an illness. The longitudinal data presented here would appear to support this suggestion, as even when women present for treatment with BN, they are likely to relapse into AN and are slower to and less likely to fully recover when compared with BN women with no AN history.
>
> (ibid.: S70)

Additional empirical evidence in favor of the notion that BN–AN is a unitary syndrome with different phases is found in reports of the occasional patients suffering from morbid obesity (MO) who develop AN after gastric reduction surgery. Atchison *et al.* (1998) have presented the cases of two adult females who experienced the MO → Surgery → AN transformation and Bonne, Bashi, and Berry (1996) have described two adult males with MO who developed AN after gastroplasty.

What is still needed, however, is a necessary and/or sufficient explanation of the dynamic factors that might account for what can be designated as the BN–AN syndrome that manifests itself in protean ways. This is what I will now attempt to provide.

Getting to the root of the Bulimia nervosa–Anorexia nervosa syndrome

The theory of the unitary nature of BN and AN is appealing because it is based on a view that the body, including the mind that reads the body, functions as a whole, which means the Hunger–Satiety drive is a part of the self-regulation of this whole. How then can we understand that a faulty perception as to whether one is hungry or not, and a similar, related difficulty in perceiving that one is full or not, represents a holistic view of the body, which is then acted upon as if it were accurate? My view that BN and AN are best thought of as manifestations of a BN–AN syndrome is based on these principles and the following etiologic assumptions: (a) psychization of the Hunger–Satiety drive during eating is always accompanied by Positive and Negative affects; (b) each episode of psychization results in the formation of an Affect-toned Hunger–Satiety drive eating complex or the increase in size of an already existing one; (c) depending on the ratio of positive to negative (or negative to positive) emotions during psychization, the resulting complex will be normal (PA > NA) or pathological (NA > PA); (d) a pathological eating complex of considerable magnitude is a necessary condition for the development of the BN–AN syndrome; (e) the onset of BN–AN in adolescence or adulthood is a measure of the time needed to construct a pathogenic complex in the individual developmental process under consideration; and (f) dissociation of the Hunger–Satiety drive, a structural aspect of the pathological complex, is a necessary condition for the BN–AN syndrome: Hunger dissociated from Satiety becomes bulimic; Satiety dissociated from Hunger becomes anorexic.

The dissociation of the Hunger–Satiety drive occurs along a continuum: The first indication of dissociation is bulimic overeating. As the dissociation progresses, a ravenous appetite appears – Hunger dissociated from Satiety predominates. With further increase in the split, anorexic self-starvation occurs – Satiety dissociated from Hunger predominates. The full pathological syndrome is now structured and we can expect the individual to fluctuate between impulses to eat too much or eat too little.

The Bulimia nervosa–Anorexia nervosa syndrome: analysis of two cases of Anorexia nervosa drawn from the literature

So let us look at a pair of actual cases that illustrate the spectrum hypothesis, even though that is not how they were first presented in the literature. Marc Miller (1991) and Giuliana Fortunato (1977) diagnosed their patients, Janey and Luigi respectively, as suffering from Anorexia nervosa. My analysis of these cases is that upon reflection both meet my criteria for the BN–AN syndrome.

Janey

The psychotherapist Marc Miller (1991) epitomizes his account of his work with anorexic "Janey," 14 years old, as "Engaging the concrete" and makes the following statement about the not untypical way I have found that eating disordered patients work their central problem through:

> Instead of talking about what therapists believe would be beneficial, anorexic patients are often preoccupied with their eating-disorder symptoms (i. e., food intake, caloric content and usage, weight loss or gain, exercise) to the exclusion of more introspective and interpersonal concerns.
>
> (Miller 1991: 85)

I do not see such preoccupations with the details of feeding and its consequences as defensive, because I do not think they originate in the ego but rather are potentially healing intrusions into consciousness of the split-off hunger drive that would naturally show an interest in eating and its effect on physical well being. In other words, I feel Janey was doing what she needed to do, even though it would look oddly concrete in a patient who did not have her problem. She needed to integrate her Hunger–Satiety drive, which was both dissociated and repressed. I have found that as the complex is integrated through what might look like obsessive attention to its issues, such preoccupations with the minutiae of eating will eventually subside. This difference in my view from Miller's does not diminish my belief that his treatment of Janey was successful. He was a shrewd enough therapist to let her find her own way of healing herself and make a space for it.

Janey began treatment with him when she was 14 years old and a high school freshman. She had already been diagnosed with AN. During the previous six months, she had lost 20 pounds (120 to 100). The way she told it, she had decided several months earlier "to do something about her 'big butt' by dieting, joining the high school track team, and exercising" (Miller 1991: 90).

Miller, a self-psychologist, reflects on the effort to improve the self by such ego-driven means, noting "that 'optimal integration' of the self is often a far cry from what has occurred in reality" (ibid.: 87). He suggests that individuals with a vulnerable self-organization may attempt to strengthen their sense of self through "concretization," a concept formulated by Atwood and Stolorow (1984), which is defined as "the encapsulation of structures of experience by concrete, sensorimotor symbols" (ibid.: 88), such as the need to diet, exercise, and look better. Miller suggests that concretization may derive from what Josephs (1989) has called the "concrete attitude," which results from an individual's failure to develop past the normally concrete attitude of middle childhood to the equally normal abstract attitude of adolescence, a shift that was first formulated by Piaget.

To be sure, Janey at first could not talk about "anything other than food and losing weight" (Miller 1991: 90). She was preoccupied with thinking about "how worried she was about what she had eaten, or would have to eat, and how much she would have to work out to use up the calories she feared would make her fat" (ibid.: 90). She had developed "an all-encompassing obsession with food, calories, exercise, and weight, which had the real potential of proving fatal" (ibid.: 90). She denied any personal problems. For Miller all this fit the pattern of "concretization."

My take on this in-therapy behavior, however, the obsessive domination of Janey's thinking and conversation by topics of food, eating, and her weight, is an example of the phenomenon of the eating complex taking the fore as the first step in its integration. Complexes, when first constellated in the treatment situation, are a bit boring and sound like nothing else than the symptoms talking. But a patient whose ego-consciousness is allowing the complex to speak is not simply rehearsing old stuff he or she has already integrated and needs to move on from. Rather, the patient is trying to integrate the complex by talking about it to someone else. Jung understood this phenomenon as "constellation," and gave it the same positive meaning as the appearance of a star in the night sky of the unconscious. As he put it, "The influence of the complex on thinking and behaviour is called a *constellation*" (Jung 1973a: 22, original emphasis). What is constellated is grist for the mill of meaningful psychotherapeutic work, but the first step in that work for a therapist is simply to let the complex emerge out of the darkness of the unconscious.

> If there is a strong complex, all progress adapted to the environment ceases and the associations revolve entirely round the complex. . . . The progress of the personality is retarded, and a large part of the psychic

activity is expended in varying the complex in all possible ways (symptomatic actions).

(Jung 1960: 93)

The complex that I am postulating involves two pathologies that have developed out of early feeding situations. First there is the excessive activation, during eating, of one or more crisis affects, archetypal emotions more usually evoked to survive danger than to accompany the satisfaction that typically attends feeding. Second, there is the dissociation of the Hunger–Satiety drive itself in response to the intensity of these crisis affects, which make feeding simply too distressing to continue in a normal way. (Babies are not so different from the rest of us in responding to strong emotion nor is it uncommon for older children or adults to experience the same type of dissociation in the face of intense affects at feeding times, so that after an argument during the preparation of a meal, one or more of the members of family may announce, "I don't feel hungry" even as other members of the same family may be stuffing themselves to bury the painful affect.) In the case of Janey, 14 years old when she came into treatment, we cannot be certain when her eating disorder complex came into being, but we can readily identify the dissociation of her Hunger–Satiety drive, and we can deduce at least one negative crisis affect accompanying that dissociation: her derogatory thinking about her "big butt" gives us a hint that the nuclear crisis affect of the complex that has induced her to starve herself is Contempt/Shame.

Faced with Janey's by now well-established pattern of compulsive thinking and talking about eating in such a strongly negative a way, her therapist felt he had to intervene:

> In view of Janey's inability to move beyond her symptoms, and because of a wish to use her expressed enjoyment of writing, [Miller] asked Janey to keep a journal as a means of helping her to open up and become more self-aware. Janey was asked to record exactly what she ate and whatever thoughts and feelings accompanied her eating and her other activities.

(Miller 1991: 91)

From a Jungian perspective, Miller has introduced Janey to the process of dialoging with her complex. So long as it occurred in the context of the ego support he was giving here, this had the potential of helping her to integrate and transform the unconscious pathogenic complex. Once Janey had begun her journal, the therapy sessions focused on what she had written between appointments: "Her early entries were lists of the food she had eaten that day, with comments and questions that expressed her fear of gaining weight" (ibid.: 91). At first, that is, Janey's ego-consciousness simply continued on the course of "concretization." Miller, however, used the journal notes to give him access to Janey's inner world, as well as "to clarify what (and how much) Janey was eating, and to examine Janey's apprehension about food" (ibid.: 91).

> Through gentle, supportive inquiry, the therapist learned, for example, that when Janey wrote that she had eaten a pita sandwich for lunch, it was not exactly a sandwich. Instead, if the pita bread was a little soggy from the lettuce, Janey ripped the soggy part off and threw it away. And if the cheese stuck out of the sandwich, she ripped off the pro-truding edge and threw it away because she did not like to eat the cheese if it stuck out. Eating brisket was also complicated. First, Janey had to cut off all the fat; then she had to blot the gravy; and then she had to cut up the meat carefully because she would eat only long, perfectly rectangular pieces.
>
> (ibid.: 91)

This may be concrete, but it was also where Janey lived while eating. Through their exchanges, the therapist became interested in "the myriad manifestations of Janey's compulsive eating and exercising rituals" (ibid.: 91). He was facilitating integration and depotentiation of the pathogenic eating complex along the lines that Jung advises when he writes, "In actual practice . . . the suitably trained analyst mediates the transcendent function for the patient, i.e., helps him to bring conscious and unconscious together and so arrive at a new attitude" (Jung 1970a: 74). Indeed, Janey now took the initiative: "She asked to have *two* notebooks so that the therapist could take one home to read the latest entries between sessions" (Miller 1991: 92, original emphasis). Their mutual effort worked:

> A few weeks after this new arrangement was initiated, Janey reported becoming aware that the writing calmed her down. Instead of using food and binging, starving, or obsessing to cope with anxiety or depression, she noticed that she found the writing itself to be soothing.
>
> (ibid.: 92)

Writing in her journal was soothing because it reduced the power the unconscious eating complex had to intrude into her ego-consciousness. In this way, she gradually overcame the dissociation of the Hunger–Satiety drive. An alteration in the course of her eating disorder followed these positive changes: "Gradually, Janey's anorexic symptoms became less pro-nounced and less life-threatening, but were nonetheless persistent, with periodic intensifications that inevitably followed real-life upsets" (ibid.: 93).

Shortly after, Janey made this entry in her journal: "The voice in my head is very annoying and scary" (ibid.: 93). In her next session, she explained, "I have these voices in my head. They tell me what to do. I don't know where they come from" (ibid.: 93). One of the voices "encouraged her to eat and the other . . . harshly and critically admonished her to eat *very* little lest she get fat" (ibid.: 93, original emphasis).

Miller offers this explanation:

> The voices in Janey's head can be understood as auditory concretiza-
> tions of two opposing, unintegrated aspects of her self-experience,
> perhaps corresponding to her incompatible experience of one (or both)
> of her parents, at times the caring, supportive, "feeding" parent, and at
> other times the rejecting, depriving, "starving" parent.
>
> (ibid.: 93)

He continued with an explanation for the appearance of these "voices" at this particular time:

> In therapy, in the presence of the (relatively) consistent empathic
> selfobject, which Janey experienced as "a new object separate and
> distinct from the dreaded parental imagoes" (Stolorow *et al.*, 1987, p.
> 44), she was able to talk about these formerly dissociated experiences
> for the very first time.
>
> (ibid.: 93)

These "voices," in my opinion were those of the eating complex itself, that is, they were complex-constellations, and can be taken as additional evidence in favor of my view that an eating disorder like Janey's can be diagnosed as the Bulimia–Anorexia (BN–AN) syndrome. For such impera-tives to appear from within, normal eating had to have been preempted by a dissociation of the Hunger–Satiety drive. The voice that encourages her to eat is Hunger dissociated from Satiety; the one that tells her not to eat is Satiety dissociated from Hunger. The archetypal Affect that promotes dissociation of the Hunger–Satiety drive into component parts that the ego can identify with or reject is Contempt/Shame. We know from Janey's report that one voice "harshly and critically admonished her [Contempt] to eat *very* little lest she get fat" [Shame].

Janey remained in therapy four years, through her high school gradu-ation. She "slowly and painfully began to get in touch with her long-dissociated anger toward both her parents, whom she now could experience as depriving and selfish" (ibid.: 93). Naturally, we have to assume that this was rejection talking, but it is certainly the way Janey felt. Their manner of relating to her had in some way triggered an archetypal affect, Shame/Contempt.

When Janey went away to college, she kept in telephone contact with Miller, the frequency gradually diminishing.

Janey recently reported that she is now able to enjoy eating and that she feels much more in control in relation to food. She belongs to a sorority and is definitely interested in boys, despite some acknowledged anxiety about becoming sexually active. When under stress, she does think about feeling fat and has an impulse to stop eating, but so far has successfully resisted this old pattern.

(ibid.: 94)

From my perspective, this sounds like someone who is now in good-enough contact with the healthy affective basis of her personality.

Luigi

Luigi was the only child of his Italian family, which lived in a small town where the father worked as a bookkeeper in a large factory. Luigi was 14½ years old when he came to the Department of Child Psychiatry where Giuliana Fortunato was a psychotherapist. Luigi has suffered from a digestive disorder since he was 13 years old, which, after thorough assessments and some drug treatment, had been diagnosed as Anorexia nervosa: "For periods the boy had refused to eat for fear of 'indigestion' and at other times ate in such a haphazard way that his weight had fallen as low as 29 kilos [63.8 lbs]" (Fortunato 1977: 111). He also complained of headaches, constipation, and nausea. Before starting outpatient treatment, Luigi spent two months in a nursing home, where he received feedings, transfusions, and some psychotherapy. After his discharge, the nursing home followed his medical state.

At the clinic, Luigi's treatment developed in three phases: (1) weekly sessions for three years; (2) biweekly sessions for an additional six months, ending in termination; and (3) two returns to the Clinic during the six months following the termination. My discussion will focus on the first five months of therapy during which his eating disorder was largely resolved.

During his first therapy visit, Luigi recounted his continuing fear of "indigestion," the symptom that had marked the onset of his eating difficulty. At the same time, he was very thin and was starving himself. I am postulating that both Luigi's "fear of 'indigestion'" and his "starving himself" are complex-indicators, that is, they are conscious manifestations that originate in an unconscious, pathological eating complex marked by a dissociation of the Hunger–Satiety drive. Due to this dissociation, Hunger, lacking regulation by Satiety, has become bulimic and, if acted upon, could cause actual indigestion. Due to this same dissociation, Satiety, lacking regulation by Hunger, has become anorexic, so that Luigi imagines he is full when he is not.

During this early period of therapy, Luigi recalled a family he had met – a mother, Emilia, a father, and a little girl, Angela. He spoke "with strong emotion" about the mother who had "'taught him to eat' bread, butter and salt" (ibid.: 113). We need to be "taught" to eat when the natural functioning of the Hunger–Satiety drive has been compromised. Does Luigi's recall of this memory at this point in his treatment indicate that he has begun to integrate dissociated Hunger? And does it express Luigi's hope that Fortunato will be the "mother" who can restore his capacity for healthy eating?

He now reported his first dream: "One day an angel [an Angela] asked me to make a wish, and I wished to eat and drink continually" (ibid.: 113). Although this can be understood as a typical wish-fulfilment dream, I think it expresses more than that. I find in it confirmation of my conjecture that Luigi has begun to integrate into consciousness the previously dissociated, and therefore bulimic, Hunger in his Hunger–Satiety drive. Although Fortunato does not always make clear the timing of events in therapy in relation to the changes in Luigi's behavior, it was about now, at the beginning of the fifth month of psychotherapy, that she was able to comment: "In the meantime his appetite had become almost normal; his weight had risen to 48 kilos [105.6 lbs – gain of 41.8 lbs], and he was growing very rapidly" (ibid.: 113). This is additional evidence that integration of the dissociated Hunger–Satiety drive was under way.

It was also around this time, however, that Fortunato wrote that his sessions began to trouble her. She tells us only that while for Luigi his father was still "the best," he was frequently irritated with his mother and spoke of her as "boring" (ibid.: 113). Whatever the tension that emerged between Luigi and his therapist at this phase of his treatment, Fortunato says it was relieved by two dreams he had in the same night, this being the first: "I was on the point of being swallowed by an enormous plant, a plant that was all mouth, like a huge slit mouth, like a colossal palate as big as this room" (ibid.: 113).

Now there can be no doubt that the integrative process is in full swing. I think the impressively threatening symbol may be thought of as an expression of the return of the repressed, the formerly dissociated and now therefore bulimic Hunger that in the course of being integrated into consciousness now threatens to devour his ego. But, looking a bit deeper, it may also be considered an expression of the maternal imago, which has taken the archetypal form of a devouring Terrible Mother. The symbol might also express Luigi's experience of the eating disorder complex itself, which had all but devoured his healthy appetite before treatment began. At the deepest level of all, the "enormous plant" is a negative symbol of the Self, the totality of the psyche, which by making itself ugly is engaging him to fight heroically against the monstrousness of the psyche so that he won't be ruled so much by his unconscious fantasies about food, which have played him false.

That is, by forcing Luigi to enter a fight for his life to overcome his own pathological orality, the Self, by sending this nightmare, is actually serving to advance his development. My overall view of the dream, therefore, is that it is progressive, integrative, and shows the strengthening of Luigi's ego that has occurred during the eventful initial period of his psychotherapy. Now Luigi was ready to confront the hero archetype.

This is the second dream of the same night:

> I was the double of Tor [a Superman type character]. In going forward I fell into enemy hands. I fell through a trap door — I mean a trap made of mirrors. The mirrors were all divided at the sides and underneath and there was a system of batteries behind, set up in such a way that if the current was lacking in one mirror, that mirror fell down and there was always one of them that was falling down so I was tossed about and half stunned. Finally Tor switched the current off and I was saved.
>
> (ibid.: 113)

The dream describes an unconscious "set-up" aimed at Luigi. Why would the unconscious want to set him up this way? Being the "double of Tor" is presumably Luigi's necessary, defensive identification with the numinous hero archetype. It is understandable that Luigi would want to appropriate the hero's power in the light of the previous dream, which found him confronted by a devouring monster, the carnivorous plant. But the usual consequence of taking such an identification with an archetype into the ego is an inflation which threatens the ego's integrity, which depends upon a proper recognition of its limits as well as of its possibilities. In this context, the trap of mirrors becomes a compensatory mechanism of the Self, which protects the psyche by causing any part of it that has become inflated to fall from inauthentic power. It's as if the mirrors are saying to Luigi's dream ego, "Who do you think you are?" Interestingly, once this compensation, painful as it is to Luigi, is complete, Tor is free to do his work of rescue by switching off the batteries, bringing the compensatory deflation to an end.

We learn that after these two dreams, Luigi experienced an intensification of headaches for several weeks. He said that the headaches "had appeared some few days before when Emilia, ever a positive mother figure for Luigi, had visited him and 'to celebrate, I ate too many cakes and got a head-ache'" (ibid.: 114). Now Luigi had become the devouring monster, making himself sick with an unwise indulgence in his usually repressed appetite. We are reminded that when Luigi first presented himself for treatment, he was suffering from headaches and also that the beginning resolution of his Anorexia was accompanied by a *worsening* of the headaches. Further, Luigi had told his therapist that his mother had suffered from severe headaches in her childhood. We might conclude that at some level his mother is the devourer in his psyche, and that identification with her, whether in anorexic withholding of food from himself or indulging in binging, is somehow at the core of his eating difficulty, viewed as the unitary BN–AN syndrome. Describing this point in the treatment, Fortunato makes the following comment, which I find insightful as to Luigi's dilemma, whether or not it is one he inherited from his mother:

> He thus seemed to be poised between a certain acceptance of his own greed, as could be seen in his improved appetite and lessened fear of "indigestion" or getting fat, along with greater awareness in the sessions of aggressive feelings towards his mother and in the maternal transference, and on the other hand, a greater awareness of the anxieties connected with the greed.
>
> (ibid.: 114)

Toward the end of this month, Luigi reported another dream. He introduced it by saying it was "unimportant":

> A tall man, blond and robust, was being attacked by a lot of men and managed to defeat them all. At a certain point a sleeping pill makes him fall into a trap. When he comes to he finds himself bound. The men are asking him questions but he doesn't talk.
>
> (ibid.: 114)

Associations were to a story in a magazine, *Criminal*, about a diary hidden from the police; so presumably the hero being questioned was the man who hid the diary. The hero is the central figure throughout the dream. Luigi, who is observing, has overcome his inflationary identification with this archetype enough to watch objectively. As in the previous dream, there is a trap set for the hero, in the form of a sleeping pill. Inducing unconsciousness is one way the Self can weaken the hero's insistence on seeing only his own point of view, which is egocentric. On other hand, the hero-figure is able to maintain his autonomy, which could point to the fact that Luigi now has a relatively strong ego. The defense of "not talking" suggests that Luigi is beginning adolescent differentiation from mother and therapist.

With the dissociation of the Hunger–Satiety drive that had been at the root of his eating disorder overcome, and with a lessened identification that might insist on solving all his problems himself as the hero, we can expect the Self to be able to get its supplies to him in support of advances in his overall development. Indeed, Luigi proceeded to advance on several fronts. He passed his examinations for secondary school brilliantly. In the seventh month of treatment, he started to develop a relationship with his first girlfriend. He also became active in sports and acquired new male friends. Luigi used his psychotherapy, which he continued for several more years, to resolve personal conflicts. When his adolescent development was far enough along, with a great deal of thought, he terminated.

In the chapters that follow, I will discuss other cases of eating disorders in adolescents and young adults that exemplify my formulation of the BN–AN syndrome, as have Janey and Luigi.

Chapter 4

A life dominated by shame

Pierre Janet's case of Anorexia – Nadia

We are now ready to continue to put the conception of BN and AN as two aspects of one eating disorder to the test, by looking at the notes of one of the most focused of the original psychotherapeutic pioneers, himself always looking for the basic processes creating the different psychopathologies. If there is indeed a BN–AN syndrome, caused by dissociation of the Hunger–Satiety drive, Pierre Janet's case report of Nadia must surely help bear that out. Let us recall my hypothesis before we start: dissociated Hunger becomes bulimic; dissociated Satiety becomes anorexic. And I would ask the reader to recall that my suggestion as to the cause of this dissociation was to postulate a pathological turn in the emotional psychization of the Hunger–Satiety drive, specifically by archetypal crisis affects (Fear, Sadness, Anger, Shame/Contempt) during a child's stages of development prior to adolescence. I argued, in Chapter 3 of this book, where this formulation can be found, that the disturbance introduced into a child's development by the flooding of his psyche with crisis affects during feedings results in the formation of a pathological eating complex of sufficient magnitude to cause the dissociation of the Hunger–Satiety drive itself. Using the cases discussed in that chapter, Janey and Luigi, it was possible to demonstrate dissociation of the Hunger–Satiety drive, but I found it difficult to identify the crisis emotions in the pathogenic complexes documented in these case reports.

That is where Janet's meticulous method of case study has proved invaluable, even though it is now over 100 years since he made the observations I am going to summarize here. In *Les Obsessions et la Psychasthenie*, Pierre Janet (1903) presented the case study of his patient, Nadia, in which he provided empirical evidence to show that Shame played a prominent part in her Anorexia. Ludwig Binswanger (1958), as we shall see, when we review his contribution to our understanding of this problem, was interested in comparing Nadia with his patient Ellen West (see Chapter 6). He included in his article translations of Janet's comments on the importance of Shame in the pathogenesis of Nadia's eating disorder. Pope, Hudson and Mialet (1985), who re-examined Janet's report 25 years ago, noted that it is one of the first detailed descriptions of a patient with Bulimia, but they did not include Janet's discussion of the importance of Shame in the etiology of the condition. In my own analysis of Nadia's eating disorder, I will draw upon the papers by Binswanger and Pope *et al.* (a) to show that Janet's case provides further support for my BN–AN hypothesis and (b) to emphasize the part played by Shame in its pathogenesis.

Nadia was 22 years old when she was referred to Janet with the diagnosis of Anorexia. She was the daughter of an affluent and distinguished French family and was an accomplished artist and musician, fluent in four languages. The onset of her eating disorder occurred during puberty.

Nadia's eating disorder

Binswanger noted that the "onset of menstruation, the growth of pubic hair, and the development of her breasts made [Nadia] half-crazy" (Binswanger 1958: 333). Pope *et al.* indicate that she was "horrified" by this event. As these changes in her body began to unfold, Nadia insisted on eating alone, as if hiding something disgusting: "She felt, in her own judgment, like someone who is asked to urinate in public; when she ate too much she reproached herself as for something indecent. She was terribly ashamed when surprised in the act of eating bonbons" (ibid.: 332). This observation describes Nadia's concern about overeating, which suggests that Hunger has already been split off from regulation by Satiety and become bulimic. Her concern about eating included not only being seen but also being heard: "Her chewing – only her own chewing – caused a particularly ugly and mortifying noise. She was willing to swallow the food, but people should not think they could force her to chew it" (ibid.: 332). Mortifying is an interesting word for a life-sustaining activity like eating. Among the synonyms for *mortifying* are degrading, humiliating, embarrassing, shaming, and abasing. Nadia's Shame over being seen or heard to eat originates, in my judgment, in an unconscious, pathological eating complex. It also suggests that Shame/Contempt was the archetypal affect that dominated the psychization of her Hunger–Satiety drive and led to the formation of the complex.

At about the age of 15 or 16, Nadia decided not to eat to stop her physical growth: "'I didn't wish,' Nadia said, 'to become fat, or to grow tall, or to resemble a woman because I always wanted to remain a little girl.' And why? 'Because I was afraid of being loved less'" (ibid.: 333). Nadia's decision to stop eating originates in Satiety dissociated from regulation by Hunger. Her decision was also influenced by her adolescent bodily maturation, which in Nadia's mind could be stopped by self-starvation and would save her from humiliating Rejection. (The reader may recall that Rejection is the life stimulus that triggers the archetypal affect Shame/Contempt, or what is also experienced by the person suffering from the influx of such emotions, Humiliation/Disgust.) Nadia suffered from intense body-Shame, and I believe this originated in an unconscious, pathological body complex. Faced by what she felt her body and its actions looked like when this complex was constellated, Nadia said she would like to don a cloak of invisibility.

Pope *et al.* report that Nadia developed a vast repertoire of obsessional rituals to prevent herself from growing any further. Some acts were forbidden: "If I touch a given note on the piano four times during the course of the same piece, I am consenting to grow bigger and never be loved again by anyone" (1985: 740). Some acts were prescribed:

> Nadia would promise herself to begin the same prayer 5 times or 10 times, or to jump 5 times on one foot. Then, recognizing this behaviour as absurd, she would resolve not to perform such acts, only to be thrown into torments as to which course – to act or not to act – was superior. Eventually, even the most trivial detail of her existence became enmeshed in an elaborate web of compulsions.
>
> (ibid.: 740)

Both the proscribed and the prescribed obsessional behaviors were complex-indicators. I feel they are motivated by the same unconscious, pathological complex, built around the archetypal affect, Shame. She was constantly being warned by the unconscious that in her vulnerable psyche Shame had the power to overtake her at any moment.

Nadia also attempted to conceal her sex by dressing and wearing her hair in such a way as to give a masculine impression. Until she was 20 years old, she also pulled out her pubic hair. These attempts to hide or prevent her sexual development were, in my opinion, also motivated by her unconscious, pathological Shame complex.

Nadia's childhood

Nadia's shame encompassed every aspect of her body. From the time she was four years old, Nadia was "ashamed of her figure because she was told she was tall for her age" (ibid.: 333). We are told that from this age "she had manifested bizarre obsessive-compulsive symptoms" (Pope *et al.* 1985: 739). By the time she was eight years old, she was ashamed of her hands, "which she found long and ridiculous" (Binswanger 1958: 333). When she was ten years old, she "became obsessed with the ugliness of her hands, her feet, her hips, and her hair" (Pope *et al.* 1985: 739):

> About her eleventh year she rebelled against short skirts because she thought everyone was looking at her legs, which she could no longer

endure. When she was allowed long skirts she was ashamed of her feet, her broad hips, her fat arms, etc.

(Binswanger 1958: 333)

In these observations of Nadia's Shame over her body in childhood, we can observe the beginning structuralization of what Janet will subsequently refer to as pervasive body-Shame, in archetypal affect terms, a Shame–Body complex. Throughout Nadia's developmental history we can find experiences that reinforced her disturbed view of her own body, which by the time of adolescence shaped her decisions around eating. Unfortunately, there is no comparable series of observations of her reactions to eating during her childhood. What is also missing from these developmental observations are descriptions of Nadia's encounters with environmental stimuli, beginning with her family, that shaped these views of herself.

Course of Nadia's eating disorder

Nevertheless, we can pick up the trail as adolescence begins. Binswanger records that from its onset in puberty her eating disorder was rapidly exacerbated by her adolescent body's development. When she was 18 years old, shortly after her mother's death, she devised a diet that in both articles is described as "bizarre": "Two bowls of clear bouillon, one egg yolk, a spoonful of vinegar, and a cup of tea with the juice of an entire lemon added" (ibid.: 740). Her motive for this diet was "fear of becoming fat" and on this regimen she was able to reduce her weight. Any attempts by others to change it caused "terrible scenes." Her diet was, in my opinion, selected by the unconscious pathogenic complex and may have symbolic meanings, which, without her associations, we cannot entirely decode. We can, however, mention the themes that Janet uncovered and that Binswanger later summarized.

Her fear of becoming fat was found to be fear of becoming like her mother: "Nadia was afraid, it seems, of becoming fat like her mother. She wanted to be thin and pale, as would correspond to her own character" (Binswanger 1958: 332). As Binswanger writes, Nadia was not concerned about being fat "for reasons of coquetry, for she had no wish to be pretty; in the eyes of the patient it was something immoral . . . abhorrent" (ibid.: 332). These observations suggest that the pathological complex we have been tracing is closely linked in its beginnings with her mother complex.

Up to this time, Nadia has been viewed as a "food-restricting" anorexic, without bulimic compensations. But now, a ravenous appetite began to alternate with self-starvation, and at times her hunger was so great that she devoured everything in sight. These food binges were followed by great remorse, and redoubled efforts to seduce herself back into austerity:

She herself admitted that it cost her a great effort to keep from eating, so that she felt like a heroine. At times she would think only of food for many hours, so great was her hunger, she would swallow her saliva, bite her handkerchief, and roll on the floor. She would search in books for descriptions of banquets, in order to participate mentally in them and to trick herself out of her own hunger.

(ibid.: 332)

Nadia, however, was now experiencing the emergence into consciousness of her dissociated Hunger drive, which would inevitably result in Bulimia. This ravenous state of mind would alternate with dissociated Satiety, which would always lead her back to anorexia. The appearance of this dual pattern in consciousness provides further empirical evidence in support of my thesis that BN and AN are manifestations of an underlying unitary syndrome, which I link semiotically as BN–AN, a condition that has its roots in dissociation of the Hunger–Satiety drive.

Shame in Nadia's life

We need to consider the relation of Shame to dissociation. We have just seen that from four to 11 years of age, Nadia experienced Shame in relation to various parts of her body. During her adolescence her fear of becoming fat, her wish to remain a child, and her eating behavior were all conditioned by Shame:

If she were ever to get fat, she would be ashamed to be exposed to anyone's gaze, both at home and in the street. . . . Only in regard to herself was being fat "shameful and immoral." And this judgment applied not only to being fat but also to everything connected with eating.

(ibid.: 332)

In addition to Hunger and Satiety, Nadia had dissociated her interest in relating to others, and settled for a world in which she managed to live without affects occasioned by human objects. From age 22 to 27, she led a isolated existence: "At the time of Janet's case report, she had lived for 5 years sequestered in a small apartment, seeing virtually no one, leaving her home only at times of the most dire necessity, and then only at night" (Pope et al. 1985: 739). Nadia's sequestration is due to complex-sensitiveness and its purpose is to avoid dialogues with others that might constellate desire for them, which could produce Shame because she thought she looked ridiculous to others and intensely unattractive to them, when she showed any need of them. But, as Binswanger shrewdly concludes from the case report, "the real reason that Nadia was afraid of being ugly and ridiculous is, according to Janet, the fear that people would mock at her, not like her any more, or find her different from the others" (ibid.: 333). I see Nadia's condition as the constellation of a complex composed of Rejection + Alienation leading to a flooding of her psyche by toxic emotions: her childhood experiences of relating, composed of the perception of Contempt from others and Disgust within herself, both conducive to Shame, has pursued her into her adult life.

Janet thought that the Shame Nadia experienced in relation to her eating disorder was only part of a much more pervasive body-shame, and that this was the subconscious fixed idea she was suffering from. This raises the following question: Is it possible for an individual to develop an eating disorder if the life stimulus for Shame, Rejection, has been directed at his/her body as a whole and not specifically or especially at his/her eating behaviors? We do not know the answer to this question, which must await further study. My assumption is that for an eating disorder of any consequence to develop, the individual needs more than disturbed object relations based on toxic shame. The person must consciously experience mealtimes that are flooded with crisis affects in the presence of a deficit in the regulators of such emotions, the positive affects of the life instinct (see Chapter 8).

Nadia's treatment

About the time Nadia was entering young adulthood, she was hospitalized for six months and a refeeding program was carried out; but this produced only temporary improvement and her anorexic behavior quickly recurred. This is the summary by Pope *et al.* of Janet's treatment of Nadia, which began when she was 22 years old and ended five years later.

> Janet describes some success in treating Nadia by separating her from her family, then gradually helping her to re-establish a more normal eating pattern and to forsake some of her compulsive rituals. But the process was tedious: years elapsed before the patient would play the piano in Janet's presence, or would even allow herself to be seen in full light in her room. At the time of the case report, the prognosis remained guarded at best.
>
> (Pope *et al.* 1985: 741)

I don't see the denouement of her treatment quite so negatively. Nadia's becoming more "visible," at least to Janet, indicates significant integration and depotentiation of the pathological complex. Nadia's rapport with Janet allowed her to apologize to him "in innumerable letters" when she had eaten chocolates on an impulse. We can imagine that these expressions provided her with considerable relief from the Shame she experienced after her "transgressions." As with other conditions, symptoms that arise and are discussed within the context of a psychotherapeutic relationship are much more prone to dissolution than are rigid, unreflected repetitive behaviors that belong to the isolated world of the patient who is stuck with them all alone.

With these hints, the case of Nadia must rest, barring the publication of a word-for-word translation of Janet's case study or the discovery of additional material.

Chapter 5

Healing regression to the first three months of life

Marguerite Sechehaye and her patient Renee

Two accounts of a remarkable case were published in 1951: *Symbolic Realization* by the therapist, the Swiss psychologist Marguerite Sechehaye (MS) and the other by the patient, Renee, whose version was published as *The Autobiography of a Schizophrenic Girl*. Renee was 18 years old and markedly regressed when she first met with MS, who made the clinical diagnosis of schizophrenia, which we might question today. It was only later that MS realized that Renee also had an eating disorder. After the first six years of a ten-year period of treatment, Renee was cured of both conditions.

When I reviewed the details of the now famous treatment, I came upon unexpected parallels to certain demonstrations that I made in my own first book about normal development in the first few months of life. I concluded that during the course of her therapy with the receptive MS, Renee had regressed to the neonatal phase of infancy in order to initiate a new beginning of her psychological development, which then could proceed along normal lines. The symbolic steps in Renee's rebirth were the same as those I had identified within normal parent–infant interaction in the first three months of life (*The Symbolic Impetus*, 2001). I propose in this chapter to bring this parallel into as sharp focus as I can, so that the reader can appreciate just how important for the healing of an eating disorder is traversing in the right way this symbolic entry into thriving outside the womb.

It is also possible on the basis of what the reader of this book will come to know about the role that archetypal affect complexes play in emotional development to see that Renee's treatment was challenged throughout by the existence of an unconscious, pathological Affect-toned complex, the "System," which had begun to be constructed during the first three months of her infancy. By the time Renee entered therapy, this complex had attained sufficient intensity to produce a block to her psychological development. This block was expressed in states of "Unreality." Renee's cure resulted from reductive resolution of the "System" accompanied by the activation and synthesis of healing forces in her unconscious, forces that a

Jungian reader will recognize as archetypal. Indeed, what is activated illustrates a principle of Jung's, that the archetypes appear when the instincts are in danger. Re-reading the case with these formulations in mind actually makes its instinctive rightness, as a therapy co-created by patient and therapist, all the more clear.

The "system" as an affect-toned complex

Renee's persecutory "System" first appeared to her consciousness in mid-adolescence. Around the time she turned 16, while working on her lessons at school, she began to draw "strange geometric figures in her copybooks, and explained to her intrigued classmates that this was the 'System' . . . a machine which could blow up the world" (Sechehaye 1951: 28). From our perspective, it was Renee's ego-complex that was in danger of being exploded, the "world" of her self and object relations.

The first image of the threatening "System" that MS saw was as part of a drawing Renee made during the first few weeks of her psychotherapy (see Figure 5.1).

The female figure in the center of the drawing is Renee's drawing-ego, which she regularly refers to as the "Little Personage" (LP). This drawing includes both a geometric image of the "System" and personifications of its voices, which Renee called her "Persecutors." The abstract geometric representation of the System appears in the upper right hand corner of the drawing. One head of a Persecutor is just above the System and three heads of the Persecutors appear behind the LP. The 12 arrows that emanate from the "System" express the intense energy that is concentrated in this complex. There is the suggestion of supercilious expressions on the faces of the three "Persecutors," who are even more clearly mocking in subsequent drawings, that provide support for my conclusion that they are nothing other than the "voices" Renee was intermittently hearing. The lines from their eyes express their contemptuous glances, a visualization of the tone of the voices. Contempt is one pole of the archetypal affect Shame/Contempt, but in Renee's case the Contempt leveled at her was experienced as near-total Humiliation. There are three other elements in the drawing that deserve our comment. First there is a sort of animal, with its snout at her pelvis, which she called "the beast of sensuality". Then there is a crowd of people, smaller than she, who are seeking her help. Renee feels obligated to help them in their suffering. (This correlates with some inflated religiosity in Renee's background, since during the first part of her adolescence she had been quite impressed by the Christian doctrine of the "community of saints" and had begun to feel responsible for the suffering of the world.) The third element is two little people with a string drawn taut between them, which represents the energy field of the complex itself, a tension arc

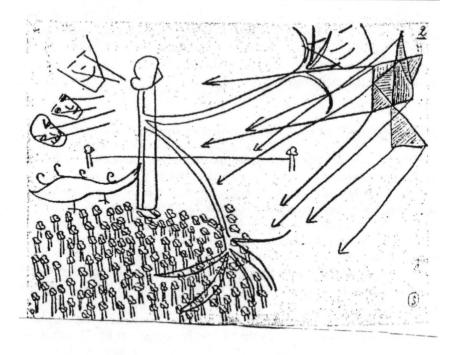

Figure 5.1 The "Little Personage" defends herself against the "System" and the "Multitude" (Sechehaye 1957: 976).

originating in the intense persecution of the System. As for the LP (Renee herself) we have to note the rigidity of her posture, and the degree to which she feels the need to protect herself from both the System and the Sufferings of the World. One of Renee's gigantic hands is fending off the persecutory System while the other is pushing away the demands of those who are seeking to dump their suffering on her. One can see how little of her is left to connect to the world in a normal way.

Shortly after starting treatment, Renee became aware of two states of mind that she could not explain to herself – one was "a guilt infinite and awful," the other was a hostility she harbored toward everyone. She gave expression to the latter in dreams and waking fantasies, where "[she] constructed an electric machine to blow up the earth and everyone with it" (Renee 1951: 27). With this machine, she could "rob all men of their brains, thus creating robots obedient to [her] will alone. This was [her] greatest, most terrible revenge" (ibid.: 27).

She wrote the following description of her "guilt," which she realized did not have an actual object:

It was too pervasive, too enormous, to be founded on anything definite, and it demanded punishment. The punishment was indeed horrible, sadistic — it consisted, fittingly enough, of being guilty. For to feel oneself guilty is the worst that can happen, it is the punishment of punishments. Consequently, I could never be relieved of it as though I had been truly punished. Quite the reverse, I felt more and more guilty, immeasurably guilty.

(ibid.: 27–8)

Puzzled by these unknowns, she set out to discover "what was punishing me so dreadfully, what was making me so guilty" (ibid.: 28).

One day I wrote a letter of entreaty to the unknown author of my suffering, to the Persecutor, asking him to tell me what evil I had done, that I might finally know. But because I did not know where to send my letter, I tore it up.

(ibid.: 28)

This charming confession was what led her to realize that the "Perse-cutors" were part of the "System," which had not been fully clear to her before. Now she thought of the System as a vast world, encompassing everyone: "At the top were those who gave orders, who imposed punish-ment, who pronounced others guilty" (ibid.: 28). Those who gave orders were also guilty because "a formidable interdependence bound all men under the scourge of culpability" (ibid.: 28). Although everyone was part of the "System," only some were aware of this. In almost Kafkaesque lan-guage, she summarized her condition in this way:

[To] enter into it was to become insensible of everything except culpability, the supreme punishment, freely granted by the System. I was guilty, abominably, intolerably guilty, without cause and without motive. Any punishment, the very worst, could be imposed on me — it could never deliver me of the load. Because, as I have already said, the most dreadful punishment was to make me feel eternally, universally culpable.

(ibid.: 29)

How the "System" developed

Renee's experience of "guilt" suggests that it began at a pre-ego stage of development. I say this because it is without cause and without motive, eternal and universal, and originates in a "System" that encompasses everyone. It is, therefore, not surprising to learn from the developmental history that MS was able to obtain that the construction of the "System" began during the first three months of Renee's life. This is a time when the infant's level of consciousness has been referred to by various authors as unconscious identity (Jung), primary unitary reality (Neumann), adualism (Piaget), and non-recognition (Fraiberg).

The normal pattern of development during these months is not entirely intrapsychic. The psyche field is shared between the infant and the infant's caregivers. The archetype of the "Wonder-child" is constellated in the psyche of the parents and projected upon their newborn. The emotional components that enable the infant to live up to the projected infant symbol of the wondrous, magical baby are the archetypal affects of the life instinct, Interest and Joy, along with their respective dynamisms, curiosity/exploration and fantasy/play. Beginning with their projection of this image, a flow of affects from the unconscious expectations of the parents to the unconscious of the capabilities of the infant is established. This is the parent–infant bond. Without awareness of their origin, the infant will begin to experience these emotions through a process of emotional contagion. Love for an infant is contagious under optimal circumstances; the infant as a new individual and everything the infant does is regularly cradled in a numinous aura of Interest and Joy. Among the many effects of such a parent–infant bond is the healthy psychization of the Hunger–Satiety drive. The result is happy feedings. It is also inevitable that the infant will be exposed to the crisis affects of Fear, Sadness, Anger, and Shame/Contempt, both through contagion from parents' negative emotions and by parental behaviors that constellate these affects in the newborn. Hopefully, in the context of a robust circulation of Interest and Joy, these negative emotions will be modulated and integrated.

The first three months of Renee's life, so far as it can be known, stand in stark contrast to this pattern. At birth, Renee was very definitely greeted by her mother's Rejection: "The delivery of this first child was very difficult, but the baby was healthy and beautiful, and the object of admiration of the nurses at the clinic. Only the mother found her ugly" (Sechehaye 1951: 21). The archetypal affective pattern that I believe has been activated in Renee by her mother is Rejection + Alienation → Shame/Contempt–Humiliation/ Disgust. The reaction of the nurses certainly puts mother's response in question. Mother's Rejection was toxic, particularly because it extended to her daughter's feedings. As mother felt unable to breast feed Renee, she fed her from a bottle. But, mother put too much water in the milk, and Renee refused the bottle and cried continuously. By three months of age, when we would expect her to be a rosy, smiling and laughing infant, her "body had the appearance of a skeleton, [she] was about to starve to death" (ibid.: 22). A pathological eating complex is being constructed. Renee now has the appearance of an infant suffering from the eating disorder of infancy referred to as Failure to Thrive (see Chapter 2). It is evident that the psychization of her Hunger–Satiety drive has been conditioned by crisis emotions.

A first question, then, is whether mother's Rejection was an initial step, however negative, toward developing a positive maternal orientation or whether it was the manifestation of a persistent negative attitude toward her daughter. If the former was the case, we might expect the Rejection to be modulated and integrated over time. If the latter was the case, we should expect the magnitude of the initial Rejection to increase over time. There is certainly evidence for the persistence of a negative attitude toward her daughter.

When Renee was 13 years old, she was shocked when her mother told her that she "had been an unwanted child; that she had been annoyed at her birth, and had considered her a hideous baby" (Sechehaye 1951: 27). On frequent occasions, her mother embellished these criticisms:

> The mother reproached her for not loving her enough, and for going to Church too often. She accused her of tendencies toward inversions, because the girl looked for protection by older and maternal friends; she accused her also of other "shocking" tendencies such as dressing more meticulously for a visit to the doctor.
>
> (ibid.: 27)

The mother would demand exclusive, unconditional love from Renee and threaten to return after death and punish her if she ever loved someone else. During an interview with MS when Renee was in treatment, the mother said she had told her daughter the following:

> "I have an absolute right over you; if I wanted to, I could kill you; I could make you steal or do any wicked thing without the right of anyone to interfere." Or, "I know everything you are thinking; it is my right to know, even what you dream. And at night in my room, I know if you are moving in your bed; your body, your mind, your soul are mine; you have absolutely nothing."
>
> (Sechehaye 1956: 88)

It is clear that mother's Rejection of Renee at her birth was the expression of an attitude toward Renee's autonomy and very existence that persisted until Renee was an adult.

Renee's father also made a contribution to Renee's Rejection complex. At the end of infancy and beginning of early childhood Renee was sleeping in her parents' bedroom. When she woke in the morning and asked to be fed, this was her parents' response:

> But the parents laughed at her, deliberately made her wait, called her the "Little Corporal" and threatened to give her nothing at all if she

continued to cry. The father made Renee understand that he would take the mother away from her, because the mother belonged to him. He could beat her and eat her, if it pleased him. He then would pretend to bite the mother hungrily.

(Sechehaye 1951: 22–3)

When Renee was 14 months old, she had as a playmate, a little white rabbit, which she adored. One day, the father, in an act of senseless Rejection, killed the rabbit, in Renee's presence. From then on, Renee asked constantly and with persistence for her rabbit: "'Coco, bobo?,' and she refused to eat" (ibid.: 23). We don't know the inner dynamics for this negative psychization of Renee's Hunger–Satiety drive. When Renee was two years old, her father directed his ridiculing Rejection at her body: "Renee's father liked a good laugh, and to amuse himself would lift up the little girl's clothing and tease her about her nakedness" (ibid.: 23).

I believe that these empirical observations indicate (a) that Renee was raised in a family in which Rejection from both parents was a leitmotif and (b) that this experience was no joke to Renee; rather it was structuralized as a pathological, monopolistic systematic persecution of her very being – this was imaged as the "System." The nuclear archetypal affect of this rejection complex is the crisis affect Shame/Contempt–Humiliation/Disgust. This was the feeling-tone that dominated the "voices" of the "System," the "Persecutors."

Erich Neumann: the primary feeling of guilt

There are characteristics of Renee's experience of "guilt" that confirm it began during the pre-ego stage of development, when the infant has few defenses against environmentally induced emotions. It is without cause and without motive, eternal and universal, and originates in a "System" that encompasses everyone. Erich Neumann's conceptualization of the origin of a primary feeling of guilt in infancy will help clarify this connection.

He speaks of a primal relationship by which he means the parent–infant relatedness during the first year of life:

[T]he primal relationship is cosmic and transpersonal because the child has neither a stable ego nor a delimited body image. It is a unitary reality not yet separated into inside and outside, subject and object. It is all-encompassing. In this primal relationship the mother too, lives like the child in an archetypally determined unitary reality, but only a part of her enters into it, because her relationship with her child governs only a part of her total existence. The infant, however, is totally embedded in this realm, in which the mother represents for it both world and Self.

(Neumann 1990: 12–13)

A disturbance in this relation produces the primary feeling of guilt:

> Surprising as it may seem, the need to counteract the lack of love resulting from a disturbed primal relationship causes the child not to blame the world and man, but to feel guilty. This type of guilt feeling appears in an early phase and is archaic . . . The primary guilt feeling, it goes without saying, is not a matter of conscious reflection in the child, but it leads to the conviction, which will later play a determining role in the child's existence and development, that not-to-be-loved is identical with being abnormal, sick, "leprous," and above all "condemned."
>
> (ibid.: 86)

Since the mother is all, her Rejection leaves the child utterly alone. She may, on the other hand, "become an enemy or persecutor, a representative of the Terrible Mother. Life, as the Great Mother, has turned away and only death remains. In the context of the archetype's affects, the Terrible Mother is comprised of crisis emotions – Terror, Anguish, Rage, and Humiliation/Disgust, whereas the Good Mother expresses the life-enhancing emotions, Interest and Joy. As the symbolic Mother of the primal relationship is a goddess of fate, "her attitude is the supreme judgment, so that her defection is identical with a nameless guilt on the part of the child" (ibid.: 87).

As the primary guilt feeling originates in the pre-ego phase, it appears to the adult ego as present from the start: "A primary guilt feeling leads a child to associate the disturbance of the primal relationship with its own primordial guilt or original sin. . . . In this case the child lays its misfortune to only one cause: its own guilt" (ibid.: 87). If this complex is not resolved, it undermines the personality throughout life, unless it is resolved later on:

> It would seem that virtually the only way in which this primary guilt feeling and its consequences can be reduced and resolved in the first half of life is through a situation of transfer that reconstitutes the primal relationship and regenerates the damaged ego-Self axis.
>
> (ibid.: 88)

One such "situation of transfer" is the psychotherapeutic relationship, which Freud and Jung both felt depended fundamentally on transference. As I will show, a transfer of Renee's attachment to a new parental figure, a therapist who could assist Renee in reconfiguring her basic worth, is what MS and Renee accomplished during the first six years of Renee's treatment.

"Unreality"

Renee later wrote that during the first year of her treatment she realized that madness was not an illness, but the perception of Unreality: "Madness was finding oneself permanently in an all-embracing unreality" (Renee 1951: 24). "Unreality" was a country, in our terms a psychic image, opposed to Reality, and having the following characteristics:

1. It was a state of extreme tension that permeated everything in this land: "It was as if an electric current of extraordinary power ran through every object . . ." (Renee 1951: 24).
2. In spite of this enormous energy, everything is unchangeable, congealed, and silent. There is a stasis of life. Over the entire landscape, there is an implacable, pitiless electric light that casts no shadows. Objects and people have lost relatedness and meaning: "Objects are stage trappings, placed here and there, geometric cubes without meaning. People turn weirdly about, they make gestures, movements without sense; they are phantoms whirling on an infinite plain, crushed by the pitiless electric light" (ibid.: 24).
3. When she inhabits this country, Renee experiences unbearable emotion, absolute isolation, and utter desolation: "I am terrifyingly alone; no one comes to help me" (ibid.: 24). A brass wall separates her from everybody and everything. The lunar landscape on which she must try to live is limitless, flat, rocky, and cold. If there were to be an event in this lifeless land, it could only be an explosion in which everything was destroyed.

Psychogenesis of "Unreality"

"Unreality" like this has a history. Renee wrote that she first experienced this state in a recurrent nightmare from her childhood. As we will observe in Renee's drawings, she cannot draw herself, whom she designates as the "Little Personage," without adding a wire through the body or mind. This wire expressed the "tension of unreality and at the same time recalled the nightmare of the needle in the haystack" (ibid.: 25). In her autobiography she often refers to the wire as "the Straw" so as to remind herself of the hay in that dream. It was a dream that recurred often around the time Renee was five years old, especially when she was feverish; it caused her considerable Fear. Here is the dream:

> A barn, brilliantly illuminated by electricity. The walls painted white, smooth — smooth and shining. In the immensity, a needle — fine, pointed, hard, glittering in the light. The needle in the emptiness filled me with horror. Then a haystack fills up the emptiness and engulfs the

needle. The haystack, small at first, swells and swells; and in the center, the needle, endowed with tremendous electrical force, communicates its charge to the hay. The electrical current, the invasion of the hay, and the blinding light combine to augment the fear to a paroxysm of terror and I wake up screaming, "The needle, the needle!"

(ibid.: 5–6)

The threatening "needle" seems to me to be a symbol of the Self, the totality of the personality that unfolds in the course of development. Its tremendous energy charge, however, is unwelcome, not unlike the way Renee's own unfolding self was unwelcome in her parents' home. That it is also unwelcome to Renee herself reflects the dangerous damming up of libido that Renee is unable to deploy for adaptation and development. The "haystack" which hides the needle depicts a dissociation that is growing between a conscious conformity to her parents' expectations and the unconscious need to develop her own autonomy, initiative, and agency. It is a deeper dissociation that is the actual cause of the block to development in my opinion. That dissociation is between the flat, joyless, bland effort to accommodate her parents on the one hand and anything in her real affective life that could take joy in such an accommodation. The "Unreality," in other words, is the fact that everything she has to do to keep her parents happy has no basis at all in what feels good to her. The illumination, the walls, the spatial immensity, and the lack of human activity are additional expressions of the depersonalization and derealization of the compromise she has accepted and the dissociation of affect involved in making it. This is the real basis of the developmental impasse and stasis that Renee is experiencing by the time she is first seen for treatment. Her life has long since ceased being her own, because the heart of her affect is not in it. In Jungian terms, what has been completely dissociated is Eros, so that all that is left is a dull, lifeless conforming Logos. That Logos, however, enabled her to do quite well in her studies, so that to outward observers she looked for a while like an excellent student, and it only gradually dawned on others that something was "haywire" in the model pupil.

During a recess at her elementary school that Renee describes in the *Autobiography*, she experiences, side by side, a more affectively energized Reality, and the growing "Unreality" pervading of the life she is living at school.

I kept close to the fence as though I were indeed a prisoner and watched the other pupils shouting and running about in the school yard. They looked to me like ants under a bright light. The school building became immense, smooth unreal, and an inexpressible anguish pressed in on me. I fancied that the people watching us from the street thought all of us were prisoners just as I was a prisoner and I wanted so much to escape. Sometimes I shook the grating as though there were no other way out, like a madman, I thought, who wanted to return to real life. For the street seemed alive, gay and real, and the people moving there were living and real people, while all that was within the confines of the yard was limitless, unreal, mechanical and without meaning: it was the nightmare of the needle in the hay.

(ibid.: 6–7)

The "fence" is a symbol of the barrier against genuine affect creating the dissociation in Renee's developing personality.

That Renee's development is blocked rather than arrested is suggested by the healthy world on the other side of the fence and it is demonstrated by Renee's normal symbolic advances in middle childhood and adolescence. As she entered the former, Renee experienced the emergence of a Symbolic Community, and on her entry into the latter, a Religious cultural attitude developed (see my *The Symbolic Impetus*, 2001). And, although Renee made little effort to make friends at school, she did well academically and ended her primary grades with three prizes, two of them firsts. We have to assume that some part of her genuine affective life provided the symbolic impetus for these achievements, and that she took at least some satisfaction in them. We can verify that in terms of the energy she brought to her religious development as described by MS (Sechehaye 1951: 26).

Looking for "the mother"

When Renee was three months old and starving to death from being underfed, a grandmother arrived, took over her care, and restored her to physical health. But she left abruptly when Renee was 11 months old. Renee was stunned by her departure: "She cried, hit her head and looked everywhere for the grandmother" (Sechehaye 1951: 22). The grandmother's leaving occurred at a particularly inopportune time, for Renee was at that stage of infant development when she had begun to develop interpersonal relationships and the construction of object constancy, which at that age requires the presence of an actual permanent object. The resulting archetypal affect is structured by Loss (Life Stimulus) + the Void (Primal image) leading to Agony, which produces an abandonment complex.

When Renee was 18 months old, a sister was born. Renee responded by spitting at everyone, especially her baby sister and the grandmother, who had returned just long enough to be present at the birth. Renee's spitting was a telling expression that originated in the unconscious and was a complex-indicator, that is, it is an expression of other-Disgust, just as it would be in a much older person. It was directed, not surprisingly, at two prototypical figures that she associated with her feelings of Rejection.

Kovacs, Mahon, and Palmer (2002) have discovered that chewing and spitting is a common symptom in all patients with eating disorders, but is more frequent in patients with anorexia nervosa.

Contempt for these problematic others was not, however, Renee's only affective expression. At five years of age, Renee was looking everywhere to find the "constant object" that she had been denied by her grandmother's abandonment of a continuous role in her life, as well as by her parents' lack of empathy for what she was experiencing throughout her infancy and early childhood. MS records that when Renee went walking with her mother, she looked in every garden for "the mother" (Sechehaye 1951: 24). Renee will find that mother in MS herself during the first phase of her psychotherapy.

The first three months of analysis: Renee finds a "mother" and makes three drawings

In her initial interviews with MS, Renee is uncertain whether or not she should accept analysis. She feels that if her psychological problems are her fault, then she must solve them herself. She thinks, on the other hand, that she should engage in therapy. There is a definite interest in the punishment involved because it is bound to be both difficult and humiliating to accept help. She resists, however, developing a positive relation with MS because "she would be humiliated by loving, which is an enslavement; and anyway, sensitive people are laughed at" (ibid.: 36). Renee's fears of humiliation, domination, and ridicule indicate that the therapeutic situation has been at least partly assimilated to the Rejection complex.

Renee is afraid she will be "punished by humiliation" (ibid.: 34) for her vengeful fantasies and the hate which she harbors toward people. She does want, on the other hand, to hold on to the possibility of vengeance because it is justified by all the harm that has been done to her. As MS says, "she can only have pleasure in harming, biting off heads, crushing, dominating, commanding, bending others to her will (because this is worse than biting off heads)" (ibid.: 36).

Such fantasies can be explained on the basis of the eating-disorder dynamic we have been tracing. When the self-regulatory Hunger–Satiety drive is dissociated, the Hunger pole becomes "uncivilized," that is, animalistic. The basic issue of nutrition, eating or being eaten, that every culture has to face, Jung views as "one of the deepest chords in the human psyche . . . human sacrifice and ritual anthropophagy" (Jung 1970c: 222). They are characteristics of Kali, as the devouring Terrible Mother. Renee's retaliatory cannibalistic fantasies are expressions of the Humiliation/Disgust complex that arises when the archetypal fantasies evoked by this Terrible Mother image invade normal eating, which is then experienced as a disgusting devouring rather than a happy feeding in which mother and child are united around something good, rather than something shameful. Renee's reactions to having such fantasies indicates that a vicious circle involving the poles of the complex has been established: "She feels cowardly, impure, miserly, mean, and because of this, inferior to everybody" (Sechehaye 1951: 36). This is the Humiliation pole. Everything she does is bad and punishable. Renee believes that in her everyday life the safest stance is to lie in bed without moving, without light, without food, and without sleep. This is Renee's first reference to self-starvation, which also may in part be a defence against the cannibalistic fantasies. The emergence of devouring images into conscious-ness or at least her willingness to describe them to MS in therapy, even though she has to redouble her efforts to defend against them, indicates that Renee is beginning to resolve the dissociation.

As these pivotal first three months of treatment drew to a close, there were two further important and unexpected advances. After leaving her sessions, Renee began to jump up and down in the street shouting: "I have a mother! I have a mother" (ibid.: 38). Surely this registered MS's ability to hold and metabolize Renee's primitive material, something Renee's own mother could not do. At the same time, Renee made three drawings – A, B, C – and brought them to a session. This meant that the ability to symbolize was at last able to proceed. MS noted that a positive transference was clearly established from this moment on (the drawings being at least in part gifts to MS) and that from then on Renee made drawings during her sessions, and that they calmed her.

Individuation, according to Jung, has two principal aspects: a process of objective relationship and an internal, subjective process of integration. A sign that the arrest of Renee's psychological development has been restarted is that the blocked state itself can be depicted and its poignancy for Renee symbolically conveyed. In Drawing A (Sechehaye 1951: 146), Renee is imprisoned behind an electric fence and longs for the freedom of the human figures standing next to her. In Drawing B (Sechehaye 1951: 148), a leafy tree has had its crown cut off. In Drawing C (Sechehaye 1951: 150), a woman has had her head cut off. In short, Renee's individuation, Renee's ego, and Renee's feminine self have all been terribly restricted. Now Renee has a vantage point from which to examine what has happened to her devel-opment, and a way to tell her therapist how bad she feels about that.

The next nine months of analysis: Renee becomes Sechehaye's "wonder-child"

Once the full level of Renee's wounding had been registered within the therapy, a compensatory sequence of a new beginning needed to occur with MS. To undo the traumatic sequences in her life, installed in the "System," it was necessary for Renee to experience, as if for the first time, mother–

infant bonding and a willingness on the part of the new mothering figure to take these emotions as valid.

Renee reaped many benefits from her rapport with MS – her therapist's voice and touch were soothing and seemed to make it safe for Renee to start to display emotion again. Before treatment began, Renee always felt "cold" inside, but now she began to feel warm. Renee continued to struggle, of course, with object constancy: she was in Agony when MS was away, for then she thought she actually ceased to exist.

Within the security of their rapport, however, Renee found herself able to continue to bring the "System" to consciousness. She no longer believed her "guilt" has an actual objective basis, and she became interested in discovering what it was that made her feel this way.

> Some time after, I discovered that the Persecutor was none other than [an aspect of] the electric machine, that is, it was the "System" that was punishing me. I thought of it as some vast world-like entity encompassing all [human beings]. At the top were those who gave orders, who imposed punishment, who pronounced others guilty. But they themselves were guilty. . . . Everyone was part of the System. But only some were aware of being part.
>
> (Renee 1951: 28)

This advance in conscious integration of the complex that was at the root of her eating disorder was quite important. Her understanding of the magnitude of the "System" that did not want her to thrive made it possible for Renee to achieve an insight into how this System had succeeded in making her unconscious enough of herself to be unaware of basic innate drives such as hunger that were her birthright:

> At this moment the ring closed: the Land of Enlightenment was the same as the System. That is why to enter into it was to become insensible of everything except culpability, the supreme punishment, freely granted by the System. I was guilty, abominably, intolerably guilty, without cause and without motive. Any punishment, the very worst, could be imposed on me — it could never deliver me of the load. Because, as I have already said, the most dreadful punishment was to make me feel eternally, universally culpable.
>
> (ibid.: 29)

As I have noted, Renee's description of her "guilt" is strikingly like Jungian analyst Erich Neumann's primary feeling of guilt. It is an affect that replaces any positive affects, including those surrounding the Hunger–Satiety drive, making them irrelevant to the person, who is no longer able to entertain such life-supporting psychological activities as enjoyable eating. The characterization of Renee as feeling too guilty to deserve such pleasures is consistent with my view that the "System" is an unconscious, monopolistic Rejection + Alienation → Shame/Humiliation–Contempt/Disgust complex which began to be structuralized in Renee's earliest infancy. We recall that Renee nearly died from Failure to Thrive-induced starvation in the first three months of her life.

A new foundation: Renee becomes MS's "Wonder-child"

Despite this grim history, by the end of the first year of treatment, MS had concluded that Renee could be cured if she could understand and resolve her pattern of self-punishment. By this time, however, both she and Renee had agreed that the interpretive method usual to psychoanalytic work had made Renee's "guilt" worse. As Renee's diary puts it:

> In the beginning, she analyzed everything I said, my fear, my guilt. These investigations seemed to me like a bill of complaints, quite as though in looking for the cause of my feelings, they became more at fault and more real. As if to say, "Find out in what instances you are guilty, and why." . . . From these sessions, I went home more unhappy, more blameworthy, more isolated than ever, without any contact, alone in my own unreal world.
>
> (Renee 1951: 33)

Renee's lack of object constancy had also made the use of the analytic couch, at that time the *sine qua non* of "deep" work, counterproductive. When MS was seated behind her, as good psychoanalytic technique required, Renee thought she was not there.

MS's first strategy in establishing a therapeutic alliance with Renee that would have a chance of defeating the System was to modify her seating: "I therefore have her sit next to me on the couch; she then observes that she is being listened to and that she has a partner. She feels less lonely and more protected against fear" (ibid.: 42). This new beginning positioned MS to begin to confront Renee's "guilt" in a more healing way. She now felt free to put her arm around Renee and "to resolutely take the side of the ego against the unconscious self-punishment, in thrusting aside the accusations, in condemning the punitive System and in associating myself with Renee's protests against it" (ibid.: 42). She reported that Renee felt relieved each time she did this.

Here is Renee's report of how she reacted to this radical change in MS's therapeutic stance:

Only near her I felt secure, especially from the time when she began to sit next to me on the couch and put her arm around my shoulders. Oh, what joy, what relief to feel the life, the warmth, the reality! From the moment I left her at the end of the session, I began to count the hours and the minutes; only twenty-four hours, only twenty-three and a half hours, only eighteen hours.

(Renee 1951: 25)

When Renee does enter into "Unreality" during a visit, MS now has the power to help her return to Reality.

What MS does not quite say in her discussion of this case is that Renee's symbolic development depended upon her becoming the "Wonder-child" to MS's loving "Mother" in the transference. In her day, a debate raged as to whether a corrective emotional experience was truly psychoanalytic, and she took pains to emphasize the degree of "symbolic realization" that she believed was at the root of Renee's recovery. Today, we can say that such symbolic development is impossible without the experience of being someone's "Wonder-child," and thus that MS did exactly enough to ensure that Renee would have that.

MS was certainly ahead of most psychoanalytic writers of her time in emphasizing the emotional influences on Renee's cure, for instance stating: "Naturally, too, the therapist's profound interest in the patient implies the determination to persevere to the end in order to find the real solution, and in this sense, her interest guides her search" (ibid.: 130). If we identify the root of MS's "maternal love" in the therapeutic situation as constellating within the therapeutic couple the archetypal affect of Joy, and then combine this with her obvious Interest in the patient, which also evoked the patient's Interest in herself, we can suggest that a healing archetypal field composed of the twin affects of the life instinct, Interest and Joy, was now embracing both her and Renee. This is no more than what is to be expected when an authentic mother–infant bonding has occurred (see my *The Symbolic Impetus*, 2001, Chapter 1). MS is human enough to admit a measure of ambivalence toward her difficult patient, which yielded to this newly constellated archetypal field. She says that her interest in Renee might have dropped off "without the responsibility which this affection gave me . . ." (ibid.: 130).

At this point, MS made another change in her approach to her patient: she began to speak to her in a different way. This is an example of this new approach:

Then Mama's sweet voice sounded in the midst of this madness and she was saying, "Little Renee, my little Renee needn't be afraid when there is a Mama. Renee is not alone. Mama is here to take care of her. She is stronger than everything else, stronger than the 'Enlightenment.' Mama will take Renee out of the water; we will win. See how strong Mama is, she knows how to protect Renee." And she passed her light hand over my head and kissed my forehead. Then, her voice, the caress on my hair, her protection, began to exert its charm.

(ibid.: 31)

Renee analyzes what is was about this speech modification that was beneficial to her:

What did me the most amazing good was her use of the third person in speaking of herself, "Mama and Renee," not "I and you." When by chance she used the first person, abruptly I no longer knew her, and I was angry that she had, by this error, broken my contact with her. So that when she said, "You will see how together we shall fight against the System," (what were "I" and "you?") for me there was no reality. Only "Mama," "Renee," or, better still, "the little personage," contained reality, life, affectivity.

(ibid.: 32)

One way to understand the effectiveness of MS's new form of verbal address is from a developmental perspective. At the beginning of early childhood (Chapter 3 of my *The Symbolic Impetus*, 2001), children use the impersonal pronoun "You," or their name, in self-reference, while at its close they employ the personal pronoun, "I." This is true of English and French speaking, as well as blind children (Huxley 1970; Fraiberg and Adelson 1973; Halliday 1975). Jung was aware of this pattern:

I wouldn't call the ego a creation of mind or consciousness, since, as we know, little children talk of themselves first in the third person and begin to say "I" only when they have found their ego. The ego, therefore, is rather a find or an experience and not a creation. We rather might say the empirical existence of an ego is a condition through which continuous consciousness becomes possible. For we know that the sort of impersonal consciousness observed in little children is not continuous but of a dissociated and insular character.

(Jung 1973b: 254–5)

It is understandable that in her regressed state, Renee prefers to be handled by MS as a young child. In this way, she is returned to a period of development before ego and shadow had been firmly distinguished enough to create responsibility. This relieves her from having to assume so much responsibility for the persecuting parental voices of the "System," whereas the earlier analytic technique had made her feel that there was something to be discovered that she had actually done which would explain why the voices were so accusatory.

As this first year of therapy drew to a close, Renee noted that the advances she made in her sessions had begun to last beyond the visits and MS's presence:

> Once in the street, however, I saw again the pasteboard scenery of unreality. Nevertheless, I did not suffer from it as I had at the beginning of the session for I still kept a little of Mama's warmth, her words in my heart. Particularly, I no longer struggled to break the unreality but submitted to the odd perception without trying to change it. As for the way home, the people, or the objects I passed, I experienced no further pressing need to enter into contact with them as with Mama.
>
> (ibid.: 32–3)

Renee's level of object constancy has improved. She can now hold "Unreality" in consciousness without entering into this desolate land with a feeling of responsibility for it. That freed her more mature ego for other tasks in the real world. MS wrote that a sure sign of improvement during this first year of therapy is that Renee obtained a school certificate and was immediately employed in an office.

The second and third years of analysis: MS becomes Renee's "Mother-sun"

Renee is 19 years old as she begins her third year of treatment, and she is continuing to struggle, with MS's help, against permanent entry into the barren land of "Unreality," that is, madness. Through the "voices" of its "Persecutors," the "System" often laughs derisively at her. Renee also reports experiencing a continuation of the devouring fantasies that she found so disgusting:

> It seemed that my mouth was full of birds which I crunched between my teeth, and their feathers, their blood and broken bones were choking me. Or I saw people whom I had entombed in milk bottles, putrefying, and I was consuming their rotting cadavers. Or I was devouring the head of a cat which meanwhile gnawed at my vitals. It was ghastly, intolerable.
>
> (Renee 1951: 37)

I see these morbid, "bulimic" fantasies as originating in the Hunger pole of a dissociated Hunger–Satiety drive. When Renee identifies with the dissociated Hunger drive, others are cannibalized; and when she detaches herself from it, she herself is attacked. But this other-directed and self-directed drive aggression is accompanied by the nuclear archetypal affect of Disgust, which continues to structure the eating complex in a grisly, pathological way. It's appearance in consciousness, on the other hand, indicates the dissociation is being overcome.

Other libidinal investments were also under attack during this period of her therapy. Her work as a secretary was disrupted by orders from the "System" to burn her hand. When she succumbed to this command and burned herself slightly, she was admitted to a rest home. During the first two weeks there, she lost ten pounds, for the "System" would not allow her to eat. Her dissociated Satiety drive had evidently trumped her Hunger drive. She had to be transferred to a psychiatric clinic for three weeks before she could return home and resume analysis with MS.

Renee now was no longer able to work, and she spent most of her time at home in a trance-like state:

> For the greater part of the day I sat in a chair, gazing fixedly before me, or plunged in the absorbed contemplation of a tiny spot; a spot which, no bigger than a grain of pepper, could hold me for an hour without any urge to shift my eyes from their absorption in this microscopic world.
>
> (ibid.: 56)

I believe she was now beginning to introvert and regress, which led to projection of the Self, the totality of the psyche, into the "spot." It was as if, to paraphrase Blake, To see the world in a grain of pepper.

"Mother-sun"

Renee is now 20 years old and eating hardly anything. She has terrible nightmares. Unconsciously motivated stereotypic behaviors begin and are repeated endlessly: taking three steps forward followed by three steps back; hitting a wall for hours; circling of a table; singing a Requiem continuously. I think that the circling helps us to imagine the point of such repetitive rituals: Renee is being driven to concentrate her introverted energies on the creative center of her psyche, the Self. That this circumambulation is successful in stimulating unconscious creative fantasy is shown by Renee now making Figures 5.2 and 5.3, a Requiem being an important element in the latter figure.

Figure 5.2 again shows an animal, an LP, and the System. It is divided into upper and lower sections. In the upper section, the LP stands with the "System" behind her, a line from it entering her head. In front of the LP is a figure who appears for the first time in one of her drawings, a figure she refers to as "Mother-sun." "Mother-sun" is smiling. She has both upper

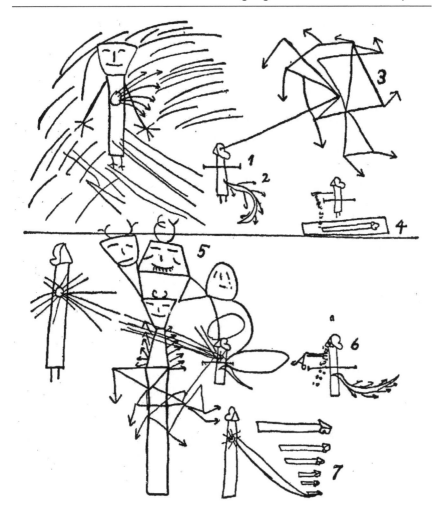

Figure 5.2 The "Little Personage" enters the body of "Mother-sun" (Sechehaye
         1951: 152).

and lower extremities and a circular heart with six radiant emanations.
"Mother-sun" is surrounded by what MS has learned to understand as
attack lines. There is an enigmatic scene in the lower right corner consisting
of the LP holding the "scissors" of hostility dripping blood and standing on
a coffin that has a dead woman inside it.

"Mother-sun" is that type of transpersonal image that Jungians refer to as
a positive mother imago, meaning the symbolic mother image achieved by
an imprinting of a positive mothering experience onto the mother archetype

itself, the structuring properties of which enable the image to form around the experience. When, in earliest infancy, this imago is constellated in the infant on the basis of positive and affirming experiences in the hands of a nurturant, caregiving mother figure, it can then be projected onto the personal "mother" and the basis for an infant–parent symbolic bond is established. Once established, this symbolic bond will persist throughout infancy and perhaps beyond, giving both self and world a transcendent, nurturing aspect. The archetypal affects that attend this vital engagement with the nurturing possibilities of existence are Interest and Joy, i.e. "mother," and Interest, i.e. "sun." The hyphen in "Mother-sun" expresses the fact that their relationship is a dialectical one. As the dynamism of Interest is curiosity/exploration and that of Joy is fantasy/play, it is apparent that the mother archetype, far from being a static image suggestive of a single, consistent mental state, is a dynamic center of psychological development with a process of its own.

The activation of the symbolic mother imago occurred at this moment in Renee's treatment because (a) the "System," the pathological complex that had been causing the dissociation of her personality, had been partially dissolved by its integration into consciousness and thus could not interfere so much with Renee's long put off healthy symbolic development (b) the positive maternal imago, beaming Interest and Joy at Renee's return to such development, was Renee's natural need at this moment in her regressive search for symbolic rebirth. In terms of emotional development, what the constellation of the "Mother-sun" in Renee means is that she is now in touch with the healthy, affective basis of her personality and that a new beginning of her ego development on a fully embodied basis may be possible. This is the promise of the upper half of Figure 5.2. But the lower half of this drawing, which depicts the shadow of all this positivity – the devouring mother complex still dominating her unconscious life, and now, as ever, threatening to swallow her ego and smother her consciousness – reminds that Renee's awareness of the healthy basis of her personality was, for now, to be short-lived.

For, in the lower half of Figure 5.2, a transformation of the scene in the upper half has occurred. Although "Mother-sun" and the LP still face each other, in between them is a formidable "System" that has reached a powerful, dissociative proportion. It has three heads, each a mocking "Persecutor" with horns; it has an elongated neck with six arrows projecting energy outward on each side; and the torso of the figure is the "System" itself. Above the LP are a sad face and a cloud, while she is carrying a bag of "guilt." Behind this LP is another LP holding scissors, but now sobbing. Nevertheless, the loss of a healthy relation to her birthright, the archetypal affect system that offers so many more feelings than guilt and sorrow, is not complete. The configuration at the lower right of this half of Figure 5.2 suggests that in this part of the drawing, at least, the dissociation has been overcome. There, "Mother-sun" stands unencumbered. Before her, lying in mid-air, are six LPs that grow smaller and smaller in descending order. The two lines extending from the smallest figure to the heart of "Mother-sun" indicate that this LP has entered her body, which means that she can be reborn. The motif clearly suggests that Renee's rebirth from the mother archetype is still a possibility. Figure 5.3 renews this promise.

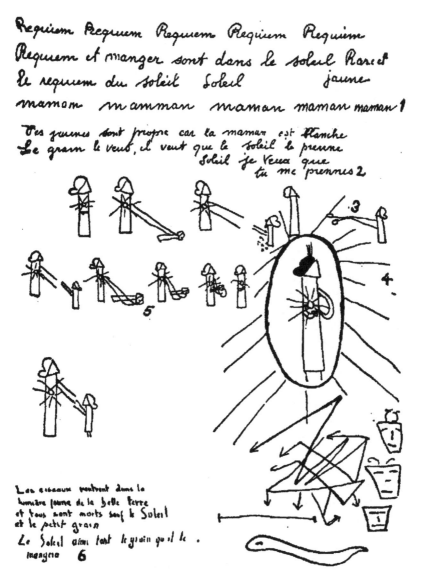

Figure 5.3 The "Little Personage" again enters the body of "Mother-sun" (Sechehaye 1951: 154).

Across the top of Figure 5.3 is written, in French, the "Requiem," which Renee has been finding herself singing incessantly. Invented by Renee, I think to say farewell to the wounded infantile self that must be transformed through rebirth, the symbolism of the Requiem involves a "white" mother, the "yellow" sun, and "eating" as a function of the latter. Renee explains to MS that Requiem means the inside of "Mother-sun," where she would like to live and be fed. LP stands before "Mother-sun," reaching out her arms to her. Next, there are two sequences, one above the other, in which the LP, now the "grain," is taken into the "Mother-sun." At the end of these depictions stands "Mother-sun," now with a radiant aura and holding the LP closed to her heart. To the right of "Mother-sun" stands the LP holding the "scissors," with these lines written at the bottom of the drawing:

> The scissors enter into the
> yellow light of the beautiful earth
> and everyone dies except the Sun
> and the little grain.
> The Sun loves the little grain so much
> that he will eat it.

(Sechehaye 1951: 55)

Once again, Jung seems to have been present at the creation of such symbolism. He writes, "Every sun myth shows the strange idea of becoming a child again, of returning to the parental shelter and of entering into the mother in order to be reborn through her" (Jung 1967: 223–4).

In the lower right hand corner of Figure 5.3, the "System," the heads of three "Persecutors" as well as two other figures, the "Straw," and the "Beast," are collapsed on top of each other. The writing to the left indicates that it was the "scissors" that accomplished this feat. This was why Renee wanted to hold onto her revenge, that is, to vanquish the pathological complexes. They appear, happily, depotentiated of their energies. This is a graphic presentation of the dissolving of the "System" complex en route to its integration into consciousness, i.e. the end of the dissociation that has so often interrupted Renee's development as a person.

This is not, however, the moment for Renee's rebirth. She is transferred to a rest home for her protection, where she makes several suicide attempts as well as beating, biting, and banging her body unmercifully. Once again the "System," that is, the pathological eating complex, is forbidding her to eat. A significant transformation, on the other hand, of the land of "Unreality" has begun. Renee now is the Queen of this desert country, the Unreality in which she has once more taken up residence, and she no longer suffers from being unloved. Although she still lives in complete solitude there, the necessities of life are now provided, especially (and for the first time) warmth.

When she refuses to feed herself, perhaps expecting to be fed in the oasis she has managed to transform into a more nourishing environment, she is transferred to a psychiatric clinic. She lapses into indifference and only rouses herself to write MS or to draw. In one letter, she asks: "Who constructed the System? It built itself and I entered into it" (Sechehaye 1951: 46). This is correct. In another letter, she wrote she hates her life and wants to enter MS's body. This rebirth fantasy signals that her hope for renewal is still alive. At any other time, this would be have been a reason for rejoicing and the end of crying. She is concerned, however, that she is getting younger and may reach the age of zero! But soon this regression becomes her goal. She now makes Figure 5.4.

In Figure 5.4, the "System" and the "Persecutors" stand resurgent above the LP and "Mother-sun," who face each other but are firmly separated by an ominous black barrier. The solid wall between them is a symbol of the dissociation of Renee's personality when the System takes over. That the "System" appears to be kicking up its heels, while the "Persecutors" rain their ridicule upon the LP, suggests that she has not yet fully integrated the negative in a way that can work for her; hence, it is free to interrupt the connection with MS that has been facilitating her connection to the archetypal affect system, that is, "Mother-sun," in a positive, well-modulated way. The overstimulated LP, again pierced by the revitalized electric wire or straw (in other words, raw negative affect that is not modulated), is sobbing. Below this tableau of primitive agonies, we see the "Beast," which has grown in size. This is Renee's sensuality, which has often threatened to overwhelm her from below, just as her System does from above, by making her feel unfit to live. Two little figures, however, hold the ends of another "Straw" without a barrier between them. And, in the lower right hand corner a new kind of image has emerged, two "flowers" ["Mother-sun" and Renee] with only a "nettle" between them.

When the head psychiatrist finds Renee quiet enough, MS finds a boarding house for her in the country where she is made comfortable and is able to see MS every day.

The miracle of the apples

Renee is now 21 years old. Her eating disturbance has begun to exhibit a new pattern. The "System" now forbids her anything salted or sweetened. She is able to eat only green vegetables and green apples, which do not cause feelings of guilt because they are products of the earth. The apples are to be picked directly from the tree, for that confers upon them the status of breast milk. Ripe apples that have fallen to the ground are "boiled cow's milk," not suitable for human consumption. The fact that "good" and "bad" apples appear in consciousness simultaneously suggests that the dissociation of the Hunger–Satiety drive is closer to resolution.

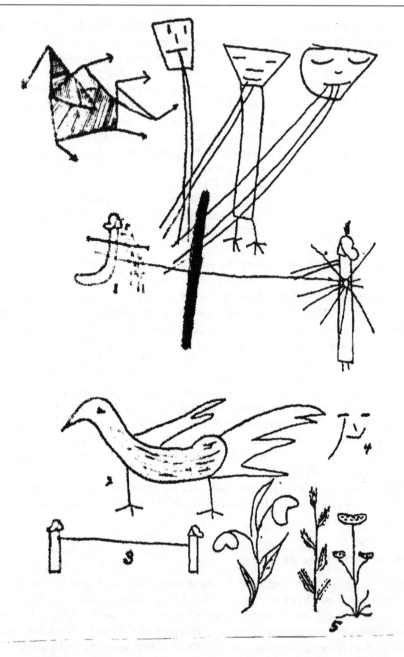

Figure 5.4 The "System" separates the "Little Personage" and "Mother-sun" (Sechehaye 1951: 156).

Renee picks green apples from the tree in the neighboring farmer's orchard and eats them voraciously. Her autobiography records:

> In taking these apples I had no sense of guilt for the tree was part of my country, the land of Tibet I called it, of which I was the queen. Indeed, I had the clear impression of living in a desert country, desolate, rocky, unreal, where I had one right — to eat the apples of my tree. Nevertheless, despite the tree, I was abandoned, miserable, left only the right to eat the apples; everything else was denied me.
>
> (Renee 1951: 73)

Renee's ego is at least now strong enough to allow the voracious, long dissociated and repressed Hunger drive full sway. She is also describing an important advance, for an oasis, "the right to eat the apples" (as significant as water rights in the Arabian desert), has been created in the stony wasteland of "Unreality."

MS takes full advantage of this reprieve and brings Renee pounds of the most beautiful apples she can find. Renee, however, always refuses these store-bought apples. Renee at this time finds herself losing contact with "Mama" and the withdrawn libido goes to stoke the fires of the "System." Once again, she fears that she will be changed into a starving cat forced to eat decomposing cadavers in cemeteries. She is continually being mocked and jeered by the Persecutors, who say "Ah, ah, wretched creature, eat, eat, only eat, do eat!" As she describes them at this time in her autobiography, "They kept urging me to eat, knowing it was forbidden and that I would be severely punished if I acceded to their prompting" (ibid.: 74). In other words, one aspect of the "System" encourages her to eat, while another part prohibits it. Again, however, the ability to symbolize her unconscious conflict as opposites she can actually experience suggests that both poles of the dissociated Hunger–Satiety drive are now present in consciousness and thus available for integration.

Then, a crisis occured. One day when Renee went to pick apples, the farmer's wife accused her of stealing, and said she must stop. Renee ran home in great turmoil and hid in her room. Under the force of this shaming confrontation, her own self-blaming, persecutory "System" was activated and she experienced insupportable Shame and Rage that she nevertheless somehow tolerated. Her one remaining sanction, that she can feed herself with apples from a tree, has been torn from her – the implacable authority of the "System" now wishes her dead because she has abused this privilege. Renee is desolate and cries out for her apples. This outraged cry of pain is highly significant. She is able to experience a healthy, surging wrath at the farmer's wife, who she feels has taken away her right to live. The next day, she runs away but returns home on the advice of a kindly woman she met on the road. There she found MS, who was critical of her behavior; that evening, her nurse forced her to eat dinner with the others. Following these setbacks, "The longing for [her] apples reached such a peak that [she] did not know what was to become of [her]" (ibid.: 78). In desperation, she runs away again, this time to the nearby home of MS, whom she thinks of as "Mama."

> In a state of distraction, strangeness and unheard of anguish, at nine o'clock that evening I ran on foot to Mama's house. In my ears the voices sneered, threatened me with death. My hands, like cat's paws, filled me with fear. At the same time I seemed to grow smaller and the nine centuries weighed heavily on my spirit. A tempest of horror, of desolation, of unreality, of hopeless abandonment roared in my soul. The voices were screaming, crying out that I ought to throw myself in the river. But I resisted with all my strength as I ran to Mama.
>
> (ibid.: 78)

MS tries to calm her, but without much success. This dialogue then takes place between them:

> Why [MS] said, "don't you take the apples I bring you?" "I can't do that, Mama," I answered. And while in my heart I was outraged that Mama too wanted to force me to eat, my eyes fell to her bosom, and when she insisted, "But why don't you want the apples *I* buy you?" I knew what I was yearning for so desperately and I was able to bring out, "Because the apples you buy are food for grown-ups and I want real apples, mama's apples, like those," and I pointed to Mama's breasts.
>
> (ibid.: 78–9, original emphasis)

The embodied transference that does have the potential for healing is obvious: Renee has now projected the image of "Mother-sun" onto the very person of MS, who immediately accepts the totality of the projection upon her without interpretation but claiming the full freedom the projection grants her to speak to Renee exactly as a mother would to her infant:

> She got up at once, went to get a magnificent apple, cut a piece and gave it to me, saying, "Now, Mama is going to feed her little Renee. It is time to drink the good milk from Mama's apples." She put the piece in my mouth, and with my eyes closed, my head against her breast, I ate, or rather, drank my milk. A nameless felicity flowed into my heart. It was as though, suddenly, by magic, all my agony, the tempest which had shaken me a moment ago, had given place to a blissful calm; I thought of nothing, I discerned nothing, I reveled in my joy, I was fully

content, with a passive contentment, the contentment of a tiny baby, quite unconscious, for I did not even know what caused it.

(ibid.: 79)

The constellation of the archetypal affects of Interest and Joy are evident. MS's resonance to the symbolic transference radiating from Renee's own image of her therapist as "Mother-sun" is allowing the affects associated with this image to enter Renee's consciousness. They now belong to her, as does the imagery that evoked them. MS's acceptance of Renee's projection also confirms Renee's status as her "Wonder-child," but it is Renee's psyche, not MS's skill as a therapist, that is leading the process at this point. MS is wisely accepting the energy that Renee's psyche is bringing to their relationship, and what she enacts allows Renee to claim it within their relationship. Symbolic patient/infant–therapist/mother bonding has become a psychological reality, something Renee can retain and build upon.

Following this breakthrough, which MS referred to as "the miracle of the apples," MS makes "feeding" Renee a regular part of her appointments. In MS's part of the account of the therapy, she writes, "Now my task is well mapped out; I must bring Renee a piece of raw apple and give it to her at regular intervals. She eats it gravely at [the part of] each of our 'sessions,' which represent the feeding hour" (Sechehaye 1951: 52–3).

We notice that during Renee's eating of a piece of raw apple, positive emotional psychization of her Hunger–Satiety occurs. That this is healthy serious eating is indicated by her "eating it gravely." (Meals, of course, often have this grave aspect for many people; they are sacred occasions, marked in many homes at the outset by the saying of grace.) The transformative effects of realized patient/infant–therapist/parent bonding have become expanded into a religious ritual. But not all is solemn. There is also a general relaxation within Renee's ego, the "System" is in abeyance and the fantasied cat invasions (surely an image of the intrusive devouring mother) have subsided: "And even more startling, Renee has the sensation of reality for the first time (though still fragmentary). She feels transported with joy and astonishment, as one born blind, seeing the light for the first time" (ibid.: 53). This means that the rituals within the mother–infant transference have provided a symbolic impetus to healthy, discriminating ego development out of the devouring, fantasy-driven unconscious.

In addition, the archetypal affects of Joy and Interest are bringing color to Renee's experience of reality. Renee's perception of MS alters accordingly:

Mama too had changed in my eyes. Before she had appeared like an image, a statue that one likes to look at, though it remains artificial, unreal; but from this moment on she became alive, warm, animated, and I cherished her deeply. I had an intense desire to remain near her, against her, to preserve this marvelous contact.

(Renee 1951: 81)

Both Renee and MS are now contained in an archetypal field characterized by the continuous flow of Interest and Joy from each to the other.

Resolution of the eating disorder continues, strong evidence for this book's hypothesis that a problem with eating reflects blocked positive affective development and tends to disappear when the affects that are required to enjoy the hunger drive become available. After the raw apples, Renee began to take apple sauce and could progressively eat real milk and porridge, "something unheard of, for until that day I detested milk. But at that time it seemed altogether natural to drink milk" (Renee 1951: 82). And MS placed on the mantelpiece "two beautiful apples representing the maternal breasts given me by Mama to protect me. At the least anxiety I ran to them and at once was reassured" (ibid.: 82). The apples are, for Renee, symbols of "Mother-sun."

Intrapsychic developments associated with this therapeutic breakthrough are recorded in drawings H (Sechehaye 1951: 159) and I (ibid.: 160) that Renee made at this time. At the top of drawing H are the "Apples," as well as a benevolent "sun/star," which are keeping watch over little Jesus (Renee herself), who sleeps in a crèche. Beneath the crèche, there are mythological hieroglyphics and, below them, is a hymn of adoration to her apples. A "Divine child," a symbol of the Self, has been born in Renee's psyche. In Drawing I, Renee takes her revenge on the farmer's wife, who carries the projection of the archetype of the Terrible Mother. She is drawn with horns and is shown attempting to prevent the LP from picking and eating green apples. The LP, however, goes ahead anyway and claims the tree as her own, and she is thus free to eat as many apples as she chooses. The LP's final act of self-assertion, to assure her right to satisfy her appetite, is to rain curses on the horned, negative mother imago. At this point, then, the "tree of life," shown severed in Drawing A (see p. 74), has been fully restored within Renee's psyche.

Third, fourth, and fifth years of analysis: Renee floats in the "green sea"

We have just observed Renee recapitulate with MS the infant–parent bonding, the miracle of the apples, that follows the earlier mother/MS–infant/Renee bonding when Renee became MS's "Wonder-child." During this phase of treatment, there is a strong parallel between Renee's advance during therapy – Renee–Self bonding – and the third step in earliest symbolic development – infant–Self bonding.

After the miracle of the apples, Renee's struggles with "Unreality" and the "System" decreased. During this phase of therapy, however, there were more frequent hospitalizations. These were necessary to protect Renee from her self-destructive behaviors and to provide her with a supportive milieu for her continuing introversion and regression.

In Late Thoughts, Chapter XII of *Memories, Dreams, Reflections*, C. G. Jung states that as a psychiatrist, a "doctor of the soul," he was always primarily interested in how he could help his patients recover the healthy basis of their personalities, which for him was always to be found in their spontaneous emotions, which he understood to be expressions of an innate, Archetypal affect system. The emotions, he believed, were expressions of the life instinct within the person. Of the Archetypal affect system itself, he wrote:

> On this complicated base, the ego arises. Throughout life the ego is sustained by this base. When the base does not function, stasis ensues and then death. Its life and reality are of vital importance. Compared to it, even the external world is secondary, for what does the world matter if the endogenous impulse to grasp and manipulate it is lacking? In the long run no conscious will can ever replace the life instinct. This instinct comes to us from within, as a compulsion or will or command, and if – as has more or less been done since time immemorial – we give it the name of a personal daimon we are at least aptly expressing the psychological situation.
>
> (Jung 1961: 348–9)

Coming at the same phenomenon from the standpoint of the personality structures Jung had postulated for the individuation of the human personality, Erich Neumann defined the relation between ego-consciousness and the healthy basis of the personality as the ego-Self axis:

> This relationship between the ego and the Self is of crucial importance for the development and sound functioning of the psyche. We call it the ego-Self axis. When we say that the ego is based on the Self or that the ego is a derivative of the Self, we are again referring to the function of centroversion. In other words, we are stating a condensation of the phenomenon that the total personality (for which the Self stands as a necessarily hypostatized center) directs, controls and balances all the processes leading to the emergence of the child ego and its development into an adult ego.
>
> (Neumann 1973/1990: 20)

Reconstruction and construction of the ego-Self axis, which in her drawings was symbolized by the "tree of life," was the task that confronted

Renee during this period of her treatment. The symbol of "Mother-sun," realized during the previous phase of treatment and projected upon MS, was a radiant symbol originating in this healthy basis of Renee's personality and one that provided the support that enabled the ego-Self axis to become healthy and to bear fruit.

At this point in her treatment, Renee moved from the country home, where the miracle of the apples occurred, to MS's residence. There, two setbacks occurred. The psychiatric nurse, who cared for Renee in the rural setting and moved to MS's home with her, left abruptly. This was a great shock to Renee: "All night long I sobbed in anger and grief; my whole world had fallen to pieces. Her absence was simply unbearable and my suffering was cruel" (Renee 1951: 85). The nurse's departure constellated an unconscious abandonment complex in Renee, which seems to have first been formed when her grandmother left her abruptly when Renee was 11 months old. The complex gathered unpleasant similar experiences into itself and thus increased in magnitude and severity each time her parents threatened to abandon her. It became frank pathology when her father actually did abandon the family.

In Drawing K (Sechehaye 1951: 162), Renee expressed her reaction to the loss of her nurse, which she protested loudly to MS with a diatribe against the now absent nurse, "Elise." Renee shamed her by giving her horns and covering her with spit, lice, and dirt. Renee stated that the nurse was mean, a liar, detestable, and shameful – in a word, a witch. She said she wanted to kill her. There is no doubt that the proximal cause of this spasm of archetypal Contempt and Disgust was the nurse's departure. The deep trigger of the complex, on the other hand, was the memory preserved in her unconscious of the primitive agonies she had felt upon the sudden departure of her grandmother when she was 11 months old. The complex formed around these events appeared to combine Loss with Rejection, the latter fantasy predominating in the drawing she made after her nurse suddenly left her. It is useful to recall that when her grandmother did return to the home when a sibling was born, Renee met her with a spray of spit. In the drawing around her nurse, Renee seems to have a much broader emotional vocabulary for expressing her negative archetypal affects, which indicates strengthening of her ego-complex.

A related type of reversal was Renee's experience of MS's other patients as they came to and left the office in which she saw people at her home. This evoked the rivalrous rage Renee had directed toward younger siblings whom their mother had favored. By this time, Renee was beginning to perceive MS ambivalently, on the one hand as Mama, the Queen, the Goddess, the source of life and of Renee's joy, and on the other, as a source of frustrating deprivation. As she put it in her diary, "This Goddess was unfair, giving of her sacredly precious milk to the undeserving [the other patients] whose need was not as pressing as mine" (Renee 1951: 86).

Renee expresses these feelings graphically in Figure 9 (Sechehaye 1957: 988). At the top, "Mother-sun" is presenting the symbolic pair of apples to Renee's therapeutic "siblings," with her back to the LP, who turns away from her sobbing. At the lower left, "Mother-sun" has returned to present the two life-giving apples to the LP, who now is much too angry to accept them. In the last scene, Renee is struck by lightning when she realizes that one of her rivals has usurped her place at the breasts of "Mother-sun." Renee is horrified that her place has been taken. When MS rebukes her for her complaints about the other patients, Renee is strong enough, however, to draw up bills of indictment in which she points out her Mama's iniquitous behaviors.

During this trying period, Renee had to be hospitalized twice under guard of a nurse to prevent her from hurting herself. Kept drowsy with sedatives and hot baths, Renee fell into a stupor for the next six months. Her inability to feed herself recurred and she had to be tube fed. One day, when she saw Mama again and recognized her, noticing she was crying, Renee at last felt some reason to move out of her stupor in MS's direction. MS immediately understood the gesture, took her home, and got Renee to eat a little. Although at first dissociation of the Hunger–Satiety drive persisted, MS was able to frame the possibility of eating with enough positive emotions that Renee was actually able to resume eating. So far as Renee's psychosis was concerned, reestablishing her rapport with MS allowed Renee to countermand the order from the "System" that she not eat, which represented a significant degree of reversal of the basis of the recurrent dissociation of the Hunger–Satiety drive.

For the next year, Renee was able, off and on, to continue to live with Mama, but only because a great deal of her time was spent at the hospital. There she lay in a near-catatonic state, with her knees up and her head turned toward the wall. The accompanying monotonous psychic state of "congealed lethargy" was disrupted by episodes of self-recrimination and despair. There were also daydreams that detailed how destructive her badness had actually been: "In my fantasy, entire cities lay in ruins, rocks crushed in fragments, all a consequence of my execrable crime, the sin of Cain" (Renee 1951: 89–90). An image of these demolitions appears in Figure 10 (Sechehaye 1957: 989).

My own understanding of this material is based on Renee's previous descriptions of the land of "Unreality" as a desert country, desolate and rocky, one where she had the right to eat only green apples from the special tree. This tree was rooted in an "oasis" that Renee herself had constructed by removal of some of the mineral rocks in the desert terrain of "Unreality." In terms of her psychic structure, then, the breaking up of the rocks meant that breakdown of the dissociation of her personality was in fact under way. The "rocks crushed into fragments" were, I believe, symbolic expressions of the continuation of Renee's significant attempts to do something about the dissociation of her Hunger–Satiety drive. If the "cities" and "rocks" are taken as structures associated with the pathological organization of the "System," then breaking them up suggests an attempt to undo the hold these pathological complexes had on Renee's psyche's by taking apart the associations that had helped to form them.

The danger inherent in such self-demolition of damaging internal structures, of course, is that it can go too far, and at this time in Renee's therapy, such "progress" was often accompanied by suicidal impulses, in other words the fantasy of a total self-demolition, which would make any further work on the self unnecessary. About this time, she wrote:

> Only one thing absorbed me, to annihilate, to assassinate this ignoble being, this hideous, infamous creature, myself, hated to the point of death. The voices were unchained afresh; a devastating tempest ravaged my soul.
>
> (Renee 1951: 91)

The emotional quality of the self-reproaches that led her to contemplate simply ending her wretched existence once and for all suggested the archetypal affect of Humiliation/Disgust. But these suicidal states alternated with states of detachment. At such moments, she wrote:

> Indeed, everything had become so totally irrelevant, so devoid of emotion and sensibility that in truth it was the same as though they were not talking to me at all. I simply could not react, the essential motor force had broken down. Images with whom I had nothing to do, from whom I was remote, moved toward and away from my bed. I was, myself, a lifeless image.
>
> (ibid.: 91–2)

Jung envisions a possible value in such a detached introversion, a state he understands with empathy for its self-healing potential:

> So far as I have been able to understand it, it seems to have to do with an acute state of consciousness, as intense as it is abstract, a "detached" consciousness. . . . As a rule, the phenomenon is spontaneous, coming and going on its own initiative. Its effect is astonishing in that it almost always brings about a solution of psychic complications and frees the inner personality from emotional and intellectual entanglements, thus creating a unity of being which is universally felt as liberation.
>
> (Jung 1968b: 27–8)

Getting to a unity of being took Renee, who was now 22 years of age and still in a fragmented state, another two years to achieve. It was, however, en route: MS tells us that one day she gave Renee a big, plush tiger to protect her from the persecuting voices: "The relief was tremendous for when I wanted to revenge myself against the evil-doers, it was he who took my place, loving me and biting those who would do me injury" (ibid.: 92). Renee felt she was his chosen one and this made her proud.

Again, MS had to offer the helpful symbol that could rally Renee's resilience. Renee's own internal development of her symbolic function had not reached the level where her unconscious could create in a dream or waking fantasy a "helpful" animal of the kind found in myth and fairy tale. She could however recognize and utilize one that was given to her. Jung connects this motif to constructive regression. The plush tiger, like other symbolic "helpful animals," may be connected with the parental imago, in Renee's case, the "Mother-sun." At the same time, the "System," as evidenced by its persecutory voices, had not lost its emotional hold over Renee, for she was racked by a fury of self-annihilation. Eating under such circumstances was unthinkable, and so tube feeding was again necessary.

During this difficult time, MS needed to make a change inside her home, and it became necessary to send Renee to a private clinic. Renee, naturally, experienced this as a Rejection:

> She became quickly worse, manifested catatonia, mutism, negativism, and repeatedly tore up her clothing. Again she had to be fed by tube, for a month, and put in a cell at night with three straps, as during the day. Complete disintegration and little by little total inertia with self-mutilation set in.
>
> (Sechehaye 1951: 67)

After six weeks, MS found a family with a helper where Renee could be in a home and yet under her doctor's supervision and MS could see her for two to three hours every afternoon. As Renee was still unable to eat, tube feeding continued to be a necessity. Renee knew she could not talk because (as she wrote at the time) "it is bad" but she communicated with MS through Drawing L (Sechehaye 1951: 164–5). In the top image, the LP lies terrified on a small mound below a large eye in the sky that is watching her (a line extends down from the eye to her). On her left stands a barren tree of life, with a possible eyebrow from a persecutor among it branches. In the middle of the drawing, the LP is sobbing under her burden of punishment and death. In the lower left, she kneels and sobs under a perhaps more beneficent sun, with a large question mark in front of her. In the lower part of the drawing, to the right, we find that her question is what she has done to warrant such suffering: she has stopped sobbing and raises her arms in ritual supplication to the sun, a hopeful gesture.

It is tempting to see the watching eye as ominous, along the lines of the Evil Eye in some mythic traditions, but Jung has written that the center of the total personality, the Self, is frequently symbolized by an eye, "the ever-open eye of the fish in alchemy, or the unsleeping 'God's eye' of conscience, or the all-seeing sun" (Jung 1970b: 424). He elaborates:

> The symbols of divinity coincide with those of the self: what, on the one side, appears as a psychological experience signifying wholeness, expresses on the other side the idea of God. This is not to assert a metaphysical identity of the two, but merely the empirical identity of the images representing them, which all originate in the human psyche . . . What the metaphysical conditions are for the similarity of the images is, like everything transcendental, beyond human knowledge.
>
> (ibid.: 339)

This interpretation of the celestial "eye" as a symbol of the Self, the totality of Renee's personality, suggests that the eye is not simply the paranoid gaze of the persecutory system under which Renee had been living so long, but a symbol of the remaining possibility of wholeness, still available to her, i.e. the healthy, affective basis of her personality (see also R. Pettazzoni, 1956, *The All-Knowing God*). This is in favor of my view that, even though the regressive, psychotic symptoms that were accompanying the fragmentation of the complexes that had been causing her dissociation from the healthy matrix of ego development, including the Hunger–Satiety drive, were evident, the dissociation of her personality was in fact in the final stages of being resolved.

As a corollary to this advance, Renee was able to take advantage of a new symbolic gift from MS, a doll Renee christened Ezekiel and declared was six months old. MS frequently engaged in loving symbolic play with Ezekiel, performances which Renee watched intently:

> Taking courage one day when Ezekiel was in Mama's arms, I pushed his head forward on her bosom to test whether I had the right to live. At this, Mama pressed him to her breast and let him nurse. This she did regularly several times a day so that I awaited the moment in fear of her forgetting. But Mama did not forget and I began to dare to live.
>
> (Renee 1951: 94–5)

Renee's active, imaginative entry into the Ezekiel fantasy was a significant step in resolving her problem over the right to live:

> The best way of dealing with the unconscious is the creative way. Create for instance a fantasy. Work it out with all the means at your disposal. Work it out as if you were it or in it, as you would work out a real situation in life which you cannot escape. All the difficulties you overcome in such a fantasy are symbolic expressions of psychological

difficulties in yourself, and inasmuch as you overcome them in your imagination you also overcome them in your psyche.

(Jung 1973b: 108–9)

And here is the empirical proof of this principle:

The self-destructive impulses decreased perceptibly, and instead of spending the day in bed with my head under the covers, I looked about, interested in everything concerning Ezekiel. Then I, who had always refused food, even presumed to eat. A little later when I saw how Mama bathed and dressed Ezekiel, I consented with pleasure to being bathed and dressed myself and actually enjoyed it. In busying herself lovingly with Ezekiel it was as though Mama were bestowing on me the right to live. Slowly I came out of my lethargy and grew more and more interested in what Mama said and did to Ezekiel, an interest confined strictly, however, to feeding and cleanliness. I allowed myself to enjoy it a bit; even so, the dreadful crises of guilt persisted.

(Renee 1951: 95)

Renee was at this point more securely than ever in touch with the healthy affective basis of her personality, because she had established a right to be so, and the twin emotions of the life instinct – Interest–curiosity/exploration and Joy–fantasy/play – which made their home there, now irrigated her psyche with a new zest for living. She was now ready for the last phase of her self-healing regression.

As ever, this positive development came cloaked in a painful guise. Renee fell ill, with a severe attack of pyelonephritis accompanied by agonizing kidney pain. She immediately interpreted the illness as a certain sign of her blameworthiness. She stopped eating, and her weight plummeted to 53 pounds. Her doctor thought she would die. But he was able to make an autovaccine that cured her renal infection. MS herself fell ill for several weeks at this time. Renee, seeing herself as omnipotent in her destructiveness, took this as proof of an abandonment she herself had caused and determined that she was not to go on living. The self-destructive impulses and persecutory voices awoke with fresh energy: "She refused medicine and food, and started hitting and biting herself" (Sechehaye 1951: 70). It was necessary to place pillows against the wall and attach Renee to her bed with straps on the hands and the body. When MS had recovered, she resumed Renee's treatment and six months later the straps could be removed. Renee was now 23¾ years old.

One day, when Renee was being attacked by persecutory voices, MS told her that she was going to banish the voices so Renee could sleep like Moses and Ezekiel. She proceeded to give her a sedative hypodermic injection, whereupon Renee felt herself "slipping into a wonderful realm of peace":

Everything in the room was green, green as the sea, quite like being in Mama's body. My pain assuaged, in a state of perfect passivity, without want of any kind; Mama had procured this bliss for me. Hence, I thought, she is willing to take me into her body. An immense relief flowed over me; I was in Paradise, in the maternal bosom.

(Renee 1951: 97)

Quite soon, an injection was no longer necessary. The persecutory voices returned, however, and Renee complained: "It isn't green anymore!" (Sechehaye 1951: 73). When MS put a compress to her forehead, however, Renee said: "You are making green" (ibid.: 73).

This was the new miracle. Renee wrote that "from that moment I had unshakable confidence in Mama and I loved her as never before" (ibid.: 97).

That she had received me into herself, that she had acceded to my fondest wish filled me with happiness and proved without doubt that she loved me, that I was loved. Whenever after this the suffering bore down and the voices afflicted me, by the simple expedient of sedative hypodermic and arranging the green twilight in my room, Mama placed me in the "green sea," in her felicity, safe from vicissitude.

(ibid.: 97)

MS wrote that for Renee green was the color of the bottom of the ocean and marshland, and to be in the green meant to be in the mother's body, the wished-for paradise" (Sechehaye 1951: 72–3). I understand the "wished-for paradise" as not just a recreation of an original Divine Child/Great Mother object relation between patient and therapist in the transference, but the access of the patient's ego to the pristine, emotionally alive, healthy, matrix of her personality, the archetypal affect system of the Self, now as ever alive in the depths of her psyche but no longer dissociated because, thanks to MS's care in establishing a symbolic base for it, an ego-Self axis has been constructed between ego-consciousness and the center of Renee's total personality. This axis is what gave Renee foundational confidence in the integrity of her own personality, and her right to thrive. Madness at this point was no longer a danger, and Renee's eating disturbance was resolved. As with any patient, there were fits and starts in Renee's psychological development from this point forward, but her overall therapeutic course was progressive.

Chapter 6

The Bulimia–Anorexia syndrome and suicide

Ludwig Binswanger's case of Ellen West

In 1958, as part of a book that brought Existential Analysis to the attention of American psychotherapists, the Swiss psychiatrist Ludwig Binswanger (LB) presented an English version of his 1944 case study of the life and suicide of his patient "Ellen West," whom he had diagnosed as suffering from a form of schizophrenia. A frequent critique of this courageous, empathic account of a failed psychotherapy has been that Ellen actually suffered from Anorexia nervosa (AN). Commentaries on this classic case have been published by David Lester (1971), R. D. Laing (1982), Angelyn Spignesi (1983), Carl Rogers (1990), Craig Jackson and co-authors (1990), Namah Akavia (2003), and Katrien Libbrecht (2003), among others.

In 2002, Albrecht Hirschmuller convened a conference to study the original reports of the case, including Binswanger's original notes, and new material obtained from Ellen's family. The papers presented at this meeting have been edited and published by Hirschmuller (2003) in "*Ellen West, Eine Patientin Ludwig Binswangers zwischen Kreativitat und destruktivem Leiden*," but this material has not been translated into English.

I will begin my own reformulation of this classic material, which lives in the imagination as eternally present, even though it unfolded over a period of time, by discussing the onset of Ellen's eating disorder, a moment that takes us into the life and world of Binswanger's future patient when she is 20 years old. Next, I will follow the course of her eating disorder until her death, when she is 33 years old, to show how the severity of her BN–AN syndrome, which I will document as such, was influenced by Ellen's advances into and retreats from life. I am marshalling the empirical evidence, not just in favor of my view that Ellen suffered from the unitary BN–AN syndrome I have been postulating throughout this book, but also to argue that this syndrome's pervasive takeover of a patient's life and world can be explained by a simple phenomenological reduction: it is nothing other than possession by the dissociated fragments of the Hunger–Satiety Drive, which have returned to dominate the entire life of the patient by controlling her attitude and behavior in relation to the food that keeps her alive, to the point that she must give life itself up to make herself free of their terrifying power. My basic hypothesis will be simple: Hunger dissociated from Satiety becomes bulimic; Satiety dissociated from Hunger becomes anorexic. I believe the empirical data will show that the cause of this dissociation was a pathological eating complex, with its nucleus composed of crisis archetypal affects. At the end of this chapter, I will offer a new approach to understanding her suicide, in the hope it may actually prevent similar outcomes in other BN–AN patients.

Ellen is 20 years old: an eating disorder begins

Ellen West was raised in an intact family along with an older and a younger brother. Her birth date is never mentioned in LB's report, but I believe there is enough material alluding to it that we can estimate it was in July 1897.

Just before the onset of her eating disorder, Ellen had made two advances into life. She left home and traveled to another country to help take care of her older brother who was ill. And, during her return trip, she had become engaged to a "romantic foreigner." It was then that she was forced into the first of her many retreats from this promising, emerging life: At the request of her father, Ellen broke off the engagement.

We begin to experience her dilemma, in the report, when she stops in Sicily on her way home and writes in her diary that all her fine ideas and plans are not being turned into deeds – there is a lack of self-realization. We sense that with this confession she is recognizing that she is already, by returning home, regressing into the lap of her family. The next reaction to the retreat that follows, the breaking off of her engagement, is the onset of her eating disorder. Binswanger tells us:

> Along with this, however, something new emerges now, a definite dread – namely, a dread of getting fat. At the beginning of her stay in Sicily Ellen had still displayed an enormous appetite. As a result she got so fat that her girl friends began to tease her about it. At once she begins to mortify herself by fasting and immoderate hikes. . . . When she goes home in the spring, everyone is horrified at how bad she looks.
>
> (Binswanger 1958: 242)

My speculation is that this onset came about in this way: Unknown to all, a pathological eating complex had been developing in Ellen's unconscious; it was fueled in part by an appetite for life that was being suppressed and consisted in a dissociation of her Hunger–Satiety drive. When Ellen withdrew from her engagement, the energy associated with her desire to have a life of her own fell into the unconscious where it became assimilated by this already split-off eating complex, which achieved a magnitude sufficient to produce the BN–AN syndrome. It was not just her Hunger that was split off, but her Satiety as well, so that she never knew, after that, how much food was enough. The dissociation of her Hunger–Satiety drive, the condition I find necessary for this type of eating disorder to develop, is expressed in her "ravenous appetite," that is, Hunger dissociated from Satiety, followed by a satisfaction with "fasting," that is, Satiety dissociated from Hunger.

Ellen is 21 years old

LB begins his report of this year by indicating that Ellen is constantly tormented by the idea that she is getting too fat. My understanding of an BN–AN syndrome is that when the Hunger–Satiety drive is dissociated, the unconscious, bulimic Hunger, though present and sometimes acted out, will inevitably be compensated, as night follows day, by a conscious anorexic Satiety, expressed in Ellen's case by "the idea that she is getting too fat." In my opinion, this idea could not have been present had she not regularly felt that she had already had enough to eat.

Turning to her descriptions of her emotional life, LB gives a moving account of Ellen's struggle with low self-esteem: "She feels herself to be absolutely worthless and useless. She sees herself as being on the lowest rung of the ladder that leads to the light, degraded to the status of a cowardly, wretched creature: [she even writes in her diary,] I despise myself" (Binswanger 1958: 242). These thoughts and feelings that Ellen has about herself are generated, in my judgment, by the unconscious eating complex that is plaguing her. We can hear the contempt she levels at herself as indicating that the nuclear emotion of this structure has the following constellating pattern: Rejection + Alienation → Shame/Contempt–Humiliation/ Disgust. At this time in Ellen's life, self-Disgust, which is another name for Humiliation, is present in her conscious mind, while other-Disgust is nearly entirely unconscious. In Ellen's poem, "Evil Thoughts," the same archetypal affects are expressed. LB introduces this poem by writing that Ellen sees evil demons behind every tree, who mock her, seize her, and then speak. After pointing out that all her projects lie buried, as they did in Sicily when Ellen lent the demons her voice, they attack her:

> And you've become a nothing,
> A timid earthy worm.
> . . .
> If you seek peace and quiet,
> Then we'll come creeping nigh
> And we'll take vengeance on you
> With our derisive cry.

> If you seek joy and gladness,
> We'll hurry to your side;
> Accusing you and jeering
> We'll e'er with you abide!
>
> (ibid.: 244)

What the "voices," which I believe are of the pathological eating complex, keep expressing is the Contempt half of the archetypal affect (and object relation) Shame/Contempt. As Contempt is leveled at her, she experiences the archetypal affect's other half, Shame. The "voices" also have the power to dissociate Ellen from the Interest and Joy that had previously been able to give her personality an interest in its advancement and a pleasure at the prospect of realizing that.

Ellen is painfully aware of this deficit in vitality that has resulted, and she notes the blandness that has settled over her psyche: "Everything is so uniform to me, so utterly indifferent, I know no feeling of joy and none of fear" (ibid.: 242–3). LB paraphrases one of her poems which portrays her psychic stagnation: "In a poem, grim distress sits at her grave, ashy pale – sits and stares, does not flinch nor budge; the birds grow mute and flee, the flowers wilt before its ice-cold breath" (ibid.: 242). The complex (for that is what I think it is) blocking her growth is personified as a threatening hydra: "Everything in me trembles with dread, dread of the adders of my every-day, which would coil about me with their cold bodies and press the will to fight out of me" (ibid.: 244). The image in another diary entry depicts the stunting of souls, that is, undeveloped elements of her personality, dwelling in the musty cellar hole in which she is imprisoned:

> No wonder you have got such ugly yellow souls, you who have grown up in this atmosphere. Already you have ceased to notice how hard it is to breathe here. Your souls have grown dwarf lungs. Everything about you is dwarflike: thoughts, feelings, and – dreams.
>
> (ibid.: 245)

She struggles to break free from the unconscious and is able to mobilize her energies enough to make preparations for the installation of children's reading rooms, a project that has interested her for a long time.

Ellen at 23 and 24

Ellen keeps a close eye on her weight and reduces her food intake at the first sign of weight gain: "But now dread of getting fat is accompanied by an intensified longing for food . . ." (ibid.: 245). The simultaneous appearance in her conscious self-experience of both "intensified longing for food" and "fear of getting fat" suggests that her writings have served at least one healing function: they have enabled her to partially integrate the dissociated Hunger–Satiety drive, to the extent that she can feel and think about its parts. We also see a measure of retrieval of the psychic energy tied up in the complex, her long-lost appetite for life. We have, for a brief time, reason to hope this energy will actually be used by Ellen for progression into life. She passes the teacher's examination so that she can audit courses at a nearby university during the summer semester of her twenty-third year and the winter semester of the beginning of her twenty-fourth year. LB writes that this is one of the most joyful periods in her life. In the summer, she falls in love with a fellow student.

There are, however, shadows. Although she willingly goes with her classmates on long excursions to the mountains, she cannot do so alone: she needs her old governess constantly with her. This is the first direct evidence of Ellen's mother hunger, and as well gives us a clue that she suffers from a lack of object constancy. She decides she cannot free herself of her fear of getting fat, which she now refers to as her "fixed idea." She avoids fattening foods and begins a reducing diet.

When her love affair with the student turns into an engagement, her parents once again interfere: they demand a temporary separation, and once again Ellen complies. Her joyful advance into life has once again been sidetracked into a retreat, one for which she will pay a high price. After she separates from her fiancé, she moves to a seaside resort. There, "She does everything to get just as thin as possible, takes long hikes, and daily swallows thirty-six to forty-eight thyroid tablets! Consumed by homesickness, she begs her parents to let her return. She arrives completely emaciated . . ." (ibid.: 246). Her "homesickness" is a further symptom of her retreat from life. The energy Ellen withdrew from her beloved has lapsed into the unconscious and strengthened the power of the pathological eating complex, which has now begun to devour her, in the all-consuming way of the BN–AN syndrome. Interestingly, though this is much the same dynamic we observed when she withdrew from her love affair with the "romantic foreigner," this time the engagement with the man she has withdrawn from remains in effect.

Ellen is 25 years old

However, once she reaches the quarter century mark in her life, she does break off the engagement to the student. A few months later, a cousin takes a special interest in her. They had been friends for several years and now they take long excursions together: "Although the broken engagement with the student remains an 'open wound,' a love relationship with the cousin develops" (ibid.: 247). She is able to resume activities in the children's home but is said not to enjoy them. Her fear of getting fat, however, does not dominate consciousness quite as much as it has before. This is because she is not so sure her life is full enough: libido has been retrieved from the split-off Hunger in her Hunger–Satiety complex and invested in her relationship with her cousin as a longing for a new start in life.

Ellen is 26 years old

The libido retrieved from the complex is also deployed to expand Ellen's aesthetic attitude – she develops a love for music. Again it looks as if her appetite for life will lead to actual progress in making her life more satisfying.

Ellen is 28 years old

What follows is somewhat operatic. After wavering for two years between her cousin and the student, with whom she has resumed a relationship, Ellen finally breaks off with the student for good and marries her cousin. She hopes that her marriage will cure her eating disorder, but this is not to be.

Instead, in the prison-compromise of a marriage with someone from her own family rather than from the longed for but tabooed outside world, she suffers continuously from a conflict between a wish for healthy eating and her dread of getting fat. Ellen is still able to continue to hold dissociated aspects of the Hunger–Satiety drive in consciousness, but they now lead a life of their own, and they oscillate within her in a bipolar way. Jung has drawn our attention to the fact that the experience of conflicting tendencies is a regular manifestation of an unconscious complex when it is activated by some ambiguous life experience.

> Theories apart, experience shows that complexes always contain something like a conflict, or at least are either the cause or the effect of a conflict. At any rate the characteristic of conflict – shock, upheaval, mental agony, inner strife – are peculiar to complexes.
>
> (Jung 1971: 528)

When a complex is continuously constellated, as Ellen's was throughout her adult life, it functions like an ongoing affective event, behaving autonomously, and the magnitude of the complex increases as it comes more and more to engulf consciousness.

Ellen is 29 years old

A few months after her marriage, Ellen has a miscarriage. When her doctor tells her that adequate nutrition is a prerequisite for a new pregnancy, Ellen is thrown into further conflict – will she eat to make pregnancy possible or continue to restrict her eating? When the latter wins out, Ellen begins to retreat once more from life. Now her periods stop even though she is not pregnant. When another doctor tells her that adequate nutrition is *not* a requirement for pregnancy, she resumes using strong laxatives. At the same time, she makes efforts to advance. She is able, for instance, to work energetically in social welfare on behalf of other wounded people: "She takes the warmest human interest in the people committed to her care, with whom personal relationships are kept up for years" (Binswanger 1958: 247). She frequently attends the theater and reads a great deal, both activities reflecting, in my opinion, her appetite for life.

Ellen is 31 years old

At this point, Ellen has the realization that "she is living her life only with a view to being able to remain thin, that she is subordinating every one of her actions to this end, and that this idea has gained a terrible power over her" (ibid.: 248–9). This is a recognition that her unconscious pathological eating complex has increased in magnitude and has Ellen more and more in its grip.

It may be this capitulation to the all consuming quality of her eating complex that made Binswanger decide that Ellen was actually schizophrenic. Jung, one of his first clinical teachers, was later to describe a schizophrenic patient whose associations, with a few exceptions, were nothing but expressions of her complexes: "From this we can conclude that the psychic activity of the patient is completely taken up by the complex: she is under the sway of the complex, she speaks, acts, and dreams nothing but what the complex suggests to her" (Jung 1960: 109). I am sure Binswanger would not have disagreed with my formulation that Ellen, at this point in her life, is "under the sway of [a] complex."

Or we could put it another way: the two poles of the dissociated Hunger–Satiety drive, Anorexia and Bulimia, are continuing to dominate her consciousness:

> During this entire time she has further impoverished her diet; her weight goes down to 103 pounds [this again is a sign of Satiety dissociated from Hunger]. At the same time she becomes intensely preoccupied with calorie charts, recipes, etc. In every free minute she writes recipes of

delectable dishes, puddings, desserts, etc., in her cookbook [this is the
other side of Ellen's conflict: Hunger dissociated from Satiety].

(ibid.: 249)

Both sides of this conflict belong to the eating complex that is possessing
her. The dissociation that has helped to produce it is enacted in her social
relationships: "She demands of those around her that they eat much and
well [Hunger projected], while she denies herself everything [Satiety intro-
jected]" (ibid.: 249).

A constellated complex like this, with two distinct sides, leads to rituals
of doing and undoing. She fills her plate and then secretly throws it out –
this is what happens when Satiety dominates consciousness and questions
any movement to fill the self. Alternately, when Hunger dominates Ellen's
consciousness: "Foods which she thinks are not fattening, such as shellfish
and clams, she eats with great greed and haste. Often on the way home she
eats up things she has bought for her household . . ." (ibid.: 249).

Ellen is 32 years old

As this year begins, the pathological eating complex has reached what we
might term monopolistic magnitude:

> At the beginning of her thirty-second year her physical condition
> deteriorates still further. Her use of laxatives increases beyond measure.
> Every evening she takes sixty to seventy tablets of a vegetable laxative,
> with the result that she suffers tortured vomiting at night and violent
> diarrhea by day, often accompanied by a weakness of the heart. Now
> she no longer eats fish, has thinned down to a skeleton, and weighs
> only 92 pounds.
>
> (ibid.: 249)

The observing part of Ellen's consciousness, however, is not extinguished.
She is becoming aware of the increased power of the complex:

> Ellen becomes more and more debilitated, goes back to bed in the
> afternoon, and is terribly tortured by the feeling that "her instincts are
> stronger than her reason," that "all inner development, all real life has
> stopped," and that she is completely dominated by her "overpowering
> idea, long since recognized as senseless."
>
> (ibid.: 249)

What began as a block to development when she was 21 years old has
advanced to an arrest of her individuation. She herself is certain she is

suffering from an obsessional neurosis, and she starts to seek psychological treatment.

When she is 32½ years old she begins analysis. At first she finds it energizing, but soon declares it useless: "Often I am completely broken by the conflict which never comes to an end [between the wish for healthy eating and the "fixed idea"], and in despair I leave my analyst and go home with the certainty: he can give me discernment, but not healing" (ibid.: 249). Her conflict is becoming unbearable, her terror is mounting, and she has constantly to think about food.

She has made her own analysis, which she shares with her husband, of how she projected her conflict upon him and the student during her two years of vacillation. Under this condition of projection, at first one of the men exemplified her ideal of being thin and the other stood for the life she was ready to accept after relinquishing the ideal. However, the projections were soon reversed, and so on, back and forth, as both poles of the complex were projected on each of them in an alternating fashion. It is at this point that Ellen realizes that there is something buried and hidden in her [the complex] which is the real problem. This insight leads to qualified hope, qualified because she recognizes that "The only real improvement, which must come from within, is not yet here . . ." (ibid.: 251).

Ellen and her husband have by now agreed that he will tell her parents what is the matter with her. After he does, Ellen feels a great longing for her parents, especially for her mother (this is perhaps the most direct expression in the case report of her underlying mother hunger); she feels dread, however, at the grave and serious nature of her father, which reveals the degree to which she cannot stand up to his authority.

Ellen is 33 years old

I am going to divide my reporting of the last eight months of Ellen's life into three sections. In the first, I summarize the evidence for my view that she suffers from the BN–AN syndrome. In the second part, I will point out manifestations of the unconscious complex that I believe is at the root of her eating disorder. In the last part, I will present my speculations about the possible etiologic processes in Ellen's early development.

Bulimia nervosa–Anorexia nervosa syndrome

In Chapter 3 of this book, I identified the etiology of Bulimia nervosa and Anorexia nervosa, viewed as one condition, as the symptoms that emerge when there is dissociation of the Hunger–Satiety drive. Once again, the formula is: Hunger dissociated from Satiety becomes bulimic; Satiety dissociated from Hunger becomes anorexic. The second condition compensates the first, and the first the second. Neither is primary, because both are split off, and can only appear out of the unconscious, as a compensation, when the other has overwhelmed the ego.

Certainly in August of her last year, Ellen's eating exhibited the oscillating pattern of behavior that results from such a dissociation of the motivational components of eating: "Her food intake becomes quite irregular; Ellen leaves out entire meals, to throw herself indiscriminately with all the greater greed upon any foods which may happen to be at hand. Each day she consumes several pounds of tomatoes and twenty oranges" (ibid.: 252).

Two months later, on 19 October, she had this profound insight:

> 1 don't think that the dread of becoming fat is the real obsessive neurosis, but *the constant desire for food*. The pleasure of eating must have been the primary thing. Dread of becoming fat served as a brake. Now that I see the pleasure of eating as the real obsessive idea, it has pounced upon me like a wild beast. I am defenselessly at its mercy. It pursues me constantly and is driving me to despair.
>
> (ibid.: 253 emphasis in original)

When Ellen is able to integrate dissociated Hunger for the first time, its stored up energy is very powerful. I don't want to seriously question Binswanger, who became her psychiatrist after two failed psychoanalyses and made every effort to comprehend what his patient was experiencing, with attention to the phenomenology of her condition and with a minimum of judgment as to its right to exist (the attitude of the existential analyst), but we can speculate that if his patient had been provided with both the understanding I am offering and adequate support for her struggling ego in insisting that a unity of mind was her birthright, she might still have been able to heal the dissociation of her Hunger–Satiety drive. As we know, this was not to be her fate. Two days after her insight that the pleasure of eating is in fact obsessing her, she experiences simultaneously "the uninterrupted desire for eating and the dread of eating" (ibid.: 253). Ellen elaborates: "On the days when I am not tortured by hunger, the dread of becoming fat again moves to the center. Two things, then, torture me: First, hunger. Second, the dread of getting fatter. I find no way out of this noose" (ibid.: 253).

On 7 November, she refuses food the whole day and two days later eats food ravenously. She records in her diary the intense suffering that this conflict is inflicting on her:

> The months which followed were the most terrible I have ever experienced, and I have not yet gotten over them. Now it was no longer the

fixed idea alone which embittered my life, but something far worse was added: the compulsion of always having to think about eating. This compulsion has become the curse of my life, it pursues me waking and sleeping, it stands beside everything I do like an evil spirit, and never and nowhere can I escape it. It pursues me as the Furies pursue a murderer, it makes the world a caricature and my life a hell. It seems to me that I could stand any other pain more easily; if my existence were darkened by a really heavy sorrow, I would have the strength to bear it. But the torture of having each day to tilt anew against the windmill with a mass of absurd, base, contemptible thoughts, this torment spoils my life.

(ibid.: 257)

Ellen is at this point unable to work at her desk because her attention and thoughts are constantly interrupted by a tormenting restlessness, caused by her preoccupation with whether or not to eat a piece of bread. What ego-consciousness she once had to muster outside her conflict is now undergoing depotentiation.

On 12 November, Ellen and her husband enter a clinic recommended by her internist. Once again, as with all her steps to expand her horizons, a brief psychological advance occurs, predicated on an acceptance of her appetite for life: "From the first day on she eats everything which is put before her, including things she had not touched for years, such as soup, potatoes, meat, sweet dishes, chocolate" (ibid.: 255). She audits lectures at a nearby university and in the evening goes for walks or attends the theater. Her poems show new hope and courage. I interpret this progression as a result of the integration into consciousness of her Hunger drive. Unfortunately, Satiety did not get integrated as well, because, a week later, the incessant thoughts about how she was eating too much returned, and after that her continued oscillation between the poles of her Hunger–Satiety drive never left her. It was if the complex that she could not integrate had swallowed her.

The next observation occurs after her admission to the Kreuzlingen Sanatorium on 16 January, three months before her suicide: "The patient is allowed to eat in her room, but comes readily with her husband to afternoon coffee, whereas previously she had stoutly resisted this on the ground that she did not really eat but devoured like a wild animal – which she demonstrated with utmost realism" (ibid.: 261). On 8 February, she suffers from "obsessional impulses to throw herself upon food and gulp it down like an animal (confirmed by observation). One night devoured seven oranges in succession" (ibid.: 263). This contrasts with her behavior during meals, when "ascetic impulses [force] her to deny herself this and that, especially the dessert" (ibid.: 263). The two dissociated aspects of the Hunger–Satiety drive again alternate in dominating consciousness: "I feel myself, quite passively, the stage on which two hostile forces are mangling each other" (ibid.: 264). Once again, the remarkable intensity of the newly unleashed Hunger is soon met by equally intense Satiety.

Two days later, she self-describes her gluttony "as when a wild animal throws itself on its food" (ibid.: 264). Then, of course, she reproaches herself for having eaten too much. At the same moment, she starts to want to be slender and yet makes sure not to miss a bite of the food put before her. On 22 March, eight days before her discharge from Kreuzlingen, she trembles and her whole body is covered with perspiration when "the desire to eat up everything fights within me a furious battle against the resolve not to eat everything" (ibid.: 265). We do not know how the staff dealt with this "furious battle" inside her during her stay at the sanatorium, but I can say that it is extremely difficult for most therapists not to end up colluding with one or another side of a conflict that is driven by a complex.

Complex-indicators

On 26 February of Ellen's final year of life, the unconscious dissociation of the Hunger–Satiety drive was unequivocally expressed in her dreams: "Dreams very vividly and always about food or death; sees the finest things before her, feels terrible hunger [dissociated Hunger – Bulimia], but at the same time the compulsion not to be allowed to eat [dissociated Satiety – Anorexia]" (ibid.: 263). This dream, which reveals both sides of Ellen's conflict as parts of a single complex state of mind, was generated, in my judgment, by the wisdom of the Self to reveal to Ellen, satisfying the wish for consciousness that is perhaps the strongest of all unconscious drives, the entirety of the pathological eating complex that was the root cause of the dissociation of her Hunger–Satiety drive, which mostly came at her only one side at a time.

By this point in her life, however, Ellen finds herself confronted with another seemingly inescapable problem, one she finds unbearable: "Every meal is associated with dread and agitation. . ." (ibid.: 257). This is another characteristic of an unconscious complex, according to Jung: "Everything that touches this complex, however slightly, excites a vehement reaction, a regular emotional explosion" (Jung 1966: 130). It is not surprising that the sight of food, as well as the necessity of eating it, is able to touch the pathological eating complex in Ellen's unconscious. It takes very little of the right stimulus to evoke a complex. Nor is it surprising that its victim feels caged: "I am in prison, caught in a net from which I cannot free myself. I am a prisoner within myself; I get more and more entangled, and every day is a new, useless struggle; the meshes tighten more and more" (Binswanger 1958: 258). This is no more than to say that she knows she is in the grip of the complex and that her psychic activity, together with all the energy she might have used to advance, is completely taken up by the complex: as Binswanger poignantly puts it, "What is constantly denied her is unconcern" (ibid.: 258).

Another entry in her diary gives a hint at what the nuclear affect of the complex might be:

> How often I begin a morning cheerily, in heart full of sunshine and hope, and before I am able to understand why I am so happy, something comes and strikes my mood down. Something quite insignificant, perhaps a cold tone in the voice of a person whom I love, or some other usually insignificant thing to disappoint me in someone, I see how the world darkens before my blurred vision.
>
> (ibid.: 265)

The effect on Ellen of the "cold tone" and her disappointment, that is, her feelings of rejection from and toward others, suggest that at the heart of the complex is not really appetite for life, but rejection of the self that would have such an appetite. Once again to give names to the sequence of archetypal affects that govern the complex created around the idea that others find her essentially worthless, we can supply the following formula for the evolution of Ellen's emotional state: Rejection + Alienation → Shame/Contempt–Humiliation/Disgust.

Ellen's stay at the Kreuzlingen Sanatorium, needless to say, did not change the course of her disorder; her suicide followed only a few days after her discharge.

Ellen's two psychoanalyses

What was done to provide meaningful psychological treatment to this victim of BN–AN before she became its casualty? Ellen's first psychoanalysis, which was of seven months' duration, began in February when she was 32 years old and ended "for external reasons" in August when she was 33 years old. In October of the same year, she commenced her second analysis (with a psychoanalyst Binswanger describes as "more orthodox than the first) and continued it until January, when she acceded to her internist's prohibition of further analysis and to his suggestion that she enter Kreuzlingen Sanatorium. Neither analysis, therefore, was given the chance to afford her the relief and improvement she had hoped for.

Etiologic speculation

On 21 October of the last year of her life, Ellen made these entries in her diary. In the first, she writes, "The sun shines, but there is emptiness within me" (ibid.: 253). She elaborates on her agony: "What is the meaning of this terrible feeling of emptiness – the horrible feeling of dissatisfaction which takes hold after each meal? My heart sinks, I feel it bodily, it is an indescribably miserable feeling" (ibid.: 253). She concludes these observations with this anguished statement: "Horrible feeling of emptiness. Horrible fear of this feeling. I have nothing that can dull this feeling" (ibid.: 253).

Ellen thinks that understanding this painful mood might benefit her: "Perhaps I would find liberation if I could solve this puzzle: The connection between eating and longing" (ibid.: 254). (Again, I see this as her largely suppressed appetite for life, but of course the longing is also hunger for parents, and particularly a mother, who would validate that appetite so that it wouldn't need to be suppressed.) The very sight of groceries (they are assimilated to the complex) can awaken this miserable longing. In her second analysis, Ellen and her analyst explained this psychic state in this way: "I attempt to satisfy two things while eating – hunger and love. Hunger gets satisfied – love does not! There remains the great, unfilled hole" (ibid.: 253–4).

In his notion of *balking of instinct*, Jung conceives how such an emptiness and longing might develop. He describes how this formulation applies to a patient suffering from a nervous stomach: "Analysis shows an infantile longing for the mother, a so-called mother-complex. The symptoms disappear with this new-won insight, but there remains a longing which refuses to be assuaged by the explanation that it was 'nothing but an infantile mother-complex'" (Jung 1970a: 369). His description of his patient's longing seems similar to Ellen's: "The longing is an insistent demand, and aching inner emptiness, which can be forgotten from time to time but never overcome by strength of will. It always returns" (ibid.: 369). Jung then poses the question of the source of such psychic pain and replies:

> So if, in the case of the patient with the stomach-neurosis, I were asked to name what it is in the unconscious, over and above the personal mother-complex, that keeps alive an indefinable but agonizing longing, the answer is: it is the collective image of the mother, not of the personal mother, but of the mother in her universal aspect.
>
> (ibid.: 373)

Now, Jung introduces his conception of the balking of instinct:

> Naturally the image of the individual mother is impressive, but its peculiar impressiveness is due to the fact that it is blended with an unconscious aptitude or inborn image which is the result of the symbiotic relationship of mother and child that has existed from eternity. Where the individual mother fails in this or that aspect, a loss is felt,

and this amounts to a demand of the collective mother-image for fulfilment. An instinct has been balked, so to speak.

(ibid.: 372–3)

We are left to wonder what is a maternal failure that might lead to the balking of instinct. My conclusion in the case of Trudy (Chapter 2) and of Renee (Chapter 5), which I will amplify in Chapters 8 and 9, is that the deficit is a failure of "good enough" bonding between parent and infant in early infancy.

Ellen's suicide

The literature on the relation between eating disorders and suicide is controversial (Berkman *et al.* 2007; Coren and Hewitt 1998; Herzog *et al.* 2000; Pompili *et al.* 2004). Some studies indicate a higher incidence of suicide in individuals with Anorexia nervosa than normal controls, while other studies do not report this difference. There is more agreement that patients with Anorexia nervosa have a higher rate of suicide that those suffering from Bulimia nervosa.

In my previous book, *Dire Emotions and Lethal Behaviors* (2008), I identified four conditions that must be met before individuals who are suffering from severe emotional disturbances are led to kill others, themselves, or both: social isolation, dissociation of the personality, unbearable affect, and possession by affect. I documented this view, as I have done my view of BN–AN in this book, by reviewing a series of case studies. I will now apply the formulation from my earlier book to Ellen's suicide, to demonstrate its validity in her case.

Social isolation

In the above work, I conceived of a continuum of affect-based socialization with its positive end, Social Relations Framed by Interest and Joy, and a negative one, Social Isolation. Ellen's interpersonal relationships moved back and forth along this continuum, but were never robustly positive, with the result that they were progressively moving farther and farther toward the negative end, even though they continued to oscillate throughout her life. When she was 33 years old, Ellen became aware of how her relationships had deteriorated:

I feel myself excluded from all real life. I am quite isolated. I sit in a glass ball. I see people through a glass wall, their voices come to me muffled. I have an unutterable longing to get to them. I scream, but they do not hear me. I stretch out my arms toward them; but my hands merely beat against the walls of my glass ball.

(Binswanger 1958: 256)

She made this entry in her diary on 21 November, two months before she entered the Kreuzlingen Sanatorium. On 21 December, she had another painful insight: "Life has no further lure for me. There is nothing, no matter where I look, which holds me. Everything is gray and without joy. Since I have buried myself in myself and can no longer love, existence is only torture" (ibid.: 257–8). Jung has commented on one's experience of the world when it cannot be suffused with libido:

It is hard to believe that this teeming world is too poor to provide an object for human love — it offers boundless opportunities to everyone. It is rather the inability to love which robs a person of these opportunities. The world is empty only to him who does not know how to direct his libido towards things and people, and to render them alive and beautiful.

(Jung 1967: 173)

When Ellen committed suicide three and a half months later, there had been no essential improvement in her basic pattern of isolation, punctuated by fitful attempts at relatedness that never quite panned out.

Dissociation

In *Dire Emotions and Lethal Behaviors*, I also conceived of another continuum, with a positive end, Emotional Dialogues with oneself Framed by Interest and Joy, and a negative one, Dissociation of the Personality, led usually by Shame/Contempt. As dissociation reduces the flow of Interest and Joy from the unconscious to consciousness, the *level* of these archetypal affects in circulation can be taken as a measure of the degree of dissociation. The less Interest and Joy, the greater the dissociation of the archetypal affect system, which alone can provide the libido for life. And, as a ready supply of these archetypal affects is necessary for self-realization, a block to the individuation process may also occur when there is such a split in the psyche, meaning that access to new affects in the course of development dries up. (Such Dissociation also contributes to Social Isolation, by decreasing the level of emotion necessary for optimal relationships.)

When she is 21 years old, Ellen looks at her fine ideas and plans and hopes one day to transform them into deeds instead of useless words. When she is 22 years old, her life is boring and without enjoyment: "She says she is not melancholy, merely apathetic: 'Everything is so uniform to me, so utterly indifferent, I know no feeling of joy and none of fear'" (Binswanger

1958: 242–3). She is choking in her commonplace life and the plants that thrive there – "joyless submissiveness and crude indifference" (ibid.: 244). This statement indicates a lack of Joy and Interest to vitalize her consciousness. When Ellen is 32 years old, she is tortured by the feeling that "all inner development, all real life has stopped," and that she is completely dominated by her "overpowering idea, long since recognized as senseless" (ibid.: 249). She finds no joy even in her dreams, which are closest to the healthy emotional basis of her personality.

During the intake interview at Kreuzlingen, where Binswanger assumed her care on 14 January, three months before her suicide, "she has the feeling that all inner life has ceased, that everything is unreal, everything senseless" (ibid.: 261). Her development is arrested. A week later, this note appears on her chart: "One has less the impression that she suffers under a genuine depressive affect than that she feels herself physically empty and dead, completely hollow, and suffers precisely from the fact that she cannot achieve any affect" (ibid.: 262). This deadness is the result, I believe, of her dissociation from the healthy emotional basis of her personality, where Interest and Joy still reside. At a conscious level, she has the feeling "of being like a corpse among people" (ibid.: 263).

Unbearable Affect

In *Dire Emotions and Lethal Behaviors*, I conceived a continuum of difficult affect, tolerable and intolerable, with Normal Suffering at the positive end and Unbearable Affect at the negative pole. One word that Ellen uses 16 times to describe her emotional state is "torment." She uses the word "torture" six times. "Dread," which she refers to 52 times, is a constant companion, and she says it is this, particularly, that is driving her mad: "Dread of eating, dread of hunger, dread of the dread" (ibid.: 254–5). She is boundlessly wretched. During the intake interview at the sanatorium on 14 January, after a few words "the patient bursts out into loud wailing and cannot be calmed down for a long time" (ibid.: 260–1).

Possession by Affect

In *Dire Emotions*, I also fashioned another continuum, this time of degree of consciousness with respect to the constellated affect, with Consciousness of Affect, the desideratum, as its positive pole and Possession by Affect, the basis of most psychopathology, at the negative one. Jung taught that Possession by Affect occurs when an unconscious Affect-toned complex of monopolistic magnitude and energy replaces ego-consciousness and compels the behavior of the individual. Then, there is nothing intentional about the acts that follow, raising the question of degree of responsibility for them.

Ellen's internist wrote that in the months before her 33rd birthday in July, she had had a number of depressive episodes accompanied by suicidal ideas. On 6 October of this year, her husband leaves temporarily at the request of the analyst. On 8 October, "she makes an attempt at suicide by taking fifty-six tablets [of a barbiturate], most of which, however, she vomits up during the night" (ibid.: 252). On November 6, her husband returns. On November 7, Ellen "makes her second suicidal attempt by taking twenty tablets of a barbiturate compound" (ibid.: 252). On 10 November, she "attempts several times on the street to throw herself in front of a car" (ibid.: 252). The next day, she tries to leap out a window in her analyst's office. During each of these episodes, Ellen is briefly possessed by the suicidal complex.

Ellen is admitted to the Kreuzlingen Sanatorium on 14 January, three months before her suicide. In February, a month after she enters the Sanatorium, she "offers a farmer fifty thousand franks if he will shoot her quickly" (ibid.: 263). She states that if "she knows no other way of dying, she will set fire to herself or ram her head through a pane of glass" (ibid.: 264). On 15 February, she is beleaguered by suicidal impulses after lying to her doctor about laxative intake. Her chart notes indicate that on 21 March, her "suicidal threats become more serious" (ibid.: 261). Also in March, full of self-condemnation (a present-day affect theorist would call this Disgust with herself), Ellen tries to convince her doctor and her husband of the correctness of her wish to kill herself.

The issue of suicide became the central focus of Ellen's care in this manner. Binswanger had become convinced of two aspects of Ellen's disorder – that its prognosis was hopeless and that "release from the institution meant certain suicide" (ibid.: 266). He told her husband of his conclusions and they agreed to have two consultations. Both psychiatrists agreed with his view that "no definitely reliable therapy is possible" (ibid.: 266). Ellen had been requesting to be discharged and her wish was now granted, so that on 30 March she left Kreuzlingen.

Ellen is both shaken and relieved, vowing now to take her life in her own hands. She and her husband decide to return to her home and upon her arrival, and for several days, her symptoms appear more strongly. But on the third day, she is transformed:

> At breakfast she eats butter and sugar, at noon she eats so much that — for the first time in thirteen years! — she is satisfied by her food and gets really full. At afternoon coffee she eats chocolate creams and Easter eggs. She takes a walk with her husband, reads poems by Rilke, Storm, Goethe, and Tennyson, is amused by the first chapter of Mark Twain's "Christian Science," is in a positively festive mood, and all heaviness seems to have fallen away from her. She writes letters, the last one a letter to the fellow patient here to whom she had become so attached. In the evening she takes a lethal dose of poison, and on the

following morning she is dead. "She looked as she had never looked in life — calm and happy and peaceful."

(ibid.: 267)

I believe that on the third day, Ellen was fully possessed by the suicidal complex. From that moment on, unfortunately, she is no longer inside life, but is outside it. That is why her eating disorder and its unbearable concomitants have vanished and she experiences a kind of "peacefulness." All affect has been effectively dissociated by her decision to dissociate herself from life itself by making a successful suicide attempt. Confirming that such a plan was in place at this point, and that it was linked in her mind with a final, satisfying resolution of her conflict over Hunger and Satiety, on 26 February, Ellen had the following dream, which indicates how ready she was to leave that conflict's torment behind:

Dreams that on her trip overseas she jumped into the water through a porthole. Her first lover (the student) and her husband both attempted artificial respiration. She ate many chocolate creams and packed her trunks.

(ibid.: 263)

Chapter 7

Psychological treatment of eating disorders

"Solve et coagula"

The Latin phrase "solve et coagula" (dissolve and coagulate) appears in Jung's Foreword to *Mysterium Coniunctionis: An Inquiry into the Separation and Synthesis of Psychic Opposites in Alchemy*. He comments on the use of the phrase by the spiritual alchemists of the late Renaissance, whose work he believes was the precursor to modern depth psychology's efforts to dissolve pathological personality structures so that personal character can reform in a more solid and incorruptible way. Jung makes the parallel explicit when he says:

> [T]he alchemist saw the essence of his art in separation and analysis on the one hand and synthesis and consolidation on the other.
> (Jung 1970d: xiv)

It is important, when working with eating disorders, to realize the degree to which a therapist is required to work alchemically. From the perspective of the parts of Jungian theory we have appropriated for the purposes of this book, the "unsuitable structures" that need to be dissolved are pathological feeding complexes that discharge crisis affects within and around the eating situation. These florid, repetitive complexes create whole series of crises, which often need to be reduced to the original traumas that are being reenacted, so that these can at last be worked through. Before dissolution of any complex is complete, the psyches of both patient and therapist will have to be flooded with what feels like an excess of negative affects, and the resulting Terror, Anguish, Rage, Humiliation/Disgust, and even paranoia, will produce dissociation of the personality that seems to undo all previous therapeutic work. That is why symbol-formation is so necessary in the midst of regression, because symbols often contain and advance the other category of emotions, that of affects that motivate development, Interest and Joy. Such life-affirming affects foster not dissociation, but the integration of psychic energy, and psychic energy, once available to the self, fuels ego development.

In his essays on methods of psychological treatment, Jung used adjectives such as "reductive," "analytic," and "causal" as synonyms for the alchemical *"solve"* processes, and adjectives such as "constructive," "synthetic," and "final" (in the sense of goal-driven) as signifiers of the alchemical *"coagula"* processes. As I proceed to discuss these two processes, *solve* and *coagula*, in the psychological treatment of eating disorders, I will often use the adjectives Jung has given us for how they appear in a psychotherapy.

After reviewing the analytic and synthetic aspects of two classic psychotherapeutic engagements with the problem of eating disorder that have already been examined in detail in this book, I will discuss the psychological treatment of two additional cases of patients suffering from Anorexia nervosa. With these cases, I will be emphasizing parts played by analysis and synthesis in their successful outcome.

Beth and Trudy

The focus of the treatment of Beth and her daughter Trudy (Chapter 2) was on the therapeutic dissolution of this mother's complexes surrounding archetypal themes of Rejection and Loss. The more experience-near of the emotions associated with the complexes that were interfering with Beth's ability to function successfully as a mother in feeding situations was her persistent memory of being rejected by her own adoptive mother. Farther from consciousness were the affects that must have been occasioned by having been abandoned initially by her biological mother. The simultaneous constellation of both these traumatic occurrences interfered massively with Beth's ability to concentrate on the needs of her own daughter. Synthesis followed the reduction in therapy of these complexes and focused on strengthening Beth's ability to bond with Trudy. This developed in three progressive steps: (1) Beth becoming able to recollect her experience, at the time of Trudy's birth, of archetypal "awe"; (2) the constellation in Beth of a symbolic, archetypal "Wonder-child," while she was joyfully engaging in "baby talk" with Trudy during their first successful feeding; and (3) Beth's satisfying subsequent projection onto Trudy of the imago of the "Wonder-child" while watching her daughter, confidently perched on her shoulders, in a mirror.

Renee

Analysis during Renee's psychotherapy (Chapter 5) focused primarily on the gradual resolution of a pathological "System" complex, a network of persecutory fantasies centering on the idea that she did not really deserve to live. These fantasies, it turned out, had been constellated by parental Rejection beginning almost from the moment of her birth. Synthesis consisted in a miraculous new beginning of symbolic development fostered by a gifted therapist, Marguerite Sechehaye, who was able to incarnate a positive maternal image who radiated a belief that Renee deserved to thrive. This made her both "mama" and "Mother-sun," to Renee, and this archetypal image, projected on to MS's body, especially during the healing miracle of the apples, led Renee eventually to experience her ego not just as held and fed, but floating in the "green sea," an evocation of the feminine Self that could sustain growth and development outside the therapeutic situation.

C. G. Jung treats an eating disorder

In *Jung: Man and Myth*, Vincent Brome (1978) has presented an account of a case of an 18-year-old, "Anna Maria", who Jung cured of Anorexia nervosa. The course of this treatment was told to Brome by the patient when she was 70 years old. It exemplifies the paradigm of "solve" and "coagula" that seems to have guided Jung.

The patient was 18 years old when she consulted Jung because of Anorexia nervosa, severe insomnia, and loss of her powers of concentration. She described to Brome her first meeting with him:

> He gave the impression of great power and insight and I was altogether shattered at the idea that he could see right through me, even into the sexual fantasies which were tormenting me. Tormenting is not altogether true; I also derived great pleasure from them. But he overcame my shyness by the sheer informality of his manner. He talked to me – casually – like a friend – I don't even remember him making a note – not even writing down my name. It was all very informal, and I liked that. Everyone else I had seen – and by now they seemed legion – had been so stiff, correct, professional. He conveyed the feeling of an open-minded man warmly sympathetic to me in my dilemma. . . . Slowly my shyness vanished. . . .
>
> (Brome 1978: 178)

Jung was able to establish such a relaxed rapport with Anna Maria, because his deeply sympathetic attitude helped her dissolve some of the unconscious Shame that was generating her symptomatic shyness.

Dissolving the Spider-Mother

It was apparent to Jung early on that he was dealing with "a case of mother fixation" (ibid.: 178) or what he elsewhere refers to as a negative mother complex. Jung quickly discerned that although Anna Maria was constantly struggling to assert herself with her mother, it was her mother who was making most of the big and little decisions in her life for her, even down to what to wear each day. When Jung asked the patient about her dreams, perhaps to get to a part of herself that clearly belonged to her, she had one ready at hand:

> In fact a recurring dream frequently represented a female spider sitting at the centre of the web directing what appeared to be the traffic pouring down its silken threads with signals flashing on and off as her huge eye opened and shut.
>
> (ibid.: 178)

This image of a controlling mother imago identifies unmistakably the nuclear archetypal affect at the heart of Anna Maria's negative mother complex: Restriction of Autonomy + Chaos → Anger–Rage. The patient, however, was not conscious of this. She was shocked when Jung pointed out to her how much she was in fact in the power of her mother. This was an analytic, reductive interpretation along the lines of calling a spade a spade and a successful one, for there immediately followed a release of much dammed-up psychic energy. Again, it was the patient who made this clear: "I felt as if a barrier had broken and my emotional life began to flow again" (ibid.: 179). I find it reasonable to assume that the developmental forces of Interest and Joy were the primary components of this freed-up libido.

Jung then stepped into the process to help Maria get some distance from the complex that was possessing her: he advised her to insist on having a room of her own at the hotel where she and her mother were living. Anna Maria was able to take this suggestion by applying the affective forces that had been released to firmly resist her mother's objections to letting her daughter have her own space. This cannot have been easy. As Anna Maria says, "It cost me a great effort but I had made up my own mind on a major point for the first time in years, and that made me very exhilarated" (ibid.: 179). Her mother, naturally, was furious (perhaps at Jung as well as her strong-willed daughter), but as Anna Maria had begun to eat again, she acquiesced. Jung's intervention seems to have assisted Anna Maria overcome the dissociation of her Hunger–Satiety drive by helping her integrate some of the Rage at the root of this split and enabling her to separate from her mother with a more conscious effort to experience herself as an individual source of agency, which could now include the experience of deciding what to eat as a pleasure.

Rebirth from the Earth-Mother

Anna Maria's therapy was not done, however. She now entered fully into what was to become the synthetic, constructive period of treatment. It began with a phase of deep introversion and regression. She had the feeling that "something deep inside her which belonged to the very core of her viscera had been disturbed," and it was then that "a new and much more powerful dream occurred" (ibid.: 179):

> [A] monstrous mountain in the shape of two huge female breasts . . . slowly opened and engulfed her, and she woke screaming so loudly that the other guests in the hotel reported the matter to the night porter. He came to investigate and found her sound asleep, but in the morning she hurried off to Kusnacht and poured out the dream to Jung.
>
> (ibid.: 179)

When Jung, realizing that this dream contained a vision of the Earth Mother, asked Anna Maria directly whether she had ever read any mythology or otherwise knew of the Earth Mother myth, she said no. Jung's was a synthetic move, an interpretation grounded in a symbolic or mythological amplification of the patient's dream that considered how similar motifs have functioned in the psyches of many. He may have been inviting his young patient to avail herself of the healing presence of such a positive archetype, associated throughout the world with nourishment. But instead of joining him in this celebration of an emerging positive mother complex, the patient described a new symptom that had entered into consciousness: "It was a deep, deep sense of longing – of emptiness – of craving for something I could not identify" (ibid.: 179). At first she thought it was a longing for food, for by now she was eating reasonably well and was more able to experience normal hunger. But Jung was looking for aspects of the archetype she had not yet realized.

When the Earth-Mother dream recurred, Jung was able, against her own inclination, to persuade her to encourage the dream and an extraordinary thing happened:

> Three nights in one week the same dream recurred but it was different. First a sense of being engulfed, then of being embraced and then of being reborn between those beautiful, soft, huge breasts.
>
> (ibid.: 179)

Anna Maria could then make her own tentative interpretation – that perhaps she was being reborn under Jung's treatment. Her subsequent course confirmed that this was the case:

> In the end Anna Maria put on weight, her mother-angst diminished, she was able to take up her study of English literature again and back in London asserted her independence by moving into a flat with another girl.
>
> (ibid.: 179)

The first step, prior to the patient's synthetic advance, consisted of a regression that enabled her to confront the kind of negative mother that can become too powerful and curtail the individual's autonomy. Working this through freed up energies to constellate a symbolic mother from the infant stage of development, but she, in her primordial form as a chthonic Earth-Mother, evoked the archetypal affect of Terror. Anna Maria was experiencing an unknown, primordial mother with more power than even the negative maternal imago. Her "longing" appears to express an early lack of parent–infant bonding, which she was now able to achieve with such a bountiful, symbolic mother, who would encompass the psychization of the Hunger–Satiety drive in Interest and Joy.

The next three steps in what made this phase of her treatment nevertheless progressive were the variants of the same dream in which she could experienced herself as being engulfed, embraced, and finally reborn. These were stages in assimilating the value for her own development of the initially threatening nourishing maternal archetype that had rather startling emerged to replace the coldly controlling Spider-Mother archetype she had long accommodated to. It is unlikely that she could have done this with a therapist who did not understand that accessing the energies of even a positive archetype is a symbolic achievement, earned through a sustained engagement with the image of the archetype until its positive value becomes evident.

Anna Maria told Brome, "But it was really due to a kind of alchemy Jung exerted which activated something in me from a long dead past – a past to which I belonged, but wasn't really mine" (ibid.: 179). The "past" was both the collective unconscious and the center of her total personality, the Self. It was this "past" that Jung was able to help his patient to access so that it could heal her.

Roger M. Knudson's case of Anorexia nervosa: Stephanie

> Integration of the unconscious invariably has a healing effect.
>
> (C. G. Jung, *Symbols of Transformation*)

Stephanie was 15 years old and weighed 125 pounds when she experienced the onset of Anorexia nervosa. At 19, weighing 65 pounds, she had the dream that brought about her recovery from this severe eating disorder. It came to light when Stephanie, now 22 years old and a senior in college, had volunteered to be a subject in Roger Knudson's (RK) "significant" dream research. She recounted it to him and provided the context of her illness history, the events of the summer just before her dream, and its meaningful contribution to her state of mind.

During the time between the onset of her illness and the summer in which she had this significant dream, Stephanie had graduated from high school and started college. Staying alive to do so, however, had required several hospitalizations, because of her parlous nutritional state, and she had been in and out of psychotherapy several times.

This is how RK recorded the way Stephanie described her psychic state during the three months preceding the big dream that came at the end of the summer:

> Throughout the summer leading up to the dream she was fully aware of the possibility that she might die from her disorder. Her parents, she believed, had already given up on her in the sense that they no longer insisted or even encouraged her to continue in therapy. She herself had begun to wonder seriously whether it would be possible for her to recover. She experienced herself increasingly as inhabiting a state of consciousness utterly disconnected from her feelings, from passions of any kind. She had begun to wonder whether in some sense her body had already died.
>
> (Knudson 2006: 49)

Whatever rejection or despair Stephanie may have been picking up from her parents, if we interpret her feeling that her parents had given up on her on a more subjective level, that is, as some tendency on the part of imagoes in Stephanie's psyche to withdraw from trying to influence her develop-ment, then this fantasy suggests that she is in the process of differentiating herself from their control. Often patients cannot live unless the option to die is also open to them. The fact that she has begun to "wonder seriously" about her fate is in favor of this understanding. Stephanie is surprisingly objective for an Anorexia nervosa patient about the life-threatening status of her physical condition, which attests to an increasing capacity for self-reflection (she weighs 65 pounds).

Her "utterly" affectless condition, however, suggests a dissociation of her personality and/or a state of detachment. Of this phenomenon, Jung has written:

> So far as I have been able to understand it, it seems to have to do with an acute state of consciousness, as intense as it is abstract, a "detached" consciousness . . . which . . . brings into awareness areas of psychic happenings ordinarily covered in darkness. The fact that *the general bodily sensations disappear during the experience* [emphasis added] suggests that their specific energy has been withdrawn and has appar-ently gone towards heightening the clarity of consciousness. As a rule, the phenomenon is spontaneous, coming and going on its own initi-ative. Its effect is astonishing in that it almost always brings about a

solution of psychic complications and frees the inner personality from emotional and intellectual entanglements, thus creating a unity of being which is universally felt as liberation.

(Jung 1968b: 27–8)

In Stephanie's case, this state followed her severing of relations with college, her therapist, and her parents, which confirms that she was indeed "detached." *She had taken her life into her own hands.* Viewed synthetically, the death-like condition she entered upon doing so held, paradoxically, the possibility of an entirely new line of development. From that perspective, she was unconsciously preparing, through introversion and regression, for rebirth, as described by Jung. And indeed the "significant dream" that Stephanie believed, RK believed, and I believe cured her eating disorder followed. She gave it the title, "Dad Is in a Pink Shirt and There's a Monster in My Room." Because it is complex, I will divide the dream into sections, each of which will be followed by my attempt to make sense of that particular part of it. (The dream will be presented as a whole at the end of this chapter.)

Stephanie's dream

> I sit up from my bed, the big bed I have at home. I'm in the middle and there are no stuffed animals on it – It's my room at home . . . except the furniture is arranged differently. My Peter Pan picture is behind the bed.
>
> (Knudson 2006: 44)

In this opening image of the dream, the scene is set: Stephanie has been placed in her childhood "home," i.e. her family complex. It is this that will undergo transformation as the dream progresses. The dream seems to say it is time for her to give up childish things. Her stuffed toys have been annihilated, and her Peter Pan picture (the classic image of an eternally prolonged childhood) has become a thing of the past. These changes suggest a move beyond her childhood complex. A new designer, which I would interpret as the development agenda of the Self, has rearranged the furniture. This "redecorating" seems to me to be the first step in the construction of a new attitude.

> The bed is facing my window, or where the window should be . . . the whole side wall of the room is missing. It's as if someone has torn it down, like a wrecking ball came through, and I see jagged remains of bricks and wood. I sense that something is out of place, that a wall really should be there but . . . I am more *curious* than anything else. I

know the wall is gone for a reason . . . that its absence is going to allow me to see something else. Or maybe the window was there but not connected to anything — "Dali like."

(ibid.: 44, original emphasis)

Demolition is an image of the alchemical *solve*, a deconstruction of her part of her family complex, and this opens up a new view of the world. She has become "curious" because the deconstruction has reestablished contact between her dream-ego and the healthy affective base from which her personality might develop, the part of the Self where the archetypal affect Interest–curiosity/exploration resides. She senses that she is about to be shown something novel (the life stimulus for Interest). The destruction of the "side wall" indicates both resolution of some of her dissociative tendencies (what Jung would call a "reduction" of them led by the analytic work) and a newly constructive, synthetic movement emerging out of the freed-up Self:

With the wall gone, I can look directly out into my backyard. We have a pool out there. I see this weird alligator/dragon monster. It reminds me of one of those Chinese dragons that dance around at festivals the way it's jumping around in and out of the water of our pool. Or like the Loch Ness monster. I am *terrified* of it but I don't really do anything just then. I swallow hard and am queasy looking down with the insecurity of the wall not there. I don't like *heights* so I focus on that. I'll throw up if I get near the edge.

(Ibid: 44, original emphasis)

The dream has now revealed to Stephanie an aspect of in her unconscious she couldn't see so long as the dissociative walls of her childhood complex were up, that is, her "backyard." What turns out to be there is an astonishing sight to be sure – a dragon. It reminds Stephanie, however, not of the kind of monstrous dragon from which Perseus rescued Andromeda, but of Chinese celebration-dancing dragons. Western and Eastern cultures do have quite different views of the meaning of the "dragon":

The Chinese believe in what Nietzsche called the "spirit of gravity," and the dragon, which [people in the West] like to think lives in gloomy caverns, sparkles for them in the heavens as a merry firework, and drives away the magic wrought by evil spirits.

(Jung 1970b: 498)

Considered in this context, the "dragon" may be jumping playfully in and out of the pool expressing the archetypal affect Joy–fantasy/play, which suggests that the dialectical partner of Interest is beginning to flow into consciousness and make its contribution to Stephanie's development.

The other side of the dragon, its Western connotations of something devouring and therefore extremely dangerous, like the Loch Ness monster, is not missing in this dream, however, and it should not be left out of our formulation of how this dream accomplished its healing effect. We can see from Stephanie's descriptions of the feeling the image provoked in her dream ego that the archetypal affect of Terror has been activated by an efficient symbol composed of the life stimulus, the Unknown (the alligator-like monster) and its primal image, the Abyss ("heights" of which she is so afraid). But because Stephanie is also in touch with the twin aspects of the life instinct, Interest and Joy, there is the likelihood that this Terror can be synthesized into the developmental process as a wish to grow beyond childhood.

> Before I can focus on the creature, my dad comes into my room and distracts me. He is dressed so weird, with a pink shirt on and a tie around his head. I asked him why he was dressed like that and he said he had to go to work. It looked like they were having some sort of costume day or something. He didn't seem to notice there was a problem with how he looked and was really upbeat. He totally neglected to see that the entire side of my room was missing and that there was a monster in our pool jumping around. I was so shocked by his obliviousness that I didn't even mention it. My dad left and I knew my mom was putting on her makeup getting ready for work too. She wasn't going to dress weird though. I'm still in my bed.
>
> (Knudson 2006: 44)

The dream continues its program of reductively depotentiating and dissolving Stephanie's "parent" imagoes as an inhibiting source of adult help. They don't, in fact, help her in her confrontation with the dragon. Their self-preoccupation makes clear that the task ahead, of finding a way to deal with this dragon, will need to be borne upon her own shoulders.

> All of a sudden, the creature jumps from the pool to my room — jumps in through the space where the wall should be. It takes me by *surprise* and I fall off the bed. I have one leg on the bed, one on the floor, and I freeze. With the same mentality of a child afraid of the dark and sure there are monsters in her room, I think to myself, "If I don't move, he can't see me," and I stand completely still. The creature is breathing hard and rocking back and forth just a little, but enough for me to see it is alive. It is ready to pounce, and I know it wants to eat me. *Devour me.* My eyes are open.
>
> (ibid.: 44, original emphasis)

Activation of the archetypal affect of Surprise–Reflection/Orientation has occurred, evoked again by the efficient symbol, one composed of the life stimulus, the Unexpected, and the primal image, Disorientation.

> Startle serves to centre consciousness and leads to reorientation, but it accomplishes more than that; it leads to a centering of the total organism which imposes an immediate and total cessation of any movement or sound; breathing ceases, and even the beat of the heart may be momentarily interrupted. At that moment all of the other affects are, in a very real sense, functioning as its opposite. That is, their energy is totally in abeyance, although in a state of readiness to be sure, since we know that immediately following the startle response, ego consciousness is quickly restored to a particular function, and, moreover, a specific archetypal affect may take over in response to whatever it was that led to the startle response. Startle's survival function then is to prevent, if possible, the occurrence of an inappropriate response before the threat has been evaluated (one cannot help but wonder about a relationship between startle and the physiological shock reaction). The stimulus to startle is the 'unexpected', and the dimension it characterises is that of orientation, that is the place of the ego and the organism in the world and with relation to the self.
>
> (L. H. Stewart 1987a: 41–2)

In response to the emergence in her psyche of Surprise, Stephanie has frozen and become still in order to give herself time to reflect and consider how to proceed. Initially, she is able to return to childhood defenses, but quickly realizes they will not suffice. She registers that the monster is alive, breathing, and prepared to eat her up.

There are several possible interpretations of the "devouring" attribute of the alligator/dragon monster, all of which may be partially correct. The devouring dragon-image may, first of all, be an image of her eating disorder, which at the time of her dream had claimed half her normal body weight. More deeply, it (and the Anorexia itself) may be an expression of the potential for the unconscious to overwhelm the ego, i.e. by the archetype of the Terrible Mother from which the parents have not been able to protect her. On the other hand, it may, in the paradoxical way of any potent symbol, be the first step in the motif of death and rebirth. In the context of Stephanie's Anorexia, therefore, it may be not an image of the diagnosis, which was already after all well known to her, but the first step in the healing of the disorder involved. Again, we need to spell this out in terms of the archetypal affects associated with normal eating. Up to now, Stephanie's consciousness has been dominated by Satiety dissociated from Hunger, which is one way to understand Anorexia. (Why should someone eat who already feels full?) Her heretofore dissociated, and therefore demonically bulimic, Hunger has emerged into consciousness, a return of the repressed that is part of her reorientation.

> I'm stuck. My first instinct is to call for my mother. She is right down the hall and I can see her out of the corner of my eye. She's still putting on makeup and won't know that I am in trouble unless I tell her. But I can't yell. When the creature jumped into my room and startled me, I gulped; and I can feel that nothing would come out if I tried to make a noise. I would have to swallow and clear my throat first, but even that half-second action would alert the monster. Though I know mom would come running, I also realize that she can't help me. The monster is too close.
>
> (Knudson 2006: 44)

Stephanie wants to turn to her mother for help, but the compensatory function of the dream will not accept that solution to her dilemma.

> My other option is to run. But with one foot on the floor from when I slipped and one on the bed, I know I'd have to make some huge, intentional movements to get stable, to get on some ground. I'm on the side of my bed farthest from the door, so I'd either have to run around the foot of the bed or climb over the bed and run out the door. I would really like to do this — to run — but I think to myself that I am too slow now. The monster is too fast. I don't feel weak but for some reason I just know my legs wouldn't go as quickly as I need them to.
>
> (ibid.: 44–5)

Stephanie wisely decides flight is not a solution.

> I'm still frozen. And I know that if I keep thinking about what to do — whether to call my mother or to run – I am going to start to panic, because neither option is going to work. So I stand there . . . in limbo, knowing the only thing to do is to stare at the creature and not be afraid, even if I am. I have to deal with the monster, stare it down — because I can't escape it. To get rid of it, I can't be afraid. I start to turn toward it; and then, I wake up.
>
> (ibid.: 45)

This seems to me a pivotal decision, which transforms symbolized symptom into opportunity for ego development. Having decided that the only effective approach will be to conquer her fear and confront the alligator/dragon/Loch Ness monster, Stephanie can, indeed, "wake up." Considered as a symbol of the Self, the frightening monster announces, in a Chinese way, the possibility of creative change. Jung points out in several places that in order to realize this potential transformation, we must expose ourselves to the animal impulses of the unconscious "without identifying with them or 'running away'":

> For flight from the unconscious would defeat the purpose of the whole proceeding. We must hold our ground, which means here that the process initiated by the dreamer's self-observation must be experienced in all its ramifications and then articulated with consciousness to the best of his understanding.
>
> (Jung 1968a: 145–6)

When Stephanie met with RK three years later, she was still in touch with the ability of the alligator/dragon/monster symbol to constellate her own wish to survive.

Although the dream had been a terrifying nightmare, Stephanie's first reaction upon waking up was "not fear but relief" (Knudson 2006: 49). In the dream, Stephanie felt her Terror intensely throughout her body and she felt it was this that led to her relief: "As Stephanie reported that experience, she awoke with the immediate realization that if she was capable of such intense feelings in her body, albeit her dream body, then she must not be dead just yet!" (ibid.: 49).

L. H. Stewart has indicated that the archetypal emotions form a bridge between psyche and body: "Perhaps most significant, the affects are the bridge between body and psyche, instinct and spirit. They reach back into the physiology of the body, to the chemical processes of the hormones, and neurologically to the areas of the 'mammalian' brain" (L. H. Stewart 1987b: 132).

Jung, before Stewart wrote this, had suggested that a feeling-toned complex has the tendency to form a little personality of itself:

> It has a sort of body, a certain amount of its own physiology. It can upset the stomach. It upsets breathing, it disturbs the heart – in short, it behaves like a partial personality.
>
> (Jung 1977: 72)

Hillman (1992) conceives of the Material cause of emotion as the energy of the body. Stephanie told Knudson she could hardly wait to tell her previous therapist the good news: "I am *not* incurable. I *can* still feel things in my body. I *can* recover!" (Knudson 2006: 49, original emphasis). She was able to secure an immediate appointment and she reported her dream. The therapist listened carefully and then offered her interpretation, one that I find ill-conceived:

Focusing on the image of Stephanie's precarious posture in the dream, one leg on the bed and the other foot on the floor, the therapist suggested that the dream was a representation of Stephanie's unstable psychological/medical condition. Furthermore, the therapist reportedly argued, the conclusion of the dream made it clear that Stephanie was not able to deal with the dangerous situation herself.

(ibid.: 45)

The therapist's recommendation was immediate hospitalization. This undercuts the *telos* of the dream, its ability to arouse Stephanie's own resilience in fighting for herself. The therapist's interpretation was all dissolving analysis and no coagulating synthesis. One telling evidence of this is that, as Stephanie told RK, the therapist was not interested in Stephanie's own reactions to her dream. She had tried to explain them, but after the therapist reasserted her previous arguments in favor of admission, Stephanie rejected hospitalization and any further appointments. She was determined to listen to what she felt her dream meant, that she could recover on her own, and she did: "She began to eat, gained enough weight to convince her university's administration to readmit her to school in the fall, and resumed her studies" (ibid.: 49–50). She not only resolved her eating disorder but also cleared a path for ongoing development in the form of a healthy appetite for education.

When Stephanie met with RK three years later, she told him she was still in touch with the alligator/dragon/monster. At the level of symptoms:

She reported that she had continued to gain weight; she was more comfortable with her body in public situations and felt less and less need for wearing shapeless, loose fitting clothes; she felt more comfortable as well with her sexuality and her sexual needs; and she was in a serious romantic relationship.

(ibid.: 49–50)

Not the dire outcome her former therapist had predicted, although that prediction may itself have constellated Stephanie's opposition in a constructive way. In subsequent interviews with RK, Stephanie told of continuing improvement and her determination to proceed without therapy. The dream image, which she now referred to as the "jumping alligator monster," was still very much alive as a fear-evoking fantasy image. She and RK agreed to a period of work focused on her continuing confrontation and development of the image (personal communication). RK has indicated that he will describe this period of what Jung would have called "active imagination," in a future article, which I await with considerable interest.

This is Stephanie's dream without division into sections:

Dad Is in a Pink Shirt and There's a Monster in My Room

I sit up from my bed, the big bed I have at home. I'm in the middle and there are no stuffed animals on it – It's my room at home . . . except the furniture is arranged differently. My Peter Pan picture is behind the bed. The bed is facing my window, or where the window should be . . . the whole side wall of the room is missing. It's as if someone has torn it down, like a wrecking ball came through, and I see jagged remains of bricks and wood. I sense that something is out of place, that a wall really should be there but . . . I am more *curious* than anything else. I know the wall is gone for a reason . . . that its absence is going to allow me to see something else. Or maybe the window was there but not connected to anything — "Dali like." With the wall gone, I can look directly out into my backyard. We have a pool out there. I see this weird alligator/dragon monster. It reminds me of one of those Chinese dragons that dance around at festivals the way it's jumping around in and out of the water of our pool. Or like the Loch Ness monster. I am *terrified* of it but I don't really do anything just then. I swallow hard and am queasy looking down with the insecurity of the wall not there. I don't like *heights* so I focus on that. I'll throw up if I get near the edge. Before I can focus on the creature, my dad comes into my room and distracts me. He is dressed so weird, with a pink shirt on and a tie around his head. I asked him why he was dressed like that and he said he had to go to work. It looked like they were having some sort of costume day or something. He didn't seem to notice there was a problem with how he looked and was really upbeat. He totally neglected to see that the entire side of my room was missing and that there was a monster in our pool jumping around. I was so shocked by his obliviousness that I didn't even mention it. My dad left, and I knew my mom was putting on her makeup getting ready for work too. She wasn't going to dress weird though. I'm still in my bed. All of a sudden, the creature jumps from the pool to my room — jumps in through the space where the wall should be. It takes me by *surprise* and I fall off the bed. I have one leg on the bed, one on the floor, and I freeze. With the same mentality of a child afraid of the dark and sure there are monsters in her room, I think to myself, "if I don't move, he can't see me," and I stand completely still. The creature is breathing hard and rocking back and forth just a little, but enough for me to see it is alive. It is ready to pounce, and I know it wants to eat me. *Devour me.* My eyes are open. I'm stuck. My first instinct is to call for my mother. She is right down the hall and I can see her out of the corner of my eye. She's still putting on makeup and won't know that I am in trouble unless I tell her. But I can't yell. When the creature jumped into my room and startled me, I gulped; and I can feel that nothing would come out if I tried to make a noise. I would have to swallow and clear my throat first, but even that half-second action would alert the monster. Though I know mom would come running, I also realize that she can't help me. The monster is too close. My other option is to run. But with one foot on the floor from when I slipped and one on the bed, I know I'd have to make some huge, intentional movements to get stable, to get on some ground. I'm on the side of my bed farthest from the door, so I'd either have to run around the foot of the bed or climb over the bed and run out the door. I would really like to do this — to run — but I think to myself that I am too slow now. The monster is too fast. I don't feel weak but for some reason I just know my legs wouldn't go as quickly as I need them to. I'm still frozen. And I know that if I keep thinking about what to do — whether to call my mother or to run — I am going to start to panic, because neither option is going to work. So I stand there . . . in limbo, knowing the only thing to do is to stare at the creature and not be afraid, even if I am. I have to deal with the monster, stare it down — because I can't escape it. To get rid of it, I can't be afraid. I start to turn toward it; and then, I wake up.

Chapter 8

A longitudinal study of Anorexia nervosa

Sylvia Brody's subject Helen

> Never in our meetings with them over the years had either one been seen or heard to express affection or sympathy for Helen, except once when mother, with a slight sign of regret, said that Helen had never enjoyed feeding after being weaned from the breast.
>
> Sylvia Brody, *The Development of Anorexia Nervosa: The Hunger Artists*

Helen emerged into visibility as an object of attention when, as subject in a longitudinal study of normal development from infancy on, she happened to develop Anorexia nervosa (AN) during her adolescence. Sylvia Brody (hereafter SB) has presented two accounts of this research, one from Helen's birth until she was 30 years old (Brody 2002) and the other from her birth through seven years of age (Brody and Axelrad 1978). It is the first report that describes Helen's development of AN when she was an adolescent. This account is very precious to me, because it is the only longitudinal study of the BN-AN syndrome of this scope that I have come across in the eating disorder literature. It thus presents a special opportunity to assess the etiology of this disturbance.

Helen's parents

Helen's mother graduated from college after majoring in philosophy, worked as a programmer for several small businesses, and then married Helen's father when she was in her mid-twenties. They had two children, Helen and her older brother. Helen's father had been an only child. He had failed to complete a graduate program in political science and, subsequently, failed to finish law school. During the span of the study, he was employed as an insurance agent.

Infancy: birth to 6½ months

During the first year of Helen's life, SB had interviews with both mother and daughter at three days and 1½, 6½ and 12 months. Mother came alone for interviews at four and nine months. SB observed mother feed Helen at three days and 1½ and 6½ months. These observations document that the first year of Helen's life was filled with her screams.

Three days

Mother stated that she would breastfeed Helen on a self-demand schedule. She thought "babies should have as much play as possible" but that "they should be left alone for most of the day so as to learn to be by themselves" (Brody 2002: 45). According to SB, at the time, this mother believed in "being lenient – but will not 'give in' to Helen easily . . ." (ibid.: 45). During that interview, SB did observe what she viewed as a normal breast-feeding.

1½ months

SB apparently also considered the feeding at 1½ months as normal because she wrote of Helen: "She nursed comfortably, gazing at mother's face as she played her hand on mother's breast, and making soft sounds as she looked about the room. All of her responses were smooth" (Brody 2002: 47). The Gesell Developmental Schedule was administered during this same visit, and Helen scored as advanced in all sectors of development.

Mother, on the other hand, was not content, because she did not yet have Helen on a feeding schedule. Throughout the day, mother waited to feed Helen until she was screaming and then delayed another 15 to 20 minutes, while the screaming continued, to make sure Helen was hungry enough to be fed. She was concerned that she might overfeed Helen, and so in addition to delaying the onset of the feedings, she deliberately underfed her daughter by keeping each feeding short.

After each of these delayed brief feedings, she put Helen in her crib to sleep. When "Helen soon awoke and cried, mother picked up her up and held her 'a little bit' or fed her 'a little bit,' and replaced her back in her crib; then Helen fretted and screamed before she could fall asleep again" (ibid.: 48). It was SB's impression that mother was feeding Helen as little and as infrequently as she could. Mother did not appear to be at all aware of even the possibility of the self-regulating nature of the Hunger–Satiety drive.

Already, this account by mother of the pattern of Helen's feedings, which is quite hard to read without feeling the insensitive quality of mother's imposition of restriction on the entire process, indicates to me that Helen's affective psychization of her Hunger–Satiety drive had been pathological for several weeks. In her observations at this time, SB wonders if Helen's screaming was due not only to hunger but also to mother's sparse visual, vocal, and physical contacts with her daughter, i.e. that "mother hunger" as well as "food hunger" was involved. (These are my words, not SB's, but I think they fit.) Although mother did appear to be comforted by the fact that Helen liked being held, rocked, and played with, she expressed fear that Helen might want to be rocked "for a very long time" (Brody and Axelrad 1978: 135). SB concluded her report of this six-week visit by noting that "Helen's states of hunger and distress had by now become habitual" (Brody 2002: 48).

Four months

It is ten weeks since the last interview, and mother has come without Helen; so we do not have a report of an observed feeding. SB learns that feeding at home continues to be disturbed. The morning after the previous visit, mother and her pediatrician had agreed it was time to begin bottle-feeding Helen. This turned out to mean that mother would give Helen a bottle, Helen would refuse it and then the baby was left to scream for 12 hours. After these episodes, Helen finally came to alternate between small feedings, brief naps, and more screaming. This feeding pattern, which I can only regard as pathogenic, went on for days, so that pathological, negative affective conditioning of the Hunger–Satiety drive was an everyday occurrence.

When Helen reached three months of age, her mother decided to wean her completely from the breast. Helen responded by screaming a lot for two days, and her weight gain did not satisfy mother. A week later, mother gave Helen her fruit juice in a bottle and Helen screamed as hard as she ever had. Mother now decided to place Helen on a schedule that fit her own needs, which is perhaps the regimen she had been working to put in place all along.

A few days after this four-month visit, mother phoned SB and told her, with relief and pride, "Helen was content to lie in her crib alone and unattended for hours at a time" (ibid.: 49–50). If mother were sometimes to play little games with Helen, or helped her sit up, she was happily excited. Mother did these things infrequently, however, and "father was passionately against mother's doing them at all" (ibid.: 50). (In my own experience, parents' social exploration and play with their baby and the infant's own exploration and play are activities that assist the child in modulating and integrating both positive and negative affective states; so I see this behavior as deeply disruptive to the possibility of normal integration of the archetypal affect system and the Hunger–Satiety drive.)

6½ months

It is 2½ months since the previous interview. SB observes that Helen now has an immobile, emotionless facial expression. This is what SB observes of mother's feeding of Helen during this visit:

Placed by mother in the infant seat (mother's choice) to be fed, she slumped to the side and looked away from mother as she had avoided looking at me. The feeding was slow, with many pauses and little eye contact with mother, who said she didn't mind if Helen ate little of her food — Harry [a sibling] would gladly take the rest. Toward the end of the feeding Helen began to wag her head from side to side affectlessly. Quickly mother said this had never happened before — at least never during feeding. But yes, she had seen it during a diaper change — maybe it was getting to be a bad habit — in fact, once mother had been very annoyed by it and shouted at Helen to stop it.

(ibid.: 52)

Mother added that Helen sometimes "stimulated herself to vomit by pushing her finger, or the handle of a small bell, back toward her throat, again adding casually that Helen vomited once a day" (ibid.: 53). The outcome of this clearly pathogenic feeding foreshadows the development of purging, one of the characteristic behaviors of adolescents and adults with an eating disorder. Much more disturbing to me than Helen's rejection of this way of being fed is the evidence of such minimal emotional contact between mother and daughter. The flagging of Helen's appetite and her affectless head wagging are ominous signs that she has begun to dissociate herself from affect, including Interest and Joy, altogether. One wonders about the incipient dissociation of other parts of her psyche, including her ego's maturational agenda. Gesell testing showed a decline in all sectors of development.

At this stage of Helen's life, when feeding Helen at home, mother was continuing to wait for Helen's screaming to feed her and, as before, to give her small amounts of food at frequent intervals. Not surprisingly, this pattern of feeding continues to be accompanied by crying. Mother is also underfeeding semi-solids because she is afraid that otherwise Helen won't drink her milk.

Mother told SB that "she felt the baby was too young to be played with or encouraged to notice [explore] objects in the environment" (Brody and Axelrad 1978: 142). Mother considered it a good day when Helen played by herself: "She loved to be sat up or picked up, or kissed and talked to, said mother, who complied with these wishes for a minute or two. But Helen 'never asked' her to do these things . . ." (Brody 2002: 52). SB thought this indicated mother's aversion to engaging in social play with Helen and mother herself said that she seldom had time to play with her. On bad days, Helen fussed, was demanding, and screamed a lot. Recently mother left Helen with her grandmother at which Helen "screamed uncontrollably and vomited" (ibid.: 52). She also occasionally had fits of screaming that lasted one to two hours. There is no evidence that mother is moved to help Helen modulate her agony.

In the study by Ainsworth and Bell (1969) of interaction between 26 mothers and their infants in the feeding situation during the first three months of life, I found patterns similar to those between Helen and her mother. Those ten mothers who produced "unhappy feedings" regularly delayed feedings, insisted their infants cry before feeding, and terminated feedings too soon; they fed in instalments, underfed their babies, and shifted the schedule about. Unfortunately, we don't know what guide to infant nutrition these mothers were following, or whether any of these infants developed eating disorders later in life. But it does seem as if a cultural complex around indulging a child's appetite was affecting not just Helen's mother.

By the time Helen was 6½ months old, there was, in my judgment, a reason for her screaming beyond mother's persistent insensitive feeding of her. I believe she had already internalized this attitude toward her hungry self and developed a pathological, affect-toned eating complex, so that her disordered eating was conditioned not only from without by her mother's insensitivity but now also from "within" by this complex.

There is support for my hypothesis in a study by Bell and Ainsworth (1972) of infant crying during the first year. Bell and Ainsworth found that during the first three months, the most responsive mothers ignored 4 percent of their infants' cries while the least responsive mothers ignored 97 percent. There was, however, no correlation between the number of episodes of crying ignored and the frequency of crying in this first quarter. The normal nursing still observed in Helen at six weeks of age, in the face of pathological home feedings, is comparable.

In fact, Bell and Ainsworth discovered that it was only in the third and fourth quarters that there was a significant positive relationship between episodes ignored and more frequent crying: "From the beginning of the fourth month on [babies] tend to be more insistent in their crying as a consequence of the history of mother's ignoring tactics" (Bell and Ainsworth 1972: 1180). My interpretation is that only by the third and fourth quarters do affect-toned crying complexes reach sufficient magnitude to influence the frequency and duration of the baby's cries in addition to the mother's unresponsiveness. If these findings are applicable to the development of patterns of eating, then they would help explain the fact that, despite the deprivation, both nutritional and emotional, that was being meted out to her, Helen's first observed pathological feeding was at 6½ months, the beginning of the third quarter.

On the other hand, we should not assume that Helen was not distressed about the way she was being fed long before she developed the pathological eating complex that tended to co-create the mishandling of her normal Hunger–Satiety drive. Gaensbauer has conducted a series of studies focused on the effects on infants of traumatic events that occurred in each of the quarters in the first year of life. This is his summary statement about the first quarter: "The clinical and research data indicate that possibly in the first weeks of life and certainly by two to three months of age infants are able to recognize stimulus cues associated with a traumatic experience and show expectable distress reactions and behavioral responses" (Gaensbauer 2002: 267). We do know that Helen's "unhappy feedings" had begun before she was two months old. This is Gaensbauer overview of the second quarter: "By three to four months of age such recognition and distressed responding can persist for weeks to months" (ibid.: 267). Helen's continued crying suggests that feedings continued to distress her throughout her second quarter. But we cannot say she has already developed an eating complex.

Gaensbauer contrasts the effects of similarly traumatic events during the third and fourth quarters, when the affective basis for the formation of complexes, internalization and memory, begins to operate:

> By the second half of the first year, and especially from nine months on, there is evidence for internal representation of traumatic events that can be expressed in the form of sequentially meaningful play reenactments at subsequent periods of time involving months and even years. Over the course of the second year, even before the onset of language fluency, memory capacity becomes all the more impressive.
>
> (ibid.: 267)

It was during her third quarter that Helen was first observed during a feeding that was significantly disordered. The lag between toxic psychization of the Hunger–Satiety drive and manifestations of pathological complexes so induced reminds me of one of the cases Gaensbauer reports, a boy who was "severely physically and sexually abused by his father over a one-week period at seven months of age" (ibid.: 265).

> At the age of eight years, in a therapy session with the therapist and his adoptive mother, the child suddenly entered a frenzied, dissociated state during which he dramatically reenacted with his own body the experience of being abused. This included screaming in fear, wiggling on the ground with his buttocks in the air, attempting to crawl under the couch to get away from the therapist (whom he was experiencing at that moment as his father), and using words to describe how he was being hurt.
>
> (ibid.: 265)

Helen's "unhappy feedings," which resulted from repeated pathological emotional psychizations of her Hunger–Satiety drive, were a trademark of her entire infancy. I have, therefore, little reason to doubt that in Helen's case a pathological eating complex was structured during her infancy and reached sufficient magnitude to contribute to her disturbed eating by the time she was 6½ months old.

Infancy: 9 to 12 months

Two more interviews with mother will complete her account of Helen's infancy. At nine months, mother came alone and reported that Helen continued to scream in the early morning and after lunch, but only "when she was very, very hungry" (Brody and Axelrad 1978: 144). The mother's reference to home feeding was brief but telling. At meals Helen slumped in her high chair, ate little, dawdled, and wanted more urging than mother was willing to offer.

Mother brought Helen to her interview at 12 months, but again there was no observed feeding. I believe feedings had become minimal affairs, even though Helen's reaction to them continued to be maximal. Mother said that Helen's screaming continues and "on one day it had been so intense that her face got bright red for at least 20 minutes" (Brody 2002: 55). When SB asked if mother ever tried to hold her when she was screaming, mother replied that Helen would just push her away. Helen had now begun to also push food away or throw it into the air. Her recent, age-appropriate attempts to use a spoon and a fork simply irritated mother. These reports provide additional empirical evidence that construction of a pathological affect-toned eating complex was continuing, and developing in ever more sophisticated ways. Her "pushing" and "throwing" are behaviors that originate in the complex, and as obnoxious and infantile as they may have seemed to Helen's mother, they were highly purposive expressions of Helen's outrage at the feeding situations that had been imposed upon her.

Archetypal affects in Helen's screams

I also have no doubt that certain of Helen's screams are expressions of archetypal affects.

> The first year of life sees the constellation of all of the innate affects in the infant's daily experience, no matter how attentive and nurturing the mother and father may be. But it is the empathic responsiveness of the "good enough" parent that provides the modulating effects which make these eruptions of the innate affects bearable and containable. Through the infant's own play and curiosity, mirrored by the parent's responsive playfulness and attentive interest, the innate affects are continually modulated and transformed. These transformed affects make up the "archetypal complexes" of the collective unconscious. It must be remembered that during this first year of life when these earliest transformations are taking place, the infant is living in a world

of relative unconsciousness. . . . This means that for that first year of development, the structures of the unconscious complexes are in archaic forms, not easily accessible to later ego consciousness.

(L. H. Stewart 1988: 15–16)

With the data available, however, we can only speculate which screams are expressions of emotions and what these emotions are.

This is not to say that the basis for making such assessments does not exist today. Virginia Demos (1982) has reviewed the methods most often used to identify the occurrence of affect in infancy. These have included (a) a focus on an assumed one-to-one correspondence between a situation or stimulus and the evoked affect and (b) a focus on expressive behaviors such as facial, verbal and vocal expressions, along with other physical demonstrations. Paul Ekman began videotaping his daughter daily for an hour, beginning with the day of her birth: "In the first hour of life he saw many complex affect expressions involving the whole face, which he continued to see weeks afterward" (Demos 1982: 547). In a personal communication to Demos, he stated the following: "I believe that from the start one can see the facial expressions of disgust, happiness, interest, distress, and startle as close to pure expressions, and blends of distress/anger, distress/ fear" (ibid.: 547). If some of the distress expressions were actually what Sylvan Tomkins calls "sadness," then Ekman had identified all of the archetypal affects in his daughter.

My premise, as the reader may have picked up in my use of the term archetypal, which is not a casually tossed in word, is that not all of an infant's affective experiences are induced by contagion from the parents, for constellation of archetypal affects by environmental factors is to be expected. I am saying that the affects have an a priori status, because they belong to a system that will develop like other systems in the baby's body according to a pre-established developmental agenda, which parental care-takers can either foster or frustrate, but did not create. This means that if we can match specific parental behaviors with the Life Stimuli that we know evoke the archetypal affects belonging to this system, then we have a method for determining the innate emotional apparatus of the infant (see Table I.1). Obviously, such a deduction is less accurate than microanalysis of videotaped expressive behaviors of babies, but it is not a failure to honor the actual affective life of the infant.

Applying these notions to Helen, we have to ask, reading her case report, whether she experiences her mother's daily delay of her feedings as a Restriction evoking Anger or does it feel to her like Rejection evoking Shame/Contempt? We should note that SB thought that Helen had very likely been experiencing "fury" before, during and after her feedings, but this comment by itself does not distinguish between Rejection and Restriction. We can ask other questions as well: Does Helen experience her mother's daily isolation of her in her crib as Loss evoking Sadness and/or Rejection evoking Shame/Contempt? Does mother's daily failure to mediate the world leave Helen alone with the Unknown and the Fear it evokes? From what we have heard of Helen's interpersonal and personal life at home, it is possible that *all* of these constellations of negative affects occurred on a daily basis, and it is not hard to imagine that several types of affect-toned complexes resulted.

Childhood: one to seven years

During the post-study visit at 14 months, it was decided to continue data collection until Helen was seven years old.

14 months

Mother and Helen came together, but this was the last visit during her childhood that Helen attended. SB learned that Helen was continuing to scream at mealtimes and angrily throw her food in the air and then push it away, just as she had done at 52 weeks. I take this stereotypy as evidence that a pathological eating complex now inhabits Helen's unconscious psyche and motivates her Rejection of yet another unhappy feeding.

When SB leaned warmly over her, Helen pulled away. Another time when SB approached her, Helen broke into wild sobbing that lasted for ten minutes, even though her mother was right there. Then she moved to her mother, laid her head on her feet, and sobbed loudly. Such behavior in a standardized Stranger Situation would be regarded as Helen's prolonged Stranger Anxiety and reflective of insecure attachment to her mother. My conjecture is that in the absence of parental complexes with Interest and Joy as their nuclear components there was no secure base for Helen to deal with the experience of an interested other. It was for that reason, I believe, that SB's overtures toward Helen, who was not used to anything like that from her own mother, constellated the archetypal pattern that follows the formula the Unknown + the Abyss → Fear–Terror. (In Chapter 9, I will discuss the relation between eating disorders and attachment status.)

For idiosyncratic reasons I have not been able to unpack, Helen's parents had kept her in a supine position throughout her infancy. It is fascinating to read, if with considerable dismay, SB's account of how Helen had adapted to this restriction: SB noted that Helen's upper body was like that of an 18-month-old, while her limbs resembled those of a nine- to ten-month-old: "She moved along on the floor at a good pace by sitting with her knees apart and heels pressed to each other, hopping forward on her buttocks" (Brody 2002: 56).

Three years

Mother came alone for this interview. At 20 months, Helen had been underweight and reluctant to walk. A neurologist diagnosed her condition as one of poor muscle tone. She did begin to walk at 22 months, but even then her endurance was limited to a block or so.

She had little appetite, ate her meals rapidly, and left the dinner table quickly, just as mother had encouraged her to do in her infancy. Mother liked it this way because it was easier for her: Helen's older sibling would eat any food Helen left. Helen had developed the habit of chewing her food and then spitting it out.

This sort of rumination is a feature of many developing eating disorders. Angela Guarda and her co-authors (2004) published an article titled "Chewing and Spitting in Eating Disorders and its Relationship to Binge Eating." They began their research with the hypothesis that there would be a positive association between chewing and spitting and binge eating. Their subjects were eating-disordered inpatients and they compared frequent chewers/spitters with those who did not regularly engage in this behavior. The researchers found that, contrary to their predictions, chewing and spitting is more closely associated with restrictive than with binge behaviors.

Let us recall at this point that Helen was to develop the restrictive form of Anorexia nervosa in her adolescence. I believe that restrictive, like ruminative, behavior originates in a pathological eating complex. In Helen's case, the first sign that this complex was in place half way through the first year of life was Helen's self-induced vomiting, reported by her mother at the 6½ month interview.

As well as the complex that involves internalization of arbitrary parental taboos, there is also a complex that asserts the child's self against such pathogenic parenting. When she was two years old, Helen reacted to any restriction, toilet training being one example, with horrible tantrums. When mother sent Helen to her room, she refused to stay there. She was very talkative and became angry at interruptions. Mother now said Helen had been moody since birth, neatly ignoring any implication that Helen's behavior was a reaction to her own or Helen's father's.

Fourth and fifth years

Mother complained about Helen's behavior at mealtimes, reporting that she fidgeted and ate rapidly while half sitting and half standing. Father, who by now considered Helen a general nuisance, added that she "slobbers" over her food.

Mother and Helen were in such conflict by this point that SB likened their relation to a civil war, with defiance, recriminations, and rage on both sides. Both parents, moreover, seemed pleased to tell SB that they were able to isolate themselves from Helen. They did not connect this success at disavowing Helen's presence with Helen's constant demands that mother stay with her.

Helen, at this age, was reported to be very attached to her blanket, which mother threatened to take away as a disciplinary measure. Both parents teased her about the blanket, even when it upset her, because they thought she looked so "cute" when she was angry. The parents' ridicule augments what I hypothesize as a Shame/Contempt complex that is increasing in magnitude.

Sixth and seventh years

Mother said Helen was now "picky" about food. This too rings a bell for the student of the development of eating disorders. Margaret Marchi and Patricia Cohen (1990) conducted a prospective study of eating disturbances in childhood and their relation to Anorexia and Bulimia in adolescence. One question they posed was: "Are early troublesome eating behaviors related to the later development of eating disorders?" (ibid.: 112). Their study investigated problematic eating behaviors in children over a ten-year period from early and middle childhood to late childhood and adolescence. Their subjects consisted of the families of 326 girls and 333 boys: "Families were interviewed three times, when the children were ages 1 through 10, when they were 9 through 18, and 2.5 years later when they were pre-dominantly 12 through 20" (ibid.: 113).

Out of the numerous potentially pathogenic factors they could identify in these interviews, the researchers identified four for purposes of analysis: (1) Problem meals (which included unpleasantness at mealtimes and struggles over eating); (2) Pickiness (a spectrum of disdain for most food that included eating little, pickiness per se, eating slowly, and a generally low interest in food); (3) Pica (which included eating dirt, clay, laundry starch, paint or plaster, or other non-food material); (4) Digestive problems (which included frequent vomiting, diarrhea, constipation, or stomach aches.

These researchers found that "picky eating in early childhood was a *protective* factor (against the development of) bulimic symptoms in the 12- to 20-year-olds" (ibid.: 116). Their conclusions in regard to Anorexia nervosa were as follows: "Digestive problems [frequent vomiting, diarrhea, constipation, stomach aches] in early childhood, on the other hand, were predictive of elevated symptoms of anorexia nervosa in adolescence and picky eating even more so" (ibid.: 116). They added: "We do not have data that would indicate whether this mechanism is associated with lesser feelings of hunger, increased ability to ignore hunger, or learned patterns of food avoidance following discomfort" (ibid.: 116). In my view, picky eating

joins chewing and spitting as a likely indicator of an unconscious, pathological eating complex accompanied by increasing dissociation of the
Hunger–Satiety drive.

Post-study interview with mother and father

Both parents would have preferred to talk about their marital problems,
which often focused on major disagreements they harbored regarding child-
rearing. Father, for instance, was continuing his ridicule of Helen, and
Helen's mother did not approve. Helen's body was now his focus: he would
tell her her backside was not shaped well. He pursued his teasing, which
was rarely disguised as funny, even when she was in tears, and said he was
surprised she was upset because he was only speaking about her body.
Helen's image of her body was also being conditioned by an internalized
Shame/Contempt complex.

This was SB's summary comment about Helen's parents:

> Never in our meetings with them over the years had either one been
> seen or heard to express affection or sympathy for Helen, except once
> when mother, with a slight sign of regret, said that Helen had never
> enjoyed feeding after being weaned from the breast.
>
> (ibid.: 66)

Under such circumstances of near total lack of empathy, we can expect
that, in addition to her eating disturbance, Helen's ego development, her
capacity for object relations, and the subjective integration of her personality would be seriously compromised. And they were.

Nursery school and kindergarten

3½ years

Helen was described as either moving around the nursery schoolroom like a
robot or sitting still fingering her nose or mouth: "She was an aimless joyless
wanderer" (ibid.: 62). What is striking about the toddler so described is her
lack of emotional vitality, lack of excited curiosities, and lack of joyful
social and individual symbolic play.

Five years

She had become expressionless, on edge, and self-conscious. Her only social
contact was with one other girl, whom she imitated awkwardly; her voice
was tremulous and high-pitched. When the teacher invited her to join a

group rhythmic activity, she jumped and flounced about, occasionally giggling. She was, however, still making an effort to socialize.

Six years

Helen continued to be expressionless, stony-faced, and staring vacantly (as she had when she was 6½ months old). She had a relation with one girl, who was similar to the one in nursery school, but her affect was inappropriately labile, her social behavior markedly immature, and her cognitive activity restricted. She thoroughly enjoyed fine motor activity, however.

Intelligence testing

These were the results of her yearly intelligence testing: 3 years – 136; 4 years – 135; 5 years – 134; 7 years – Verbal 110, Performance 121, Full scale 123. She approached the tests soberly and uneasily. She refused all gross motor tasks but readily carried out fine motor tasks and could work competently alone. Her abstract thinking was superior. She withdrew from difficult tasks and seemed close to anger. I am not sure that Helen's actual intelligence had declined. Rather, I would postulate that the threat of failure-induced Shame (self-Contempt) was too great to allow Helen to take on the difficult questions, and so she scored below her level. Functionally, however, the result was a restriction of her intellectual capacity.

Middle childhood

There is now a three-year break in the longitudinal study of Helen that we have been following until she has an individual interview with SB when she is 18 years old. During this visit, she will give an account of her life from the time she was ten years old.

To bridge this developmental gap I would like to insert what I learned about the stages of childhood and adolescence, for which we have no direct evidence in Helen, from an article by Debra Miller and her colleagues (1993) that includes retrospective reports of grim mealtimes in childhood by bulimic patients.

The authors note that the onset of Bulimia nervosa in adolescence has tended to assume and focus investigation on an etiology in the adolescent stage itself rather than on a search for possible earlier childhood precursors. They argue for a new focus on the attitude toward food itself, which obviously can have developed well beyond the sexual and behavioral changes associated more exclusively with adolescence: "The other issue of possibly critical importance in uncovering the origins of this disorder is why food becomes the focus for these young women as opposed to other types of self-destructive behaviors, such as alcohol abuse or sexual acting out" (Miller *et al.* 1993: 622). These authors also point out that none of the etiologic theories explains why food itself has become the focus for the bulimic patient: "One area that has received scant attention, however, is the actual childhood mealtime experiences of adolescent and young adult bulimics. The purpose of the present study was to investigate whether the presence of such experiences would differentiate bulimics from nonbulimics" (ibid.: 624).

Unfortunately, this research did not obtain detailed developmental histories, but, nevertheless, its findings were very interesting. The researchers applied The Childhood Family Mealtime Questionnaire (CFMQ), which assesses mealtime experiences up to 13 years of age, to 60 subjects who qualified for the bulimic group, 55 women in the repeat dieter group, and 368 women in the nonbulimic group.

They found that women with bulimia reported more negative early mealtime and food-related experiences than did women who were nonbulimic or repeat dieters.

As reported by women classified as bulimic, conversations held during family meals were often conflictual. Interpersonal grievances and hostilities were frequently raised, parents tended to dominate or control the conversation, and children were stifled in their attempts to express opinions. This stressful, controlling posture extended to the act of eating itself. Women with bulimia reported that their families paid a great deal of attention to eating habits. They felt pressured to eat meals rapidly, to "clean their plates," and to finish dinner at the same time as other family members.

(ibid.: 631)

A second feature distinguishing the family mealtimes of bulimic women was the use of food as an instrument of reward or punishment: "The effect of this early experience was long-lasting, and women with bulimia reported that they would still feel stressed or guilty if they refused food offered by a family member" (ibid.: 631). The final feature distinguishing the early mealtime or food-related experiences of bulimic women was the great importance attached to weight, physical appearance, and attractiveness by their families.

The authors conclude their research report with a suggestion I would echo: "Longitudinal studies of family transactional patterns, particularly surrounding food and physical appearance, are needed to determine the validity of these preliminary findings" (ibid.: 632). My assumption is that there is a tableau of family mealtimes in childhood that will be found to be characteristic for those adolescents who develop the Bulimia–Anorexia (BN–AN) syndrome, and that it is a mistake to assume that faulty eating is a reaction to the stresses of adolescence per se, because the disturbed mealtimes well predate the emergence of adolescent issues.

Helen develops an eating disorder

When Helen was 18 years old, she gave her own retrospective report to SB of her adolescence. SB described Helen at this point as a tall, thin young woman with a bland facial expression and a mechanical smile. Although thoughtful and friendly, she was tense and humorless. On the other hand, she was highly verbal, even expansive. Her body, however, was tightly controlled. SB learned that from the time Helen was ten until she was 17 years old, the family made six residential moves. During this time her grades fell from superior to average. Her primary academic interest became art.

Helen said that she began menstruating when she was 13 or 14 years of age, but was not bothered by this: "Soon after, however, she got into the habit of having 'gigantic snacks,' which belied her easy acceptance of maturation" (Brody 2002: 69). As we have seen with other cases in this study, Helen's eating disorder begins with a ravenous appetite, which I believe is an expression of dissociated Hunger.

> At that time in her life, she said, mother fussed constantly about what everyone in the family was eating [out of] worry about overweight, kept watch on the contents of the refrigerator, and scolded anyone for taking anything from it instead of waiting for mealtimes.
>
> (ibid.: 69)

Mother's goal, in other words, had continued to be underfeeding, just as it was in Helen's feedings in her infancy. At the time of the interview, Helen's mother was warning Helen that if she ate freely she would get flabby arms like mother's: "[These] warnings . . . revived the misery Helen had felt at age 11 when a friend used to tease her about having 'thunder thighs' and an expectable middle-age spread" (ibid.: 69).

> At 15 she began to diet and lose weight and "got carried away." She would have a slice of Melba toast for breakfast, walk five miles, swim 30 laps, have a green pepper for lunch, and a light dinner. She liked being underweight and did not mind that menses stopped when she was 16. She attributed [this] recent change in her eating habits to an intense fear of being overweight, as her parents now were.
>
> (ibid.: 69)

Helen by this point was clearly struggling with dissociated Satiety, that is, an intrusive feeling of having already had enough that was leading to self-starvation. This is additional evidence of dissociation of both poles of the

Hunger–Satiety drive, which I regard as a necessary condition for the BN–AN syndrome. Her obese parents, however, never even noticed her extreme weight loss. Helen took a part-time job at a food shop.

Helen explained to SB that there was no cohesion among the members of her family. Mother yelled a lot, always wanted her own way, and occasionally hit Helen. Father had temper tantrums: he had once chased Helen out of the house and ran after her in a fury. Helen had begun to hit both her parents back when they picked on her.

Helen's friends were not welcome in the home at any time as mother and father felt this would intrude upon their own privacy. They were very critical of Helen's social activity, which was minimal enough.

Psychological testing: 18 years of age

Although Helen's Full Scale IQ on her intelligence test was 128, there were indications that extreme self-criticism had impinged on her judgment, even during the test. This finding is the manifestation of an unconscious Self-Rejection–Shame complex, and it suggests that it had led Helen not to accept, let alone live up to, her actual potential. There were parts of her self that emerged as undomesticated and undeveloped. Her Rorschach record indicated crude oral aggression, bizarre confusion of body parts, and loss of body boundaries. Incongruous combinations represent an unstable sense of self and an extreme departure from reality testing, manifest in a massive defensive effort to ward off anxiety. This brief interpretation tells me that the psychization of Helen's body had been as pathological as that of her Hunger–Satiety drive. Her functioning, one learns, had an "as-if" quality, and at that time this was the tentative diagnosis: "Principal Diagnosis: Borderline with Anxiety, Dysphoria, and Narcissistic trends" (ibid.: 72).

22 to 30 years: telephone interviews

By the time Helen entered college, she was trying to eat normally, but then she began to have stomach cramps, a result, she thought, of having done foolish things, such as eating only vegetables. At this time she was eating no breakfast, a salad for lunch, and a regular dinner. There were lingering symptoms of her eating disorder.

Her parents continued to change their place of residence innumerable times within the city, the state, and the country. Helen did not recall her mother ever showing emotion. Let us recall that during Helen's infancy, the only motives for Helen's screaming that mother was willing to acknowledge as valid were hunger, gastrointestinal pain, and lack of sleep; Helen's affects did not exist for her.

Marriage at 25 to a young man with whom she had lived in her senior year of college made no change in her life. She felt bored both with her husband and with her job teaching art in a small college.

30 years of age: SB's last interview with Helen

A few years ago Helen had had a nightmare that had disturbed her very much: "A big bird was *vomiting* on a train, she had to jump over the tracks to reach another platform, she jumped but fell on the tracks and was electrocuted. Then she floated upward and looked down on her body" (ibid.: 76, original emphasis). The dream speaks to me in a very understandable idiom. The bird, I believe, is a personification of Helen's pathological eating complex, which has caused a dissociation between Helen's consciousness and her body (the floating state), which she experiences as "death." It appears to me that over the past 12 years, the natural healing forces of the psyche and the environment have assisted Helen in integrating the pathogenic eating complex into consciousness, so that she no longer suffers overtly from the BN–AN syndrome.

During this interview, Helen signaled that she was well aware of her parents' deficiencies "in many areas," and with muted affect expressed her rejection of their actions and attitudes.

> They never should have had children, she said, because they could not love them, their own comforts always came first. Never, really never, had they shown any sympathy or offered any help when she was unhappy or ill or troubled about anything at all. They rather blamed her for any discontent she voiced, or laughed at her, or teased her about being so upset they would have to call an ambulance to take her away.
> (ibid.: 75)

These observations by Helen at 30 years are consonant with SB's summary of the family atmosphere when Helen was seven years old. Her marriage had improved, as she felt grateful to her husband for his support of her chosen career in painting. She did not want to have children because raising them would detract from her career.

Speculations

This ends my review of Sylvia Brody's remarkable (and also singular) longitudinal study of someone en route to developing the BN–AN syndrome. The study, for Helen, extended from her birth until she was 30 years old, and it captured, by happenstance, her experience of an eating disorder during her adolescence.

I think that research now needs to be directed toward determining whether or not construction of a pathological eating complex in infancy is a necessary condition for the development of an eating disorder in adolescence. On the basis of the case of Helen, my tentative answer to this question would have to be in the affirmative. There is little doubt, on the other hand, that a pathological eating complex constructed in infancy can be resolved before adolescence if favorable forces supervene throughout childhood. I think these considerations are not just academic. They can also be employed to direct our efforts toward the primary prevention of eating disorders.

Chapter 9

Primary prevention of eating disorders

Interest and Joy in infancy

In previous chapters of this book, I have presented my understanding of how eating disorders develop in adolescents and young adults, and how they may be treated in psychotherapy, a complex but gratifying process. We now must ask how we can prevent such disorders from arising in the first place. Although the answer I give in this final chapter has to be a tentative one because it hasn't been tested systematically, I am convinced that it follows from all that has gone before. I present it in the hope that we can actually learn from clinical experience to forestall the worst psychological handling of the normal Hunger–Satiety drive, which the reader will not be surprised to know I think is a precious asset in our emotional lives, not to be taken for granted. In Chapter 8, we observed that the inadequate care provided Helen by her parents during her infancy and throughout her childhood was followed by the onset of AN in her adolescence. Resolution of this eating disorder seemed to have been brought about by the natural healing forces of the psyche. In Chapter 5, we observed that the inadequate care provided Renee throughout her infancy, childhood, and adolescence was followed by the onset of the BN–AN syndrome when she was a young adult. In Renee's case, cure of her eating disorder occurred during a therapy that supported her healing regression to the first three months of life and new symbolic bondings with her therapist as a new "mother" and her Self, which allowed her to redevelop as if she had reborn. I was surprised to find, though perhaps I shouldn't have been, that Renee's renewal occurred in the same sequential steps that I had previously demonstrated to be characteristic of the normal bonding process between parents and infants during the first few months of life (*The Symbolic Impetus*, 2001), and that gave me a clue as to the way an eating disorder might be forestalled in the first place by healthy handling of the infant's appetitive self. My review of the eating disorder literature, however, failed to turn up case studies with comparable developmental histories against which I could test this hypothesis. I decided, however, to take the hint presented by the cases of Helen and Renee and to explore the premise that primary prevention of eating disorders in adolescents and young adults required "good enough" bonding between parents and their infants during the neonatal period when feeding is such a central part of the adult–child interaction. This made sense to me, because I had already shown in Chapter 2 that faulty parent–infant bonding in earliest infancy was a primary factor in the etiology of infant Trudy's Failure to Thrive.

I had also realized that the profound importance of these early bonding processes between parents and their babies can only become clear when we understand their emotional aspects in a way that does not exclude the symbols that inevitably attend the emergent emotions. The first event in the series, which occurs at or around birth, is the development of a mother–infant symbolic bond, in which the infant becomes the "Wonder-child" of an archetypal "Mother." (In fact, both parents are instrumental in the bonding processes that constellate this archetypal object relation, but I will refer only to mothers for ease of presentation.) The emotional component of this bond, those affects that make it a bond, are archetypal, and we have met them before as the affects of the life instinct, Interest and Joy. From the moment these affects are constellated, a link to life itself and everything life-giving is created. But this process, though it suffuses the baby, starts in the psyche of the mother, which, like her immune system, is shared with the baby, whose own affective system is still developing. That means that there is a continuous flow of Interest and Joy from the unconscious of the mother that embraces her baby. Her infant has, so to speak, acquired a nimbus and become an endlessly fascinating "Wonder-child." The second step in the sequence, which occurs one to two months later, is the first emergence of an infant–mother bond, meaning an affective linkage that both participants can fully partake in. When this development is achieved, Interest and Joy start to flow from the unconscious of the infant to suffuse its nascent ego and to envelop the mother, who then acquires a radiant aura and thus has become, to all intents and purposes, the Great Mother Goddess. In this preverbal world of archetypal object relations, the personal mother and her infant, whatever their actual human limitations, are now fully contained in an archetypal field of Interest and Joy that lends its divinity to both of them. The accompanying sense of being really special sustains their relatedness and makes it a field for growth-promoting play and exploration. The third step in this succession is the formation of a symbolic bond between the baby's nascent ego and the Self, the dynamic center of the whole psyche. It involves some perception on the baby's part that he or she is indeed special, and therefore has distinctiveness itself to draw upon. Neumann refers to the basis of this confidence as the ego-Self axis – "the basis for the tendency to compensation and balance between the ego and the unconscious and also between the world and the individual" (1990: 124). Since an eating disorder reflects a lack of trust in the world's feeding arrangements, and in the Self that wants to be fed, we have to conclude that somewhere along the three developmental steps I have just described something has not gone as well as it should have. In discussing the possible relation between disturbances in these early bonding processes and the development of eating disorders in stages as distant as adolescence and adulthood, I will have to rely upon both prospective and retrospective methods of analysis.

Eating disorders and attachment research

In an article entitled "Predictability of Attachment Behavior and Representational Processes at 1, 6, and 19 Years of Age," Main, Hesse, and Kaplan (2005) summarized the current findings from the Berkeley longitudinal study of attachment. They note that Secure and Insecure states of mind in adolescents and young adults are evidently related to attachment status at one and six years:

> Both secure responses to the mother in the 6th-year reunion procedure, and secure-resourceful status on Kaplan's version of the SAT, significantly predicted a secure-autonomous state of mind on the AAI [Adult Attachment Interview] when the participant had reached age 19. In addition, a significant match was uncovered between infant security (or insecurity) with the mother at age 1 and secure-autonomous (or insecure) status on the AAI 18 years later.
>
> (ibid.: 2005: 268)

These findings offer us an indirect window into psychological development in infancy, for they make clear that a secure autonomous state at 19 years, what could be called bedrock security as measured by the Adult Attachment Interview (AAI), implies secure attachment at 1 year of age as measured by the Strange Situation (SS). Secure attachment at 1 year, for me, implies healthy development of a symbolic bond during infancy. On the other hand, an insecure state of mind at 19 years as measured by the AAI implies insecure attachment at 1 year as measured by the SS. To me, insecure attachment at 1 year implies disturbed development of the symbolic bond with the mothering figure during infancy.

Attachment of adolescents and adults with eating disorders

The following three research studies, documenting insecurity of mind in adolescents and adults with eating disorders, will allow us to make inferences about the strength of the symbolic bonds that developed during the early months of their infancies.

In their literature review, "Attachment Research in Eating Disorders," Ward, Ramsay, and Treasure (2000) give an account of an Italian group,

Candelori and Ciocca (1998), who administered the adolescent version of the AAI to 36 patients on an inpatient Eating Disorders Unit. The patients ranged in age from 13 to 24 years. Twelve had restricting Anorexia nervosa, 12 Bulimia nervosa, and 12 were suffering from binge–purging anorexic subtypes. All of these patients were classified as having an insecure attachment status, although they showed different attachment subtypes.

In their paper, "Attachment in Anorexia: A Transgenerational Perspective," Ward *et al.* reported on their examination "of the attachment status of patients with severe anorexia nervosa and their mothers using the 'gold standard' Adult Attachment Interview (AAI)" (2001: 497). These subjects were 20 consecutive patients who had been admitted to their care with the diagnosis of Anorexia nervosa, along with 12 of their mothers, and all were given a structured interview using the AAI. These researchers found that "nineteen (95%) daughters and seven mothers (70%) were rated insecure on the AAI" (ibid.: 497).

In "Eating Disorders and Attachment: The Effects of Hidden Family Processes on Eating Disorders," Ringer and Crittenden (2007) administered the AAI, which they classified using Crittenden's Dynamic-Maturational Method, to 62 young women with an eating disorder (19 with Anorexia nervosa, 26 with Bulimia nervosa and 17 with Bulimia Anorexia). The results indicated that "all women with an eating disorder were anxiously attached" (Ringer and Crittenden 2007: 119). Most of the subjects were puzzled about how "parental behaviour was tied causally to their own behaviour" (ibid.: 119). One possible explanation for the puzzlement of these subjects is that the pathogenic parental behaviors occurred in early infancy when memory is primarily involuntary due to the immaturity of the ego.

As a working hypothesis for future research, I would like to generalize from these three studies in the following way: All, or almost all, adolescents and adults with BN or AN, when tested with the AAI, will be found to have an insecure state of mind. I would further postulate, pending verification from the actual developmental histories, that they already had an insecure attachment status at one year of age resulting from a disturbed development during infancy. Our task, for the future, is not just to develop research paradigms that can identify these factors. We have to act on what we already know to prevent such insecure early attachments from leading to researchable eating disorders in the first place. Let me suggest some ways we can identify the problems I am demanding we try to solve.

Maternal feeding and care during the first three months of infancy and attachment at one year

Up to now, I have been using what is sometimes called the method of recurrence (Piaget 1954: 221–2), which consists in extending in the opposite direction the lines of the genetic process revealed by the study of the last stages, to direct my analyses from attachment behaviors evident at 19 years of age to uncover what must have been going on at one year of age. I will now reverse direction to show that attachment to the mother at one year is determined primarily by the quality of maternal care and feeding the infant received during the first three months of life. I would add a developmental corollary, that the insecure attachment states of mind of adolescents and adults with eating disorders have their origins in the disturbed bonding between parents and their infants during the first months of life.

There is some evidence for these views already. In their article, "Early Face-to-Face Interaction and its Relation to Later Infant–Mother Attachment," Blehar, Lieberman, and Ainsworth (1977) studied the relation between mothers' interactions with their babies from 6 to 15 weeks and attachment of their babies at one year. During the 6–15-week observational period, mothers of infants who were securely attached at one year were sensitive to their babies' emotional states so as not to over- or under-stimulate them. They were able to deftly create extended social episodes. In addition, there "was a tendency for the mothers of the secure group to be more playful and lively than the other mothers . . ." (Blehar et al. 1977: 190). My interpretation of these results is that these mothers had clearly established "good enough" bonding with their infants. Mothers of infants who were insecurely attached at one year, on the other hand, approached their babies with silent, impassive facial expressions, engaged them only briefly, and tended not to respond to their infants' joyful attempts to initiate social engagements. Their behavior was less playful and more matter of fact. My interpretation of these findings is that the achievement of mother–infant bonding by these mothers was "not good enough." The unanswered question is whether any of the insecurely attached infants developed eating disorders during their adolescence or adulthood.

We do have information, however, as to whether eating behavior in infancy can be related to attachment difficulties. In their article, "Some Contemporary Patterns of Mother–Infant Interaction in the Feeding Situation," Ainsworth and Bell (1969) studied, in 26 mother–infant pairs, the interrelations between the quality of maternal care during the first three months of infancy, the patterns of mother–infant interaction during feeding in this same period, and infant attachment at one year.

The authors identified nine patterns of interaction pertinent to the feeding situation. The mothers considered most sensitive treated their babies as active partners from the start, and encouraged them to set the timing of feedings, the quantity of food eaten, and the ending of each meal. I would interpret these findings as evidence that psychization of the Hunger–Satiety drive occurred under circumstances of sensitive, encouraging parenting, conducive to the formation of eating complexes conditioned by Interest and Joy. The mothers designated as insensitive, by contrast, became more and more dominant in deciding when the baby was to eat, how much was to be eaten, and when the baby was satiated. The psychization of the Hunger–Satiety drive during this pattern of feedings could in my opinion only result in the formation of eating complexes conditioned by Fear, Sadness, Anger, and Shame/Contempt, the very affects that appear in relation to food in adolescent patients starting to manifest an eating disorder.

There was also a significant contrast between the *general* quality of care provided by sensitive and insensitive mothers. The former exhibited an ability to understand the baby's signals and to gratify the needs they expressed: "These mothers tended to be able to see things from the baby's point of view, to take delight in his behaviour, and to accept him with little regret over the temporary surrender of their autonomy" (Ainsworth and Bell 1969: 156; this refers to both female and male babies). The latter mothers "tended to be distorted in their perceptions of the baby, to take little or no delight in his behaviour, and to resent overtly or covertly the infringement of their autonomy by his demands" (ibid.: 156). The insensitive mothers' social interactions with their infants were often extremely inappropriate, for they tended "to tease or torment [them]" (ibid.: 1956).

Needless to say, the babies of sensitive mothers who provided optimal patterns of feeding and quality of care were securely attached in the SS at one year, and the infants of insensitive mothers were insecurely attached. This much we know from the research. It is my judgment that the sensitive mothers produced such secure attachment because they had established robust bonds of Interest and Joy with their babies *in general*, an attitude that encompassed each and every feeding, whereas insensitive mothers had not established bonds characterized by these life-enhancing affects, so that feedings were much more ambivalent situations.

To summarize, I have cited research that shows (a) that there is continuity between an insecure state of mind in adolescence and adulthood and insecure attachment at one year and (b) that a primary factor in insecure attachment at one year is disturbed parent–infant bonding in the neonatal period. I have chosen to go further than the research to speculate that faulty parent–infant bonding may play a significant part in the development of the BN–AN syndrome in later life. Let me now cite other research that may explain why I feel this is a justified leap beyond the data at hand.

Archetypal affects and attachment at one year

In the article, "Emotional Determinants of Infant–Mother Attachment," by Izard *et al.* (1991), we find more about the importance of the affective lives of sensitive and insensitive mothers during infancy. The authors studied 114 white, middle-class mother–infant dyads who had been recruited from birth announcements in local newspapers. Data for their research were obtained at infant ages 2.5, 3.0, 4.5, 9.0, and 13.0 months. Emotions under consideration were interest, joy, surprise, sadness, anger, disgust, contempt, fear, shame, shyness, guilt, and inner-directed hostility (anger, disgust, and contempt directed toward the self). The measures used to assess maternal affects were *Emotion Experience Scales* and *Emotion Expression Styles Questionnaires*. To assess mother–infant attachment, the Ainsworth Strange Situation procedure was conducted at 13 months. They found these contrasting patterns: Mothers of children with lower insecurity scores (those more likely to be classified as securely attached) "reported experiencing less negative emotion . . . and more positive emotion [optimal Interest and Joy] . . . These mothers were also more open in their expression of negative emotion around their children . . . and more sociable, nurturant, and empathic . . ." (ibid.: 912). Mothers of children with higher insecurity scores (those more likely to be classified as insecurely attached) "reported experiencing more negative emotion [less than optimal Interest and Joy] . . . but they were less open in their expression of negative emotions around their children . . . (ibid.: 912). The authors concluded that "mothers' emotion experiences, expressive behaviors, and personality traits were significant predictors of the level of security of the infant–mother attachment" (ibid.: 906). I believe, had this study been directed toward feeding behaviors, the same authors could have predicted the positive or negative affective psychization of the Hunger–Satiety drive during the 13-month period of the study.

In the article, "Sensitivity and Attachment: A Meta-Analysis on Parental Antecedents of infant Attachment," De Wolff and van IJzendoorn (1997) also emphasize the importance of the emotional life of the sensitive mother, whom I am interpreting as the mother most likely to promote optimal bonding. The authors conducted their meta-analysis of parental antecedents to attachment security focused on 66 studies with 176 mother–infant pairs. Their purpose was to address the question whether maternal sensitivity is associated with infant attachment and, if so, what is the strength of the relation. Their results appeared to support the position that maternal sensitivity is an important condition of attachment security. They cautioned that these results should not, however, be considered a replication of the original study by Ainsworth *et al.* (1978). They added:

> The current meta-analyses qualify the original Baltimore results in yet another way. Sensitivity cannot be considered to be the exclusive and most important factor in the development of attachment. Several domains of maternal interactive behavior showed effect sizes that were similar to those for the domain of Sensitivity.
>
> (De Wolff and van IJzendoorn 1997: 585)

The five interpersonal domains or relational affective/behavioral clusters identified by the authors were Synchrony, Mutuality, Support, Positive Attitude, and Stimulation. In future research, such domains could be conceptually defined in ways that include references to the affects involved. As an example of how this might be done, I offer the following conceptual definitions of the domain terms, followed by the affects involved:

- *Synchrony*: coordinated social play [the dynamism of Joy];
- *Stimulation*: affective stimulation;
- *Emotional Support*: playful interaction and mutual play [the dynamism of Joy];
- *Positive Attitude*: positive affect [Interest and Joy];
    - delight; affectionate contact; emotion expression; positive interaction [Interest and Joy];
    - attention [Interest].

This research provides a model for the kind of parenting to strive for during infancy if we want to prevent the development of a pathological eating disorder complex that will bedevil the child later, when unresolved infantile conflicts are reawakened by the storms of adolescence.

Additional support for this view comes from clinical observations that I doubt I am the first child psychiatrist to have made, though I have documented them in my previous writings. Optimal levels of Interest–curiosity/exploration and Joy–fantasy/play, beginning in the first three months of infancy and continuing throughout this stage of development, are necessary for social development, for healthy psychization of the Hunger–Satiety drive, and for secure attachment at one year. Under these circumstances of healthy psychization even high levels of crisis affects – Fear, Sadness, Anger, Shame/Contempt – can be integrated into the developmental process in such a way that they need not threaten the security and pleasure of eating.

Neonatal perception inventories

What is the evidence that maternal bonding succeeds in creating secure attachment to other humans later in life? In their article, "Maternal Perception of Newborns Predicts Attachment Organization in Middle Adulthood," Broussard and Cassidy (2010) demonstrated the predictive validity of a newborn infant's status in mother's eyes, as measured by the Neonatal Perception Inventories (NPI), and the offspring's attachment state of mind 40 years later as measured by the Adult Attachment Interview (AAI). The authors of this study also reviewed the research showing that the NPI at one month had already proved its predictive validity in follow-up studies of the same subjects' psychosocial adjustment at 4½, 10½, 15, and 19 years of age. Let us look more closely at how the NPI instrument came to be.

During pediatric clinical practice in the 1940s and 1950s, E. R. Broussard noted that mothers of healthy newborns varied in their response to their babies and their needs:

> Some mothers made a smooth transition from pregnancy to mother-hood and had pride and pleasure in raising their infants, and their infants thrived. These mothers and babies laughed and smile together, reflecting to each other mutual positive feelings. Other mothers lacked pride in their infants and had little pleasure in motherhood even though physicians had judged the infants' biological endowments to be normal and viewed these infants as appealing.
>
> (Broussard and Cassidy 2010: 168)

The reader of this book will not be surprised to learn that I believe the former mothers had developed a robust bond with their infants grounded in the archetypal affects Interest and Joy, and that the latter mothers had not. Broussard became aware that a mother's perception of her baby influenced her interactions with the infant throughout its development. These observations led her to develop the NPI to measure in a way that could be quantitatively assessed the mother's perception of her baby and then to conduct longitudinal studies of healthy neonates using this instrument.

With her partner Hartner, Broussard (1970, 1971) constructed and applied NPI that measured the mother's notion of what an average baby would be like (Average Baby Perception Inventory) compared with how she saw her baby (Your Baby Perception Inventory). Each Inventory consisted of six behavioral items – crying, spitting, feeding, elimination, sleeping, and predictability – which the mother rated in a five-point scale – a great deal, a good bit, a moderate amount, very little, none. The test was first administered to 318 women one month after they had given birth to their first child. Of the 318 women, 61.2 percent rated their infants as better than average (Low-Risk), 13.2 percent as equal to average and 25.6 percent as less than average (High-Risk).

Four and a half years later, 120 mothers brought their children for a psychiatric interview conducted by two child psychiatrists. Seventy two of these children had been viewed by their mothers at one month as better than average (these the researchers called the Low-Risk group) and 48 as not better than average (their High-Risk group). They then compared interview results with NPI results at one month of age:

> Of the 34 children assessed as needing therapeutic intervention (Group I) 70.6% had previously been categorized as having a High-Risk potential for subsequent developmental emotional deviations. Among

the 52 (Group II) who did not need intervention, 76.5% had been rated as Low-Risk group.

(Broussard and Hartner 1971: 21)

The predictive capability of the NPI was tested further with follow-up assessments at 10½, 15, and 19 years: ". . . children who had been classified as higher risk at 1 month because of a negative maternal perception of their infantile behaviors, relative to other infants, were significantly more likely to have psychosocial disorder than those who had been classified as low risk" (Broussard and Cassidy 2010: 160).

Broussard and Cassidy also observed that their once-infant subjects, when followed up at 19 years of age and assessed as well functioning, bore striking similarities to the characteristics of individuals classified by the AAI as secure/autonomous. This finding led them to embark upon a research project "to examine the predictive relation between an individual's NPI-rated risk status as a newborn and his or her adult attachment organization" (ibid.: 161). All of their healthy, first-born subjects, 14 males and 12 females, were drawn from the 1963 or 1973 populations of the Pittsburgh First-Born Program. Their mothers had completed the NPI when their babies were one month old. This is what they found:

> As hypothesized, the present study revealed that the experience of having been viewed negatively by one's mother as a newborn, as assessed with the NPI, substantially increased the risk of insecure adult attachment. The odds of having an insecure AAI for adults whose mothers had held a negative perception of them at one month old was 18 times greater than for adults whose mothers had perceived them positively.
>
> (ibid.: 165)

The authors noted that their finding of substantial continuity from infancy to adulthood converged with a study by Waters *et al.* (2000). Earlier clinical observations by Broussard (1979, 1984) indicated that infants from mothers who had held a "negative" perception of them relative to the norm would subsequently exhibit poor psychosocial functioning. Their mothers, it was found, "had difficulties recognizing their infant's signals, and lacked a flexible and effective range of responses" (Broussard and Cassidy 2010; 167–8). These are the definitional behaviors that Ainsworth and her colleagues used to characterize insensitive (vs. sensitive) mothers. (Again, the insensitive mothers turned out to be those whose infants were insecurely attached in the Strange Situation at 12 months.)

When Broussard (1979) presented her clinical observations of high-risk and low-risk babies and their mothers, she highlighted the difference in the affective quality of the mothers' interactions with their infants. Mothers with low-risk babies would say things to them like "Who's that pretty girl in the mirror?" (to a four-month-old playing happily on the floor with a mirror rattle) or "You're not ready for me to go? I'll sit here. So you can see me" (Broussard 1979: 99). Mothers of high-risk infants, on the other hand, would tell them, "'You're so bad,' 'You're a stinker,' or say to others, in the presence of the infant, things like 'She's a wild woman,' 'I feel like giving him away,' and 'Can't you leave me alone?'" (ibid.: 99). As I see it, the mothers of the low-risk infants are channeling positive archetypal affects, Interest and Joy, to them, and the mothers of high-risk infants are expressing negative archetypal affects, primarily Shame/Contempt and often enough Disgust.

With their discouraging, shaming, and sometimes repudiating communications, mothers of high-risk babies massively interfere with their infants' exploration and play, dynamisms that depend, respectively, on maternal Interest and Joy. Infants at low-risk were clearly receiving this psychic nutrition: they showed a progressive interest in the environment and engaged in prolonged play with objects. The two classes of infants also differed in recognizable affective expression: "Some high-risk infants display few signs of pleasure; others may have frozen, fixed smiles, apparently not demonstrating true enjoyment. Infants at low risk exhibit a range of affective responses" (ibid.: 99).

My interpretation of these important findings, which again can guide present day therapy as well as future research, if we take their implications aboard, is that mothers who perceived their babies as above average at one month had achieved a vigorous bond of Interest and Joy with their infants, who had acquired a radiant nimbus. Such bonding, if present at all, had occurred at a much less robust intensity in those mothers who perceived their infants as only average, and in them there was often a tendency to direct derogatory comments toward their infants. Unfortunately, we don't have information as to their attendant eating behaviors, but it would not surprise me to see those as problematic in the high-risk group.

So far as proactive initiatives to stave such conditions and other emotion-based psychopathologies go off, Broussard has described her efforts to alert her colleagues to the vital necessity of developing primary prevention programs in the first months of the infant's life:

> [Her] clinical experiences (moving from pediatrics to public health to child psychiatry and psychoanalysis) led her to urge clinicians, including primary service providers, to emphasize support systems for mothers during the early postpartum period (Broussard and Hartner, 1971). It remains the case that the existing system of postnatal and pediatric care often does not provide professional support for the mother during the critical interim between discharge from the hospital and the next

"routine" contact with the physician at 4–6 weeks. Further institution and evaluation of programs aimed at fostering support for the new mother by husband, family, caring professionals, and society appear to be indicated. Moreover, the Neonatal Perception Inventories provide an easily administered, low-cost screening measure that can identify infants at increased risk of insecure adult attachment. When a mother is identified as holding a negative perception of her newborn, additional assessments can be undertaken to better understand the dyad and to determine what course of action, if any, is to be offered.

(ibid.: 168–9)

Parent and infant bonding scales

A next step toward the primary prevention of eating disorders during the first three months of life will be the construction and application of scales to assess parent and infant bonding during this early period of development. Such bonding (as I explain in Chapter 1 of *The Symbolic Impetus*, 2001) includes the emergence of an image, emotion, and pattern of behavior, all being aspects of the same process, rooted in the archetypal affect system, and each of these features could provide the content for bonding scales. The assessment required could be approached in the form of questions: Do parents describe their baby in superlatives? Are the primary dynamic forces that constitute the parent–infant bond Interest and Joy? Do the parents show evident delight in their babies by engaging them in excited exploration and enjoyable play whenever possible? Does the infant recognize and greet the parents and others with joyful, bright-eyed social smiles? Does the infant express recognition of each advance in its individual development with robust laughter? Does the infant find others and the world endlessly fascinating and engage in social and individual exploration and play whenever possible?

Scales derived from the effort to assess these variables will show, I believe, that the quality of parent and of infant bonding lies on a continuum, with "good enough" bonding at the maximal end and "not good enough" bonding at the minimal end. One can expect that each point on the spectrum will correlate with developmental trajectories exhibiting patterns of relative normality and abnormality. One can also imagine that methods used in attachment research might be expanded to include observations intended to tap into many of the factors in the bonding scales.

The bottom line, as we consider the future of research into the emotional states that predispose to eating disorders with an eye to also correcting the maladaptive aspects now, without waiting for the studies that prove how anorexigenic and bulimigenic they are, is that the first three months of infancy are a critical period for psychization of the Hunger–Satiety drive.

This makes sense, for it is the same period in an infant's life when the archetypal affects of Interest and Joy, as motors of development itself, either are, or are not, invited by the parent into the infantile mind of the child. And it is then that eating becomes either a delightful or a disgusting experience, with power to shape the perception, the emotions and the pattern of behavior that will characterize the developing person's attitude toward Hunger and Satiety for decades to come.

References

Adelson, E. and Fraiberg, S. (1980) "An abandoned mother, an abandoned baby."
In S. Fraiberg (ed.), *Clinical Studies in Infant Mental Health: The First Year of
Life*, New York: Basic Books.

Ainsworth, M. D. S. and Bell, S. M. (1969) "Some contemporary patterns of
mother–infant interaction in the feeding situation." In A. Ambrose (ed.), *Stimulation in Early Infancy*, New York: Academic Press.

Ainsworth, M. D. S., Blehar, M. C., Waters, E. and Wall, S. (1978) *Patterns of
Attachment: A Psychological Study of the Strange Situation*, Hillsdale, NJ:
Lawrence Erlbaum Associates.

Akavia, N. (2003) "Binswanger's theory of therapy: The philosophical and historical
context of the 'Case of Ellen West'." In A. Hirschmuller (ed.), *Ellen West. Eine
Patientin Ludwig Binswangers zwischen Kreativitat und destruktivem Leiden*,
Heidelberg-Kroning: Asanger.

Atchison, M., Wade, T., Higgins, B. and Slavotinek, T. (1998) "Anorexia nervosa
following gastric reduction surgery for morbid obesity," *International Journal of
Eating Disorders*, 23: 111–16.

Atwood, G. E. and Stolorow, R. D. (1984) *Structure of Subjectivity: Explorations in
Psychoanalytic Phenomenology*, Hillsdale, NJ: Analytic Press.

Bell, S. M. and Ainsworth, M. D. S. (1972) "Infant crying and maternal
responsiveness," *Child Development*, 43: 1171–90.

Berkman, N. D., Lohr, K. N. and Bulik, C. M. (2007) "Outcomes of eating
disorders," *International Journal of Eating Disorders*, 40: 293–309.

Binswanger, L. (1958) "The case of Ellen West." In R. May, E. Angel, H. F.
Ellenberger (eds), *Existence: A New Dimension in Psychiatry and Psychology*,
New York: Basic Books.

Blehar, M. C., Lieberman, A. F. and Ainsworth, M. D. S. (1977) "Early face-to-face
interaction and its relation to later infant–mother attachment," *Child
Development*, 48: 182–94.

Bonne, O. B., Bashi, R. and Berry, E. M. (1996) "Anorexia nervosa following
gastroplasty in the male: Two cases," *International Journal of Eating Disorders*,
19: 105–8.

Brody, S. (2002) *The Development of Anorexia Nervosa: The Hunger Artists*,
Madison, CT: International Universities Press.

Brody, S. and Axelrad, S. (1978) *Mothers, Fathers, and Children: Explorations in the*

Formation of Character in the First Seven Years, New York: International Universities Press.

Brome, V. (1978) *Jung: Man and Myth*, New York: Atheneum.

Broussard, E. R. (1979) "Assessment of the adaptive potential of the mother–infant system: The Neonatal Perception Inventories," *Seminars in Perinatology*, 3: 91–100.

—— (1984) "The Pittsburgh first-borns at age 19." In R. Tyson, J. Call and E. Galenson (eds), *Frontiers of Infant Psychiatry*, New York: Basic Books.

Broussard, E. R. and Cassidy, J. (2010) "Maternal perception of newborns predicts attachment organization in middle adulthood," *Attachment and Human Development*, 12: 159–72.

Broussard, E. R. and Hartner, M. S. (1970) "Maternal perception of the neonate as related to development," *Child Psychiatry and Human Development*, 1: 16–25.

—— (1971) "Further considerations regarding maternal perception of the first born," In J. Hellmuth (ed.), *Exceptional Infant Studies in Abnormalities* (Vol. 2), New York: Brunner/Mazel.

Candelori, C. and Ciocca, A. (1998) "Attachment and eating disorders." In *Psychotherapeutic Issues in Eating Disorders: Models, Methods, and Results*, Rome: Societa Editrice Universo.

Cannon, W. B. (1929/1970) *Bodily Changes in Pain, Hunger, Fear and Rage: An Account of Recent Researches Into the Functions of Emotional Excitement*, College Park: Maryland: McGrath Publishing Company.

Cassirer, E. (1957) *The Philosophy of Symbolic Forms. Volume 3: The Phenomenology of Knowledge*, New Haven, CT: Yale University Press.

Coren, S. and Hewitt, P. L. (1998) "Is anorexia associated with elevated rates of suicide?," *American Journal of Public Health*, 88(8): 1206–7.

Darwin, C. (1872) *The Expression of the Emotions in Man and Animals*, New York: Philosophical Library.

Demos, V. (1982) "Affect in early infancy: Physiology or psychology," *Psychoanalytic Inquiry*, 1: 533–74.

—— (1984) "Empathy and affect: Reflections on infant experience." In J. Lichtenberg, M. Bornstein and D. Silver (eds), *Empathy: Volume 2*, Hillsdale, NJ: Analytic Press.

—— (1989a) "A prospective constructionist view of development," *Annual of Psychoanalysis*, 17: 287–342.

—— (1989b) "Resiliency in infancy." In T. F. Dugan and R. Coles (eds), *The Child in our Times: Studies in the Development of Resiliency*, Philadelphia, PA: Brunner/Mazel.

—— (1995) *Exploring Affect: The Selected Writings of Silvan S. Tomkins*, New York: Cambridge University Press.

De Wolff, M. S. and van IJzendoorn, M. H. (1997) "Sensitivity and attachment: A meta-analysis on parental antecedents of infant attachment," *Child Development*, 68(4): 571–91.

Eddy, K. Y., Dorer, D. J., Franko, D. L., Tahilani, K., Thompson-Brenner, H. and Herzog, D. B. (2007) "Should bulimia nervosa be subtyped by history of anorexia nervosa? A longitudinal validation," *International Journal of Eating Disorders*, 40: S67–71.

Ekman, P. (1994) "Strong evidence for universals in facial expressions: A reply to Russell's mistaken critique," *Psychological Bulletin*, 115: 268–87.

Ekman, P. and Friesen, W. V. (1971) "Constants across cultures in the face and emotion," *Journal of Personality and Social Psychology*, 17: 124–9.

Fortunato, G. (1977) "Psychotherapy of an adolescent case of anorexia nervosa," *Journal of Child Psychotherapy*, 4(3): 111–20.

Fraiberg, S. (ed.) (1980) *Clinical Studies in Infant Mental Health: The First Year of Life*, New York: Basic Books.

Fraiberg, S. and Adelson, E. (1973). "Self-representation in language and play: Observations of blind children," *Psychoanalytic Quarterly*, 42: 539–63.

Gaensbauer, T. J. (2002) "Representations of trauma in infancy: Clinical and theoretical implications for the understanding of early memory, *Infant Mental Health Journal*, 23(3): 259–77.

Gianino, A. and Tronick, E. Z. (1988) "The mutual regulation model: The infant's self and interactive regulation and coping and defensive capacities." In T. M. Fielding, P. M. McCabe, and N. Schneiderman (eds), *Stress and Coping Across Development*, Hillsdale, NJ: Lawrence Erlbaum Associates.

Gottman, J. M. and Levenson, R. W. (1999) "What predicts change in marital interaction over time? A study of alternative models," *Family Process*, 38: 143–58.

Guarda, A. S., Coughlin, J. W., Cummings, M., Marinilli, A., Haugh, N., Boucher, M. and Heinberg, L. J. (2004) "Chewing and spitting in eating disorders and its relationship to binge eating," *Eating Behaviors*, 5(3): 231–9.

Halliday, M. A. K. (1975) *Learning How to Mean – Explorations in the Development of Language*, London: Edward Arnold.

Halmi, K. A., Sunday, S., Puglisi, A. and Marchi, P. (1989) "Hunger and satiety in anorexia nervosa and bulimia nervosa," *Annals of the New York Academy of Sciences*, 575: 431–45.

Henry, J. (1963) *Culture Against Man*, New York: Random House.

Herzog, D. B., Greenwood, D. N., Dorer, D. J., Flores, A. T., Ekeblad, E. R., Richards, A. . . . Keller, M. B. (2000) "Mortality in eating disorders: A descriptive study," *International Journal of Eating Disorders*, 28: 20–6.

Hillman, J. (1972) *The Myth of Analysis*, New York: Harper & Row.

—— (1992) *Emotion: A Comprehensive Phenomenology of Theories and their Meanings for Therapy*, Evanston, IL: Northwestern University Press. (Original published in 1960.)

Hirschmuller, A. (ed.) (2003) *Ellen West. Eine Patient in Ludwig Binswangers zwischen Kreativitat und destruktivem Leiden*, Heidelberg-Kroning: Asanger.

Holmgren, S., Humhie, K., Norring, C., Roos, B-E., Rosmark, B. and Sohlberg, S. (1983) "The anorectic bulimic conflict: An alternative diagnostic approach to anorexia nervosa and bulimia," *International Journal of Eating Disorders*, 2(2): 3–14.

Huxley, R. (1970) "The development of the correct use of subject personal pronouns in two children." In G. B. Flores d' Arcais and W. J. M. Levelt (eds), *Advances in Psycholinguistics*, New York: Elsevier.

Izard, C. (1994) "Innate and universal facial expressions: Evidence from developmental and cross-cultural research," *Psychological Bulletin*, 115: 288–99.

Izard, C. E., Haynes, O. M., Chrisholm, G. and Baak, K. (1991) "Emotional determinants of infant–mother attachment," *Child Development*, 62: 906–17.

Jackson, C., Davidson, G., Russell, J. and Vandereycken, W. (1990) "Ellen West revisited: The theme of death in eating disorders," *International Journal of Eating Disorders*, 9(5): 529–36.

Jacobi, J. (1959) *Complex/Archetype/Symbol*, Princeton, NJ: Princeton University Press.

Janet, P. (1903) *Les Obsessions et La Psychasthenie*, Paris: Ancienne Librairie Germer Bailliere et Cie.

Josephs, L. (1989) "The world of the concrete: A comparative approach," *Contemporary Psychoanalysis*, 25: 477–500.

Jung, C. G. (1960) *The Psychogenesis of Mental Disease*, Collected Works 3, 2nd printing, with corrections and minor revisions, Princeton, NJ: Princeton University Press.

—— (1961) *Memories, Dreams, Reflections*, A. Jaffé (ed.), New York: Pantheon Books.

—— (1966) *The Practice of Psychotherapy*, Collected Works 16, 2nd ed., rev. and aug., 3rd printing, with corrections, Princeton, NJ: Princeton University Press.

—— (1967) *Symbols of Transformation*, Collected Works 5, Princeton, NJ: Princeton University Press.

—— (1968a) *Psychology and Alchemy*, Collected Works 12, 2nd ed., completely revised, Princeton, NJ: Princeton University Press.

—— (1968b) *Alchemical Studies*, Collected Works 13, Princeton, NJ: Princeton University Press.

—— (1969) *The Archetypes of the Collective Unconscious*, Collected Works 9i, 2nd ed., Princeton, NJ: Princeton University Press.

—— (1970a) *The Structure and Dynamics of the Psyche*, Collected Works 8, 2nd ed., Princeton, NJ: Princeton University Press.

—— (1970b) *Civilization in Transition*, Collected Works 10, Princeton, NJ: Princeton University Press.

—— (1970c) *Psychology and Religion: West and East*, Collected Works 11, 2nd ed., Princeton, NJ: Princeton University Press.

—— (1970d) *Mysterium Coniunctionis*, Collected Works 14, 2nd ed., Princeton, NJ: Princeton University Press.

—— (1971) *Psychological Types*, Collected Works 6, 2nd printing, Princeton, NJ: Princeton University Press.

—— (1973a) *Experimental Researches*, Collected Works 2, Princeton, NJ: Princeton University Press.

—— (1973b) *Letters, Volume 1: 1906–1950*, G. Adler (ed.), Princeton, NJ: Princeton University Press.

—— (1975) *Letters, Volume 2: 1951–1961*, G. Adler (ed.), Princeton, NJ: Princeton University Press.

—— (1977) *The Symbolic Life*, Collected Works 18, Princeton, NJ: Princeton University Press.

Knudson, R. M. (2006) "Anorexia dreaming: A case study," *Dreaming* 16(1): 43–52.

Kovacs, D., Mahon, J. and Palmer, R. L. (2002) "Chewing and spitting out food among eating-disordered patients," *International Journal of Eating Disorders*, 32: 112–15.

Laing, R. D. (1982) *The Voice of Experience*, New York: Pantheon Books.

Lester, D. (1971) "Ellen West's suicide as a case of psychic homicide," *The Psychoanalytic Review*, 58(2): 251–63.

Levenson, R. W. (1994) "The search for autonomic specificity." In P. Ekman and R. J. Davidson (eds), *The Nature of Emotion Fundamental Questions*, New York: Oxford University Press.

Libbrecht, K. (2003) "The diagnostic value(s) of the historical case-study of Ellen West." In A. Hirschmuller (ed.), *Ellen West. Eine Patientin Ludwig Binswangers zwischen Kreativitat und destruktivem Leiden*, Heidelberg-Kroning: Asanger.

Lynd, H. M. (1958) *On Shame and the Search for Identity*, New York: Harcourt, Brace & World, Inc.

McDonald, M. (1970) "Transitional tunes and musical development," *Psychoanalytic Study of the Child*, 25: 503–20.

Main, M., Hesse, E. and Kaplan, N. (2005) "Predictability of attachment behavior and representational processes at 1, 6, and 19 years of age." In K. E Grossmann, K. Grossmann and E. Waters (eds), *Attachment from Infancy to Adulthood: The Major Longitudinal Studies*, New York: The Guilford Press.

Marchi, M. and Cohen, P. (1990) "Early childhood eating behaviors and adolescent eating disorders," *Journal of the American Academy of Child and Adolescent Psychiatry*, 29(1): 112–17.

Miller, D. A. F., McCluskey-Fawcett, K. and Irving, L. M. (1993) "Correlates of bulimia nervosa: Early family mealtime experiences," *Adolescence*, 28(111): 621–35.

Miller, M. L. (1991) "Understanding the eating disordered patient: Engaging the concrete," *Bulletin of the Menninger Clinic*, 55: 85–95.

Neumann, E. (1973/1990) *The Child*, English translation 1973 by the C. G. Jung Foundation for Analytical Psychology, Foreword 1990 by L. H. Stewart, Boston: Shambhala Publications.

Nielsen, T. (1991) "Non-random positive and negative affect sequences in dream and waking event reports," *Sleep Research*, 20: 163.

Pettazzoni, R. (1956) *The All-Knowing God: Researches into Early Religion and Culture*, Trans. H. J. Rose, London: Methuen

Piaget, J. (1954) *The Construction of Reality in the Child*, New York: Basic Books.

Polivy, J. and Herman, C. P. (2002) "Causes of eating disorders," *Annual Review of Psychology*, 53: 167–213.

Pompili, M., Mancinelli, I., Girardi, P., Ruberto, A. and Tatarelli, R. (2004) "Suicide in anorexia nervosa: A meta-analysis," *International Journal of Eating Disorders*, 36: 99–103.

Pope, H. G., Hudson, J. L. and Mialet, J.-P. (1985) "Bulimia in the late nineteenth century: The observations of Pierre Janet," *Psychological Medicine*, 15: 739–43.

Renee (1951) *Autobiography of a Schizophrenic Girl: With Analytic Interpretation by Marguerite Sechehaye*, Trans. by G. Rubin-Rabson, New York, Grune & Stratton.

Ringer, F. and Crittenden, P. M. (2007) "Eating disorders and attachment: The effects of hidden family processes on eating disorders," *European Eating Disorders Review*, 15: 119–30.

Rogers, C. R. (1990) "Ellen West – and loneliness." In K. Hoeller (ed.), *Readings in*

Existential Psychology & Psychiatry, Seattle, WA: Review of Existential Psychology & Psychiatry.

Sechehaye, M. (1951) *Symbolic Realization: A New Method of Psychotherapy Applied to a Case of Schizophrenia*, Trans. B. Wursten and H. Wursten, Monograph Series on Schizophrenia No. 2, New York: International Universities Press.

—— (1956) *A New Psychotherapy in Schizophrenia*, Trans. G. Rubin-Rabson, New York: Grune & Stratton.

—— (1957) "Affects and frustrated needs as seen through the drawings of a female schizophrenic," *Acta Neurologica et Psychiatrica Belgica*, 57(12): 972–92.

Spignesi, A. (1983) *Starving Women: A Psychology of Anorexia Nervosa*, Dallas, TX: Spring Publications.

Spitz, R. (1951) "The psychogenic diseases of infancy," *The Psychoanalytic Study of the Child*, VI: 271.

Stevens, A. (1990) *On Jung*, London: Routledge.

Stewart, C. T. (2001) *The Symbolic Impetus: How Creative Fantasy Motivates Development*, London: Free Association Books.

—— (2008) *Dire Emotions and Lethal Behaviors: Eclipse of the Life Instinct*, London: Routledge.

Stewart, L. H. (1984) "Affects and Archetypes I and II." Paper presented at active imagination seminar in Geneva, Switzerland in August 1984.

—— (1985) "Affect and archetype: A Contribution to a comprehensive theory of the structure of the psyche." In *Proceedings of the 1985 California Spring Conference*: San Francisco, CA: C. G. Jung Institute, pp. 89–120.

—— (1986) "Affect and archetype: A contribution to a comprehensive theory of the structure of the psyche." In N. Schwartz-Salant and M. Stein (eds), *The Body in Analysis*, Wilmette, IL: Chiron Publications, pp. 183–203.

—— (1987a) "A brief report: Affect and archetype," *Journal of Analytical Psychology*, 32: 35–46.

—— (1987b) "Affect and archetype in analysis". In N. Schwart-Salant and M. Stein (eds), *Archetypal Processes in Psychotherapy*, Wilmette, IL: Chiron Publications, pp. 131–62.

—— (1988) "Jealousy and envy: Complex family emotions." In L. H. Stewart and J. Chodorow (eds), *The Family: Personal, Cultural and Archetypal Dimensions*, Boston, MA: Sigo Press.

—— (1992) *Changemakers: A Jungian Perspective on Sibling Positions and the Family Atmosphere*, New York: Routledge.

Striegel-Moore, R. H. and Bulik, C. M. (2007) "Risk factors for eating disorders," *American Psychologist*, 62: 181–98.

Tomkins, S. S. (1962) *Affect Imagery Consciousness. Volume I: The Positive Affects*, New York: Springer.

—— (1963) *Affect Imagery Consciousness. Volume II: The Negative Affects*, New York: Springer.

—— (1981) "The quest for primary motives: Biography and autobiography of an idea." In E. V. Demos (ed.), *Exploring Affect: The Selected Writings of Silvan S. Tomkins*, Cambridge: Cambridge University Press.

—— (1991) *Affect Imagery Consciousness. Volume III: The Negative Affects Anger and Fear*, New York: Springer.

Tronick, E. Z. (1989) "Emotions and emotional communication in infants," *American Psychologist*, 44(2): 112–19.

Van der Ham, T., Meulman, J. J., van Strien, D. C. and van Engeland, H. (1997) "Empirically based subgrouping of eating disorders in adolescents: A longitudinal perspective," *British Journal of Psychiatry*, 170: 363–8.

Waller, B. M., Cray, J. J. Jr. and Burrows, A. M. (2008) "Selection for universal facial emotion," *Emotion*, 8(3): 435–9.

Ward, A., Ramsay, R. and Treasure, J. (2000) "Attachment research in eating disorders," *British Journal of Medical Psychology*, 73: 35–51.

Ward, A., Ramsay, R., Turnbull, S., Steele, M., Steele, H. and Treasure, J. (2001) "Attachment in anorexia: A transgenerational perspective," *British Journal of Medical Psychology*, 74: 497–505.

Waters, E., Merrick, S., Treboux, D., Crowell, J. and Albersheim, L. (2000) "Attachment security in infancy and early adulthood: A twenty-year longitudinal study," *Child Development*, 71, 684–9.

Werner, H. (1957) *Comparative Psychology of Mental Development*, rev. ed., New York: International Universities Press.

Wheelwright, P. (1974) *Heraclitus*, New York: Atheneum.

Index

Page references in *italic* indicate Tables.

development 12–14; intensity of innate affects 8; Jung on 91; life stimuli for *see* life stimuli; and primary motivation 1–2; and the screams of an infant 140–2; the seven innate emotions 3; socialization of innate emotions 11; specifying the affects 2–3; and "universal" effects 3–4; Stewart, L. H. xi, 3, 6–7, 9, 12–14, 128, 130, 140–1

archetypal affect theory *see* affect theory

archetypes 1, 14, 19; energy of 16 *see also* energy, emotional/ psychological; the Good Mother 69; the Great Mother 69, 153; hero archetype 52, 53; identification with 52; and instincts 1, 16, 19–21, 63; mother archetype and symbolic mother imago 80–5, 88–9, 93, 95, 120; rebirth from mother archetype 83–4, 85, 122–3; and symbols 15–16; the Terrible Mother 51, 69, 73–4, 90, 128; the "Wonder-child" 33, 35, 37, 66, 74–7, 89, 119, 153

astonishment *8*

Atchison, M. *et al.* 44

attachment: of adolescents and adults with eating disorders 154–5; archetypal affects and attachment at 1 year 157–9; insecure 154, 156, 158; and maternal feeding and care in early infancy 155–7; research 154–9; secure 154, 156, 158

Atwood, G. E. and Stolorow, R. D. 46

autonomy 8; dissociation between autonomy needs and parental expectation 71; restrictions on 19, 121

avarice 2

awe 33, 119

baby talk 35, 119

Bell, S. M. and Ainsworth, M. D. S. 138

Berkely to Berkeley longitudinal study of attachment 154

binges/binge-eating 24, 43, 58–9, 143, 155 *see also* Bulimia nervosa

Binswanger, L. 55, 56, 57–8, 59–60; Ellen West case 99–117

Blehar, M. C. *et al.* 156

BN–AN syndrome *see* Bulimia–Anorexia syndrome

body-shame 55–61

bonding, parent–infant *see also* infant–parent relationship: bonding scales 163–4; failure in "good-enough" bonding 31–6, 66–8, 113, 119–20, 135–42, 156; "good enough" bonding 153, 156; interest, joy and 157, 160, 163–4; and neonatal perception inventories 159–63; symbolic mother–infant bond 30, 34, 35, 119

Bonne, O. B. *et al.* 44

Brody, S., longitudinal study of a subject who developed Anorexia nervosa 134–50

Brome, V. 120–3

Broussard, E. R. 161–3; and Cassidy, J. 159–60, 161; and Hartner, M. S. 160

Bulimia–Anorexia (BN–AN) syndrome 107–10; Anorectic–Bulimic-conflict (ABC) model 41; and anorexia cases from the literature 45–54; and Brody's longitudinal study of Helen 134–51; and emotional energy 100–1, 103, 108, 110–11, 115; etiology 39–54, 100–1, 107–8, 111–13, 135–49; and the hunger–satiety drive 44–54, 55–61, 99–117; and Janet's case study of an anorexic 55–61; literature review of BN–AN as a unitary disorder 40–4; and shame 55–61; and suicide 99–117

Bulimia nervosa (BN): and amplification of the hunger drive 24; BN–AN syndrome *see* Bulimia–Anorexia syndrome

"butterflies" 24

Candelori, C. and Ciocca, A. 155

cannibalistic fantasies 73–4, 79

Cannon, W. B. 21–3

Cassirer, E. 4

chaos 7, 121

Childhood Family Mealtime Questionnaire (CFMQ) 147

compensation 52

complexes: abandonment 72, 92; affect-drive 17–29; affects and the chronic activation of 7; affects in 9–12;

18, 44–53, 55, 56–61, 66–98,
138–51; and suicide 84, 99–117;
symbols/voices of 49, 63, 68, 78–9,
84, 85, 87, 97, 150; therapy *see*
therapy
eating disorders: Anorexia nervosa *see*
Anorexia nervosa; and attachment
research 154–9; Bulimia–Anorexia
syndrome *see* Bulimia–Anorexia
syndrome; Bulimia nervosa *see*
Bulimia nervosa; Failure to Thrive
30–8, 66, 76, 153; primary
prevention of *see* prevention of
eating disorders, primary; therapy
for *see* therapy
eating rituals 89
ecstasy *8*
Eddy, K. Y. *et al.* 43
ego-complex 6, 12, 25, 63, 92
ego development, affects in 12–14
ego functions 12–14
ego-Self axis 69, 91–2, 98, 153
Ekman, P. 3, 141; and Friesen, W. V. 3
embarrassment *8*
Emotion Experience Scales 158
Emotion Expression Styles
Questionnaire 158
emotional conditioning of the
hunger–satiety drive 17–29; affect
ratios and 24–9; lacking to negative
in an infant with Failure to Thrive
30–8, 119; negative conditioning in
Brody's subject, Helen 135–45
emotional energy *see* energy, emotional/
psychological
emotional stimulation 159; life stimuli 5,
6, *7*, 9, 14, 56, 60, 72, 126, 127, 128,
141
emotional support 159
emotions *see also specific emotions*:
affect ratios 24–9; affectlessness
114–15, 124–5, 136–7, 146, 149;
archetypal emotions as bridges
between psyche and body 130;
autonomy of 8; and/in complexes
see complexes; contagion of 5–6, 66,
141; drive–affect interactions
(Tomkins) 23–5; innate emotional
system *see* archetypal affect system;
intensity of 8; negative/crisis affects
see negative/crisis affects (NA);
numinosity of 8; positive affect *see*

positive affect (PA); possession by
affect 115–17; theory of archetypal
emotion *see* affect theory; Tomkins
and drive–affect interactions 23–5;
unbearable 70, 113, 115
emptiness 22, 70–1, 111–12, 122 *see also*
abyss; the void 72
energy, emotional/psychological 82, 89;
in abeyance 121, 128; of the
archetype 16; and the
Bulimia–Anorexia syndrome 100–1,
103, 108, 110–11, 115; and
complexes 10–11, 63–4; integration
of 118; introverted 80; levels 8;
libido 37, 71, 87, 104, 114, 121; and
life affirmation 118; and
psychological healing 121, 124–5;
release of 121; retrieval of 103; and
symbols 15–16; and unreality 70–1
enjoyment *8 see also* joy
envy 2
Eros 71
excitement *8*, 23; in the central nervous
system 23
Existential Analysis 99
exploration 14, 66, 82, 97, 126, 159
eye symbol 95–6

facial expressions 3, 4, 11, 136, 141, 148,
156
Failure to Thrive 30–8, 66, 76, 153
fantasies 11, 66; "bulimic" 79;
cannibalistic 73–4, 79; creative 80;
of destruction 93–4; dream *see*
dreams; fantasy/play 14, 66, 82,
96–7, 126–7, 159; invoked by the
Terrible Mother 73–4; and joy 14;
Jung on creative fantasy 96–7; of
persecutory "System" complex 64,
73–4, 79, 89, 92, 93–4, 119–20; and
the psychization of the hunger drive
20–1, 22; rebirth 85; revenge 64,
73–4, 92; unconscious fantasies
about food 51
fascination *8*
fasting 100, 101
fatness, fear/dread of getting fat/gaining
weight 47–8, 58, 100, 102–3, 104,
108
fear 2, *8*, 32, 36, 142 *see also* dread;
terror; "butterflies" induced by 24;
complex 9; conquering of 129;

144, 150, 157; with an unwanted child 67–8

infants/infancy: attachment research 154–9; blocking of psychological development 7, 62, 70–2, 74, 90; Gaensbauer's studies on trauma in first year of life 138–9; healing regression to earliest infancy 62–98; infant–Self bonding 90; an infant with Failure to Thrive 30–8; normal development pattern 66; screaming *see* screaming; structuring of an eating complex during infancy 18, 44–53, 55, 56–61, 66–98, 138–51; the "Wonder-child" 33, 35, 37, 66, 74–7, 89, 119, 153

inflation 52, 63

innate affect system *see* archetypal affect system

insecure attachment 154, 156, 158

instincts: and archetypes 1, 16, 19–21, 63 *see also* archetypes; balking of 112–13; Darwin 3; hunger–satiety drive *see* hunger–satiety drive; Jung 1, 4, 8, 19–21, 112–13; life instinct *see* life instinct; psychization of 19–21

integration: and affect ratios 26; of complexes 10, 12, 46–8, 75; and dreams 28; of hunger drive without satiety 109; of hunger–satiety drive 45, 51–2, 103; of mother complexes 37; of negative affects 30, 31, 32, 159; optimal 46; of psychic energy 118; in therapy 30, 31, 32; and thriving 37; Tomkins' integration model 10

interest 2, *8*, 126; as an affect of the life instinct 33, 66, 77, 97, 127, 153; bondings of 157, 160, 163–4; constellation *7*; curiosity/exploration 14, 66, 82, 97, 126, 140, 159; dissociation from 102, 114–15, 136–7; as a drive amplifier 24; and ego development *13*, 14; and emotional support 159; and the Good Mother 69; and libido 121; and neonatal perception inventories 162; and the psychization of the hunger–satiety drive 156; in the therapeutic alliance 89–90; and thriving 37

introversion 80, 91, 94, 122, 125

intuition 13, 25, 35

invasion 18–19, 89

isolation, social 113–14

Izard, C. 3

Izard, C. E. *et al.* 157–8

Jacobi, J. 15–16

Janet, P. 55–61

jealousy 2

Josephs, L. 46

joy 2, *8*; as an affect of the life instinct 33, 66, 77, 97, 127, 153; bondings of 157, 160, 163–4; complex 9; constellation *7*; dissociation from 102, 114–15, 136–7; and ego development *13*; and emotional support 159; of fantasy/play 14, 66, 82, 96–7, 126–7, 159; and the Good Mother 69; and libido 121; maternal 18; and neonatal perception inventories 162; and the psychization of the hunger–satiety drive 156; and social play 159; in the therapeutic alliance 89–90; and thriving 37

Jung, C. G.: affect theory x–xi, 1, 3–4, 7, 8, 9, 10–11, 16; on alchemists/alchemy 118, 119; on archetypal affect system 91; the archetype 1, 14, 16, 19; on complexes 7, 9, 10–11, 46–7, 104, 105, 130; on contagion 5, 6; on creative fantasy 96–7; on a detached consciousness 124–5; on detached introversion 94; on dragons 126; on exposing ourselves to the unconscious 130; on the eye as symbol of the Self 95–6; on human sacrifice 73; individuation 16, 74; instinct 1, 4, 8, 19–21, 112–13; Jungian ego functions 12–14; on libido failure 114; psychization of hunger–satiety drive 19–21; on recognition and developmental realization 34–5; on self-reference 78; on symbolism of sun myths 84; on the transcendent function 48; treatment of an anorexic patient (Anna Maria) 120–3; Word Association Test 11–12

play *13*, 135; coordinated social play (synchrony) 159; fantasy/play 14, 66, 82, 96–7, 126–7, 159; and joy 159; maternal aversion to 137; self-healing 12; symbolic 11, 96
Polivy, J. and Herman, C. P. 39
Pope, H. G. *et al.* 55–6, 57, 59, 60
positive affect (PA) *see also* interest; joy: affect ratios 24–9; and drive amplification 24; and emotional support 159; failure in emotional conditioning by PA in an infant with PFTT 30–8; maximizing 10, 25
possession: by affect 115–17; by dissociated fragments of hunger–satiety drive 99–117
prevention of eating disorders, primary 152–64; application of parent and infant bonding scales 163–4; attachment research 154–9; neonatal perception inventories 159–63
pride 2, 160
psychic energy *see* energy, emotional/psychological
psychotherapy *see* therapy
punishment 26, 65, 67, 73, 75, 87, 95, 147; self-punishment 65, 74, 76

rage *8*, 32, 34, 87, 118, 121 *see also* fury; complexes 34; and ego development 13, *13*; restriction/rage 34
rebirth 62, 82, 125, 128; from Earth Mother 122–3; from mother archetype 83–4, 85, 122–3; from "mother-sun" see Renee
regression: and confrontation with negative mother 123; to earliest infancy 62–98; and introversion 80, 91, 122, 125; and symbol-formation 118
rejection 7, 49, 60, 68, 72, 92, 95, 119, 141–2; and alienation 7, 60, 66, 76, 101, 111; by both parents 66–8, 119–20; complex 34, 67–9, 73; and development of the persecutory "System" complex 66–9, 119–20; humiliating 56–7; maternal 19, 31, 32, 33, 34, 36, 66–8, 69; unconscious 36

Renee, a patient of Sechehaye 62–98, 119–20
repression: repressed appetite 52; repressed hunger–satiety drive 45; return of the repressed 51
restriction 7, 74, 135, 142; of autonomy 19, 121; of intellectual capacity 146; of positive affect 26–7; reaction against 143; restriction/rage 34; restrictive behaviour 42, 143
revenge 2, 84, 90, 92, 95; fantasies 64, 73–4, 92
Ringer, F. and Crittenden, P. M. 155
rituals 48, 57, 60, 80, 89, 95, 106

sadness 2, *8*, 36; complex 9; constellation *7*; and ego development *13*; and the psychization of the hunger–satiety drive 157
screaming 33, 34, 122, 136, 137; and archetypal affects 140–2; Brody's subject, Helen 135, 138, 139, 140–2, 149
Sechehaye, M. 62, 66, 67–8, 76–85, 87–90, 92–3, 95, 96, 97–8, 120
secure attachment 154, 156, 158
Self: ego-Self axis 69, 91–2, 98, 153; infant–Self bonding 90; symbols 71, 95–6, 129–30
self-demolition 93–4
self-disgust 101 *see also* humiliation
self-esteem 101
self-punishment 65, 74, 76
self-recrimination 93, 94
self-reference 78
sensation, and ego development 13
sensuality 63, 85
sexual drive 23
shame 2–3, *8*, 87, 120; complexes 55–61, 57, 144, 145, 149; constellation *7*; and ego development *13*; Janet's case study of an anorexic's life dominated by 55–61; and the psychization of the hunger–satiety drive 157; shame–body complex 55–61; shame/contempt 9, 36, 49, 56, 66, 68, 76, 101, 111, 114, 144, 145, 157
shyness 2
social isolation 113–14
soul 15